Summits and Regional Governance

Despite the large number of regional and global summits there is very little known about the functioning and impact of this particular type of diplomatic practice. While recognizing that the growing importance of summits is a universal phenomenon, this volume takes advantage of the richness of the Americas experiment to offer a theoretically grounded comparative analysis of contemporary summitry.

The book addresses questions such as:

- How effective have summits been?
- How have civil society and other non-state actors been involved in summits?
- How have summits impacted on the management of regional affairs?

Filling a significant void in the literature, this volume offers an original contribution helping to understand how summitry has become a central feature of world politics. It will be of great interest to students and scholars of diplomacy, international organizations, and global/regional governance.

Gordon Mace is Professor in the Department of Political Science, Université Laval, Québec, Canada.

Jean-Philippe Thérien is Professor in the Department of Political Science, Université de Montréal, Canada.

Diana Tussie is Director, Department of International Relations, FLACSO-Argentina, Buenos Aires, Argentina.

Olivier Dabène is Director, Observatoire de l'Amérique latine et des Caraïbes, Sciences-Po, Paris, France.

Global Institutions

Edited by Thomas G. Weiss
The CUNY Graduate Center, New York, USA
and Rorden Wilkinson
University of Sussex, Brighton, UK

About the series

The "Global Institutions Series" provides cutting-edge books about many aspects of what we know as "global governance." It emerges from our shared frustrations with the state of available knowledge—electronic and print-wise, for research and teaching—in the area. The series is designed as a resource for those interested in exploring issues of international organization and global governance. And since the first volumes appeared in 2005, we have taken significant strides toward filling conceptual gaps.

The series consists of three related "streams" distinguished by their blue, red, and green covers. The blue volumes, comprising the majority of the books in the series, provide user-friendly and short (usually no more than 50,000 words) but authoritative guides to major global and regional organizations, as well as key issues in the global governance of security, the environment, human rights, poverty, and humanitarian action among others. The books with red covers are designed to present original research and serve as extended and more specialized treatments of issues pertinent for advancing understanding about global governance. And the volumes with green covers—the most recent departure in the series—are comprehensive and accessible accounts of the major theoretical approaches to global governance and international organization.

The books in each of the streams are written by experts in the field, ranging from the most senior and respected authors to first-rate scholars at the beginning of their careers. In combination, the three components of the series—blue, red, and green—serve as key resources for faculty, students, and practitioners alike. The works in the blue and green streams have value as core and complementary readings in courses on, among other things, international organization, global governance, international law, international relations, and international political economy; the red volumes allow further reflection and investigation in these and related areas.

The books in the series also provide a segue to the foundation volume that offers the most comprehensive textbook treatment available dealing with all the major issues, approaches, institutions, and actors in contemporary global governance—our edited work *International Organization and Global Governance* (2014)—a volume to which many of the authors in the series have contributed essays.

Understanding global governance—past, present, and future—is far from a finished journey. The books in this series nonetheless represent significant steps toward a better way of conceiving contemporary problems and issues as well as, hopefully, doing something to improve world order. We value the feedback from our readers and their role in helping shape the on-going development of the series.

A complete list of titles appears at the end of this book. The most recent titles in the series are:

Global Consumer Organizations (2015)
by Karsten Ronit

World Trade Organization (2nd edition, 2015)
by Bernard M. Hoekman and Petros C. Mavroidis

Women and Girls Rising (2015)
by Ellen Chesler and Terry McGovern

The North Atlantic Treaty Organization (2nd edition, 2015)
by Julian Lindley-French

Governing Climate Change (2nd edition, 2015)
by Harriet Bulkeley and Peter Newell

The Organization of Islamic Cooperation (2015)
by Turan Kayaoglu

Contemporary Human Rights Ideas (2nd edition, 2015)
by Bertrand G. Ramcharan

Summits and Regional Governance
The Americas in comparative perspective

Edited by
Gordon Mace, Jean-Philippe Thérien,
Diana Tussie and Olivier Dabène

LONDON AND NEW YORK

First published 2016
by Routledge
2 Park Square, Milton Park, Abingdon, Oxon OX14 4RN

and by Routledge
711 Third Avenue, New York, NY 10017

Routledge is an imprint of the Taylor & Francis Group, an informa business

© 2016 selection and editorial material, Gordon Mace, Jean-Philippe Thérien, Diana Tussie and Olivier Dabène; individual chapters, the contributors

The right of Gordon Mace, Jean-Philippe Thérien, Diana Tussie and Olivier Dabène to be identified as authors of the editorial material, and of the individual authors as authors of their contributions, has been asserted by them in accordance with sections 77 and 78 of the Copyright, Designs and Patents Act 1988.

All rights reserved. No part of this book may be reprinted or reproduced or utilised in any form or by any electronic, mechanical, or other means, now known or hereafter invented, including photocopying and recording, or in any information storage or retrieval system, without permission in writing from the publishers.

Trademark notice: Product or corporate names may be trademarks or registered trademarks, and are used only for identification and explanation without intent to infringe.

British Library Cataloguing in Publication Data
A catalogue record for this book is available from the British Library

Library of Congress Cataloging in Publication Data
Names: Mace, Gordon, editor. | Thérien, Jean-Philippe, editor. | Tussie, Diana, editor. | Dabène, Olivier, editor.
 Title: Summits and regional governance : the Americas in comparative perspective / edited by Gordon Mace, Jean-Philippe Thérien, Diana Tussie, and Olivier Dabène.
 Description: New York, NY : Routledge, 2016. | Series: Routledge global institutions series | Includes bibliographical references and index.
 Subjects: LCSH: Regionalism–America. | Summit meetings–America. | Summit meetings–America–Case studies. | America–Foreign relations. | Pan-Americanism.
 Classification: LCC JZ5331 .S87 2016 | DDC 341.24/5–dc23
 LC record available at http://lccn.loc.gov/2015021522

ISBN: 978-1-138-83194-0 (hbk)
ISBN: 978-1-315-73629-7 (ebk)

Typeset in Times New Roman
by Taylor & Francis Books

Contents

List of illustrations   x
List of contributors   xii
Acknowledgments   xvii
Foreword   xviii
Abbreviations   xxiii

Introduction: Summitry and governance in comparative perspective   1
GORDON MACE, JEAN-PHILIPPE THÉRIEN, DIANA TUSSIE AND OLIVIER DABÈNE

PART I
Summitry in context   11

1 Summitry, governance, and democracy   13
   JAN AART SCHOLTE

2 Multilayered summitry and agenda interaction in South America   30
   OLIVIER DABÈNE

PART II
Case studies—Americas   53

3 The Summits of the Americas process: Unfulfilled expectations   55
   GORDON MACE AND JEAN-PHILIPPE THÉRIEN

4 Presidential diplomacy in UNASUR: Coming together for crisis management or marking turfs? 71
DIANA TUSSIE

5 Summitry in the Caribbean Community: A fundamental feature of regional governance 88
JESSICA BYRON

6 The impact of summitry on the governance of Mercosur 106
MARCELO DE ALMEIDA MEDEIROS,
RAFAEL MESQUITA DE SOUZA LIMA AND
MARIA EDUARDA FERREIRA CABRAL

7 Presidential summitry in Central America: A predictable failure? 124
KEVIN PARTHENAY

8 The anti-summitry of North American governance 141
GREG ANDERSON

PART III
Case studies—World 157

9 ASEAN summits and regional governance in comparative perspective 159
RICHARD STUBBS

10 Assessing the role of G7/8/20 meetings in global governance: Processes, outcomes, and counterfactuals 177
EMMANUEL MOURLON-DRUOL

11 BRICS and re-shaping the model of summitry: Subordinating the regional to the global 193
ANDREW F. COOPER

PART IV
Practitioners' point of view 211

12 The Summits of the Americas process and regional governance: A reflection 213
MARC LORTIE

13 Some thoughts on summit proliferation and
regional governance 222
CARLOS PORTALES

14 Conclusion: Summitry and governance—an assessment 228
GORDON MACE, JEAN-PHILIPPE THÉRIEN, DIANA TUSSIE AND
OLIVIER DABÈNE

Bibliography 237
Index 239
Routledge Global Institutions Series 251

List of illustrations

Figures

2.1 SA-CSN-UNASUR summits: Participation and model of integration, 2000–13	40
2.2 SA-CSN-UNASUR summits: Participation and political shifts, 2000–13	42
6.1 Frequency of bilateral Brazil-Argentina summits, 1997–2013, and Mercosur Council summits, 1991–2013	109
6.2 Decisions taken by the Mercosur Council, divided by topic, 1991–2013	114
7.1 Evolution of Central American summits, 1986–2011	130
7.2 Evolution of unexecuted presidential mandates, 1993–2012	131

Tables

2.1 Existing sub-groups (ESG) embedded in a new regional integration process (NRIP): Types of agenda interaction	33
2.2 SA-CSN-UNASUR strategy regarding Mercosur and CAN agendas, 2000–13	36
2.3 Mercosur strategy regarding the SA-CSN-UNASUR agenda	38
2.4 SA-CSN-UNASUR ordinary and extraordinary summit attendance, 2000–13	44
3.1 Frequency of key terms in Summits of the Americas documents (1994–2012)	60
4.1 Milestones in the evolution of summits in UNASUR, 2000–14	77
6.1 Total Mercosur Council summits and number of participating states, 1991–2013	111

6.2 Comparison between Mercosur Council Decisions, 1991–2013, and Commission Directives, 1994–2013	117
8.1 NAFTA asymmetries, by GDP, 1975–2012	143
8.2 NAFTA export partners, 2012	144

Contributors

Greg Anderson is an Associate Professor in the Department of Political Science at the University of Alberta, Canada. He earned his PhD from the Paul H. Nitze School of Advanced International Studies of the Johns Hopkins University (Johns Hopkins/SAIS) in Washington, DC. His research interests broadly cover international political economy, Canada–United States relations, US foreign policy, and US foreign economic policy. From 2000–02, Greg also worked in the Office of the United States Trade Representative as a policy analyst in the NAFTA office, and he is a member of several professional associations, including the American Political Science Association, the International Studies Association, and the Canadian Political Science Association.

Jessica Byron is Senior Lecturer in International Relations and former head of the Department of Government, University of the West Indies, Mona, Jamaica. Her research interests include Caribbean and Latin American regionalism and small states/societies in the global political economy. Recent publications include "The Caribbean Community's Fourth Pillar: The Evolution of Regional Security Governance," in *The Security Governance of Regional Organizations*, ed. Emil Kirchner and Roberto Dominguez (Routledge, 2011); and with Patsy Lewis, "Responses to the Sovereignty/Vulnerability/Development Dilemmas: Small Territories and Regional Organizations in the Caribbean," in *Collectivités Territoriales et Organisations Régionales: de l'indifférence à l'interaction*, ed. Danielle Perrot (L'Harmattan, Collection GRALE, 2015).

Andrew F. Cooper is Professor at the Balsillie School of International Affairs and the Department of Political Science, University of Waterloo, Canada. Holding a DPhil from the University of Oxford, he is also an Associate Research Fellow-UNU CRIS, Bruges,

Belgium. He was Canada–US Fulbright Research Chair, Center on Public Diplomacy, USC in 2009, Fulbright Scholar in the Western Hemisphere Program, SAIS, Johns Hopkins University in 2000, and the Léger Fellow, DFAIT in 1993–94. Among his books either authored or edited are the *Oxford Handbook of Modern Diplomacy* (Oxford University Press, 2013); *Group of Twenty* (Routledge, 2012); *Internet Gambling Offshore: Caribbean Struggles over Casino Capitalism* (Palgrave, 2011); *Rising States, Rising Institutions: Challenges for Global Governance* (Brookings, 2010); and *Intervention Without Intervening? OAS and Democracy in the Americas* (Palgrave, 2006).

Olivier Dabène is Professor of Political Science at the Institut d'Études Politiques de Paris (Sciences Po) and Senior Researcher at the Center for International Studies and Research (CERI, Sciences Po). He is also the President of the Political Observatory of Latin America and the Caribbean (www.sciencespo.fr/opalc) and Visiting Professor in many Latin American universities. His main area of expertise is Latin American regionalism. His latest publications in English include *The Politics of Regional Integration in Latin America* (Palgrave Macmillan, 2009); and "Consistency and Resilience Through Cycles of Repoliticization," in *The Rise of Post-Hegemonic Regionalism: The Case of Latin America*, ed. Pía Riggirozzi and Diana Tussie (Springer, 2012), 41–64.

Maria Eduarda Ferreira Cabral is a Political Science undergraduate student. She is a CNPq grant holder and member of the NEPI/CNPq/UFPE.

Marc Lortie is a retired Canadian diplomat. During his career, he served as Ambassador to France (2007–12), Spain (2004–07), and Chile (1993–97). In 1997–98 he was at Harvard University as a fellow at the Weatherhead Center for International Affairs. In 2000 he was named Sherpa for the preparation of the Third Summit of the Americas that took place in Quebec City in 2001. He then became Assistant Deputy Minister for the Americas in the Department of Foreign Affairs. Born in Quebec City in 1948, he obtained a BA in Political Science (International Relations) from Université Laval in 1971.

Gordon Mace is Professor at the Department of Political Science and at the School of Advanced International Studies of Université Laval. He is also a past editor of *Études internationales* and past director of the Inter-American Studies Center. He has published extensively in various journals and with publishers both in Europe and the Americas. Among the books he has recently co-authored or co-edited are *Governing the Americas: Assessing Multilateral Institutions* (Lynne Rienner, 2007), co-edited with Jean-Philippe Thérien and Paul Haslam; *Regionalism and the State: NAFTA and Foreign Policy Convergence* (Ashgate, 2007); and *Inter-American Cooperation at a Crossroads* (Palgrave Macmillan, 2011), co-edited with Andrew Cooper and Timothy M. Shaw. He is the recipient of the 2008 ISA Canada Distinguished Scholar Award.

Marcelo de Almeida Medeiros received his PhD in Political Science from the Institut d'Études Politiques de Grenoble, and his Habilitation Thesis from the Institut d'Études Politiques de Paris (Sciences Po). He is Associate Professor of Political Science at the Federal University of Pernambuco-UFPE (Recife, Brazil), and PQ-1D Research Fellow of the National Council for Scientific and Technological Development-CNPq (Brasilia, Brazil). He was Rio Branco International Relations Chair, St Antony's College, University of Oxford (2015), and Simon Bolivar Political Science Chair, Institute of Latin American Studies, Université Sorbonne Nouvelle (2009).

Rafael Mesquita de Souza Lima received his Master in Political Science from UFPE. He is a CNPq grant holder and member of the Center of Comparative Politics and International Relations, NEPI/CNPq/UFPE.

Emmanuel Mourlon-Druol is Lord Kelvin Adam Smith Fellow in the Adam Smith Business School, University of Glasgow. He was previously Pinto Post-Doctoral Fellow at the London School of Economics and Political Science (LSE). He received his PhD from the European University Institute in Florence and holds a Master in International History from LSE. He is the author of *A Europe Made of Money: The Emergence of the European Monetary System* (Cornell University Press, 2012); has edited with Federico Romero *International Summitry and Global Governance: The Rise of the G7 and the European Council* (Routledge, 2014); and published various articles in journals such as *Business History*, *Cold War History*, *Diplomacy & Statecraft* and *West European Politics*.

Kevin Parthenay holds a PhD in Political Science from the Institut d'Études Politiques de Paris (Sciences Po). A member of the Center for International Studies and Research (CERI), he specializes in Central American foreign policies and regional integration. Before becoming a scholar, he worked for the French Ministry of Foreign and European Affairs, and as a consultant in strategic affairs and economic intelligence for the European Strategic Intelligence

Company (CEIS). He also worked for the Organization of American States (OAS) as an international observer of the Colombian 2010 general election. He currently supervises the Development and Partnership Division of the Political Observatory of Latin America and the Caribbean (OPALC). He is Academic Coordinator at Sciences Po and Associate Doctor at Sciences Po/CERI.

Carlos Portales is Professor at Facultad Latinoamericana de Ciencias Sociales (FLACSO), Chile (1977–90 and 2014–present). He was Director of the Program on International Organizations, Law and Diplomacy at WCL, American University, 2010–14. From 1990 to 2010 he served in the Chilean Foreign Ministry as Director-General for Foreign Policy (1990–94 and 2002–08), Director of Policy Planning and Director of the Diplomatic Academy. He was Ambassador to the UN in Geneva (2008–10), to the OAS in Washington, DC (1997–2000), where he chaired the Special Committee on Summit Management, and Mexico (1994–97). He was the Chilean Coordinator (Sherpa) of the Summit of the Americas Implementation Review Group (SIRG); Coordinator for the Rio Group, organizing the Seventh Summit (Santiago, 1993); and Coordinator of the Ibero-American Summit, responsible for organizing the Seventeenth Summit (Santiago, 1997).

Jan Aart Scholte is Faculty Professor in Peace and Development at the University of Gothenburg and Professor of Politics and International Studies at the University of Warwick. His research covers globalization, global governance, civil society in global politics, and global democracy. He is the author of *Globalization: A Critical Introduction* (Palgrave Macmillan, 2005); editor of *Building Global Democracy? Civil Society and Accountable Global Governance* (Cambridge University Press, 2011); and author of "Reinventing Global Democracy," *European Journal of International Relations* (2014). He is a former lead editor for the journal *Global Governance* and lead convener of the Building Global Democracy program. He works with many movements and policymakers on changing global governance.

Richard Stubbs is a Professor of Political Science at McMaster University, Canada. He has published widely on the regional political economy and security of Southeast and East Asia. His most recent publications include the *Routledge Handbook of Asian Regionalism* (Routledge, 2012), which he co-edited with Mark Beeson; "ASEAN's Leadership in East Asian Region-Building: Strength in

Weakness," *The Pacific Review* 27, no. 4 (2014); and "Ideas and Institutionalization," in *Oxford Handbook of the International Relations of Asia*, ed. Saadia M. Pekkanen, John Ravenhill and Rosemary Foot (Oxford University Press, 2014), which he co-authored with Jennifer Mustapha. He is currently working on a revised edition of his 2005 book, *Rethinking Asia's Economic Miracle: The Political Economy of War, Prosperity and Crisis* (Palgrave Macmillan).

Jean-Philippe Thérien is Professor in the Department of Political Science and Director of the Centre d'études sur la paix et la sécurité internationale (Center for International Peace and Security Studies) at Université de Montréal. His research interests focus on international organizations, North–South politics, and the inter-American system. His work has been published in journals such as the *American Political Science Review*, *Foro Internacional*, *Global Governance*, *International Organization*, *Latin American Politics and Society*, *Revue internationale de politique comparée*, and *Third World Quarterly*. He is the author of *Left and Right in Global Politics* (Cambridge University Press, 2008), with Alain Noël.

Diana Tussie heads the Department of International Relations at FLACSO, Argentina, and is the founder and director of the Latin American Trade Network (LATN). Her most recent book is *The Rise of Post-Hegemonic Regionalism: The Case of Latin America* (Springer, 2012), edited with Pía Riggirozzi. Diana is Co-Editor of the journal *Global Governance* and a Senior Fellow at the Centre for International Governance Innovation (CIGI). She serves on the board of the German Institute of Global and Area Studies, and on the editorial boards of several international journals as well as the National Council for Scientific Research in Argentina.

Acknowledgments

Editing a volume is like a journey because enjoyment depends on the company. In our case, the company was excellent. As editors, we feel immensely privileged for having had the opportunity to work with such a collegial and disciplined group of experts. Their intellectual rigor and their willingness to use a common analytical framework provided key material for the comparative analysis and made our work much easier.

We also want to express our gratitude to Gabriel Coulombe, Marion Giroux, and Nicolas Falomir Lockhart, who contributed enormously to the success of the workshop that was held in Quebec City in May 2014, and in which first drafts of the papers were discussed. The meeting went very smoothly thanks to their efficiency. Marion also did a great job in helping us to put together the manuscript, while Hugo Lavoie-Deslongchamps and Daniel Navarro provided much appreciated research assistance. The final version of the manuscript benefited immensely from the professional linguistic revision of Lazer Lederhendler and the meticulous copy editing of Martin Burke.

We also want to thank the Social Sciences and Humanities Research Council of Canada, the International Development Research Center, the Inter-American Studies Center of Université Laval, and the Observatoire politique de l'Amérique latine et des Caraïbes of Paris' Sciences-Po, whose greatly appreciated financial support enabled us to launch this project and bring it to a fruitful completion.

Finally, we are particularly grateful to Ambassador and respected scholar Jorge Heine for having kindly accepted to write the Foreword for the book and to the editors of the *Routledge Global Institutions Series*, Tom Weiss and Rorden Wilkinson, who welcomed our book project with enthusiasm and offered constant and efficient support until the end. We also thank the Routledge team—Paola Celli, Lydia de Cruz, Peter Harris, Nick Micinski, and Nicola Parkin—who provided help every time we needed it.

Foreword

The XXVI Asia-Pacific Economic Cooperation (APEC) Leaders' Summit took place in Beijing on 10–12 November 2014. Twenty-some of the world's most influential leaders, including Barack Obama from the United States, Vladimir Putin of Russia, Enrique Peña Nieto of Mexico and Shinzo Abe of Japan, descended upon the capital of China to be hosted by President Xi Jinping and to attempt to chart the course for the world's most dynamic region, the Asia-Pacific. The meeting was widely considered to have been a success. The impeccable organization, elegant conference halls and striking show that followed the gala dinner bedazzled visitors and confirmed Beijing's standing as a prime venue for big-ticket international conferences. The major item on the agenda, the proposal to initiate a feasibility study about a proposed Free Trade Area of the Asia-Pacific (FTAAP), was unanimously approved. In a follow-up, bilateral meeting between Presidents Obama and Xi, a major agreement on carbon emissions control was signed by the United States and China, marking a breakthrough after negotiations that had dragged on for years.

The APEC Summit in Beijing was in many ways the "coming out party" for President Xi's new foreign policy. In his scarce 30 months in office he has put forward such major initiatives as the Asian Investment and Infrastructure Bank (AIIB) and the "Belt and Road" project that aims to resurrect the Silk Road and nothing less than recreate Eurasia. Interestingly, President Xi, in this relatively short period, has already visited the Americas twice (and was to do so for a third time in September 2015). Shortly after the APEC Summit, he also hosted in Beijing the First Ministerial China-Community of Latin American and Caribbean Nations (CELAC) Forum, on 8–9 January 2015, attended by four heads of state/government from Latin America and the Caribbean, some 30 foreign ministers and 40 official delegations.

The relatively new diplomatic tool of summit meetings, i.e. those that bring together two (some say, three) or more heads of state/government, be it on an ad hoc or serial basis, has become not only a regular feature of the diplomatic calendar. Summits have also grown into a preferred "action-trigger" mechanism to move items forward on the foreign policy agenda and to "get things done," as was illustrated in the case of the APEC meeting in Beijing, as well as, in some cases, for crisis management.

Why this upsurge in summitry? What justifies the considerable cost (in money, security and, perhaps most importantly, time of the leaders) such meetings entail? Moreover, as they often become flashpoints for demonstrations by those who feel excluded from their deliberations, and/or take a stand against various items on the agenda such meetings pursue, are they really necessary?

In this book, four leading international relations (IR) scholars from three different continents have put together an impressive, up-to-date volume with chapters by some of the leading specialists on the international relations of the Americas and some other areas of the Global South. It focuses mostly on the Western Hemisphere, which over the past 25 years has become a veritable real-life laboratory for summitry, with a great variety of continental, regional and sub-regional entities holding their summits every so often. As Carlos Portales points out in his chapter in this book, ten different types of summits have come into being in the Americas, and their number has risen accordingly: whereas 31 summits were held from 1947 to 1989, 303 were held from 1990 to 2012.

Yet, this book's main contribution resides in its conceptual framework and its comparative perspective. By focusing on the various functions summits perform (socializing information, setting the policy agenda, managing crises, legitimizing/and or projecting the regional or global project of which they are part, etc.), the various chapters of the book enhance our understanding of the dynamics and the purpose served by these often maligned high-level meetings. They also open new vistas into their significance and why they have become so widespread in the new phase of globalization triggered by the Third Industrial Revolution.

Where does the term "summit" in this context actually come from? The term is attributed to Winston Churchill, who, in 1950, at the very beginning of the Cold War, and a time of great international tension, used it in the phrase, "It is not easy to see how matters would be worsened by a parley at the summit." John F. Kennedy, not too long before becoming president, put it in a slightly different way: "It is better that we meet at the summit than at the brink" (meaning at the brink of nuclear war).[1] During the Cold War, then, summits were closely associated with one-on-one meetings of the leaders of the two superpowers, surrounded by great expectations as to who would win the "*mano a mano*" such encounters seemed to entail—such as the Kennedy–Khruschev meeting in Vienna in 1961, or the one between Ronald Reagan and Mikhail Gorbachev in Reykjavik in 1986. In the West, such meetings never enjoyed much of a reputation. The February 1945 Yalta conference, arguably the first summit of modern times, with the participation of the "Big Three," Winston Churchill, Franklin Delano Roosevelt and Josef Stalin (with Roosevelt in the last throes of the illness that would take his life only a few months later), was blamed by some for having "given away" Eastern and Central Europe to the Soviet Union. The Vienna meeting, on the other hand, where Nikita Khruschev is said to have taken the measure of a much younger John Kennedy and found it wanting, was supposed to have encouraged him to put Soviet missiles in Cuba, on the assumption that the US president was not strong enough to react forcibly to such an initiative.

In addition to such (however dubious) time-bound objections, another, more systematic and lasting line of opposition to summit diplomacy arose in the 1950s and has remained to this day, and this is the one that comes from professional diplomats.[2] The argument here is straightforward. Diplomacy is a complex endeavor with many nuances, which specialists spend a lifetime mastering. Political leaders, who know little about this craft, and even less about the issues, should provide broad foreign policy guidelines, and leave its actual implementation to the professionals—i.e. the diplomats themselves. Moreover, in addition to the ignorance about procedures and the substance of the issues that hamper the leaders' initiatives in such meetings, it is said that the incentives in summit diplomacy are misaligned. The very holding of the summit meeting itself, with the heavy media coverage, is, of course, the first such "wrong incentive." During the meeting itself, various other counterproductive dynamics are said to be at work: the empathy with fellow leaders (arising from the "loneliness at the top" syndrome), and the presumed need to have something to announce to the media at the end of the meeting, would both work in favor of "closing a deal," even if it is not in the country's best interests. On the other hand, diplomats, not affected by any of these pernicious effects, would be able to carry on their *métier* quietly and effectively, away from the glittering lights of the TV cameras, not limited by any artificial deadlines, and taking whatever time is needed to defend and stand up for the country's national interest.

Largely unspoken of, but subjacent to much of this criticism of summit diplomacy is, of course, the fact that summits are highly labor-intensive tasks for the Ministry of Foreign Affairs bureaucracy, with many briefing papers to be drafted and many organizational matters to be taken care of. They are thus seen as an unwelcome distraction from the regular, routine diplomatic work of husbanding the nation's foreign affairs—what is defined as the true core of the organization's main mission.

If there ever was some basis for this argument, it has weakened over time. As summits proliferate, leaders become more proficient at mastering not just arcane diplomatic procedures, but also many key international issues. On the global stage, leaders such as Bill Clinton, Tony Blair and Vladimir Putin certainly display a remarkable command of them. In the Americas, the same can be said about scholar-statesmen such as Fernando Henrique Cardoso of Brazil, Ricardo Lagos of Chile and Ernesto Zedillo of Mexico. In turn, given the 24/7 news cycle, governments need to have public opinion on their side to push foreign policy issues forward, and nobody is better suited to do that than national leaders, something for which summits provide an ideal platform.

Yet, in some ways, the bureaucratic argument against summits has by now become academic. As this fine book shows ad nauseam, summits are not only here to stay, but, if anything, they are becoming more and more widespread. Summits today are in many ways the instrument of choice for cutting through the Gordian knot of longstanding global and international issues, of which we have more and more. There are many reasons for this development. One of them is the increased "presidentialization" of foreign policy—i.e. the fact that more and more presidents and prime ministers take the conduct of foreign policy into their own hands and appoint themselves as their own "diplomat-in-chief." This trend, though quite widespread (as made evident by the case of Prime Minister Narendra Modi in India, who in his first 12 months in office has demolished many a myth as to why Indian prime ministers could not be as active in foreign affairs as a country the size of India deserves), is especially apparent in South America. There, the Union of South American Nations (UNASUR) summits have taken not only the role of projecting a newly emerging South American identity, but also that of a mutual aid society among the region's leaders, stepping in when political survival is at stake.

Standard reasons put forward for the seemingly ever larger number of diplomatic summits include advances in air transport technology and the twin effects of globalization and interdependence—the latter, by triggering the rise of an ever larger number of "global commons" issues, which transcend the handling capacity of one or two countries, and demand wider collective action. Less remarked upon is a third, conceptual development. The demands of an ever more interconnected and interdependent world entail a shift of paradigms. Much as we are seeing a change from "club" to "network diplomacy"[3] we are also seeing one from the tried and tested notion of "the national interest" as the bedrock on which foreign policy is based, to that of "a balance of interests."[4] This means that far from being able to insist on a unilateral, narrow defense of what they see as their own best interests, states within an international system facing many complex collective challenges, are bound to bend their own priorities and preferences to accommodate those of others. The give and take of summits, events designed to bring together national leaders for an informal exchange of views on the most pressing issues of the day, are especially suited to convey and evaluate the views of others. Needless to say, the difficult task of bending those often longstanding priorities and pushing for the necessary compromises with their counterparts can only be undertaken by national leaders, who must in turn be convinced of the wisdom of that course of action.

Far from being merely expensive, time-wasting photo ops held in up-scale beach resorts to bolster the egos of the participating leaders, as they are often portrayed in the media, summits in this day and age truly respond to the manifold challenges of the complex world of the early decades of the new century. This book, with its comprehensive, yet nuanced, comparative, yet focused, approach to this important new phenomenon in diplomacy takes us a long way toward putting it in the proper perspective.

Jorge Heine
Beijing, June 2015

Notes

1 For an historian's perspective on summits, see David Reynolds, *Summits: Six Meetings that Shaped the Twentieth Century*. London: Allen Lane, 2007, from which these citations are taken.
2 Perhaps the most vocal of these opponents was former US Ambassador to the Soviet Union Charles ("Chip") Bohlen, who, ironically enough, advised every US president from 1943 to 1969. See his *Witness to History 1929–1969*. New York: Norton, 1973.
3 See Jorge Heine, "From Club to Network Diplomacy," in *The Oxford Handbook of Modern Diplomacy*, ed. Andrew F. Cooper, Jorge Heine and Ramesh Thakur. Oxford and New York: Oxford University Press, 2013, 54–69.
4 Ramesh Thakur, "A Balance of Interests," in *The Oxford Handbook of Modern Diplomacy*, ed. Andrew F. Cooper, Jorge Heine and Ramesh Thakur. Oxford and New York: Oxford University Press, 2013, 70–87.

Abbreviations

ACE	acuerdo de complementación económica (complementary economic agreement)
ACP	Asia, Caribbean, and Pacific group of states
AEC	ASEAN Economic Community
AFTA	ASEAN Free Trade Agreement
ALBA	Alianza Bolivariana para los Pueblos de Nuestra América (Bolivarian Alliance for the Peoples of Our America)
ALC/UE	Latin America, the Caribbean, and the European Union Summits
AMAE	Archives du Ministère des Affaires Étrangères, La Courneuve, France
AN	Archives nationales (site de Pierrefitte, France)
AP	Alianza del Pacífico (Pacific Alliance)
APEC	Asia-Pacific Economic Cooperation
APT	ASEAN Plus Three
ASA	Africa and South America Summits
ASEAN	Association of Southeast Asian Nations
ASEM	Asia-Europe Meetings
ASPA	Summits of South American and Arab countries
AU	African Union
Bancosur	Bank of the South
BASIC	Brazil, South Africa, India, and China group
BRIC	Brazil, Russia, India, and China group
BRICS	Brazil, Russia, India, China, and South Africa group
C4	El Salvador, Honduras, Guatemala, and Nicaragua
CABEI	Central American Bank for Economic Integration
CACM	Central American Common Market
CAF	Corporación Andina de Fomento (Development Bank of Latin America)

CALC	Cumbre de América Latina y del Caribe (Latin America and the Caribbean Summit)
CAN	Community of Andean Nations/Andean Community
CARICOM	Caribbean Community
CCJ	Caribbean Court of Justice
CCM	Comisión de Comercio del Mercosur (Mercosur Trade Commission)
CELAC	Comunidad de Estados Latinoamericanos y Caribeños (Community of Latin American and Caribbean Nations)
CHG	CARICOM Heads of Government
CMC	Common Market Council
COP	Conference of the Parties
CSME	CARICOM Single Market and Economy
CSN	Community of South American Nations
EAI	Enterprise for the Americas Initiative
EAS	East Asian Summit
ECLAC	Economic Commission for Latin America and the Caribbean
EEC	European Economic Community
ELN	Ejército de Liberación Nacional (National Liberation Army)
ESG	existing sub-groups
EU	European Union
FARC	Fuerzas Armadas Revolucionarias de Colombia (Revolutionary Armed Forces of Colombia)
FCCR	Foro Consultivo de Municipios, Estados Federados, Provincias y Departamentos (Consultative Forum for Municipalities, Federated States, Provinces and Departments)
FCES	Foro Consultivo Económico-Social (Economic-Social Consultative Forum)
FDI	foreign direct investment
FDL	Gerald Ford Digital Library
FOCEM	El Fondo para la Convergencia Estructural (Structural Convergence Fund)
FTA	free trade area
FTAA	Free Trade Area of the Americas
G7	Group of Seven
G8	Group of Eight
G20	Group of 20
GATT	General Agreement on Tariffs and Trade

GDP	gross domestic product
GFATM	Global Fund to Fight AIDS, Tuberculosis and Malaria
GMC	Grupo Mercado Común (Common Market Group)
IA	integration agenda
IACHR	Inter-American Commission on Human Rights
IASB	International Accounting Standards Board
IBSA	India, Brazil, and South Africa group
ICANN	Internet Corporation for Assigned Names and Numbers
IDB	Inter-American Development Bank
IFI	international financial institution
IIRSA	Initiative for the Integration of the Regional Infrastructure in South America
ILO	International Labour Organization
IMF	International Monetary Fund
IR	international relations
IS	institutional system
JSWG	Joint Summit Working Group
LDC	less developed country
MDC	more developed country
Mercosur	Southern Common Market
MIKTA	Mexico, Indonesia, South Korea, Turkey, and Australia group
MINUSTAH	United Nations Mission in Haiti
NAFTA	North American Free Trade Agreement
NALS	North American Leaders' Summit
NARA	US National Archives and Records Administration
NATO	North Atlantic Treaty Organization
NEPAD	New Partnership for Africa's Development
NGO	nongovernmental organization
NRIP	new regional integration process
NSA	National Security Advisor
O5	Outreach 5 process
OAS	Organization of American States
OAU	Organization of African Unity
ODECA	Organización de Estados Centroamericanos (Central American States Organization)
OECD	Organisation for Economic Co-operation and Development
PAHO	Pan American Health Organization
Parlacen	Central American Parliament
Parlasur	Mercosur Parliament

Parlatino	Latin American Parliament
PTP	Pro Tempore Presidency
RG	Rio Group
RNM	Regional Negotiating Machinery
SA	South American Summit
SADC	South American Defense Council
SAFTA	South American Free Trade Agreement
SARS	severe acute respiratory syndrome
SG	secretary-general
SICA	Sistema de la Integración Centroamericana (Central American Integration System)
SIRG	Summit Implementation Review Group
SOA	Summits of the Americas
SPP	Security and Prosperity Partnership
TAC	Treaty of Amity and Cooperation
TNA	The National Archives, Kew, UK
UN	United Nations
UNASUR	Unión de Naciones Suramericanas (Union of South American Nations)
UNFCCC	United Nations Framework Convention on Climate Change
USAID	United States Agency for International Development
WTO	World Trade Organization
ZOPFAN	Zone of Peace, Freedom and Neutrality

Introduction
Summitry and governance in comparative perspective[1]

Gordon Mace, Jean-Philippe Thérien, Diana Tussie and Olivier Dabène

- **What we know about summitry**
- **What is this book about?**
- **The structure of the book**

The rise of summitry is one of the most important changes in modern diplomacy of the last 40 years. Presidents and prime ministers everywhere have found it essential to hold face-to-face meetings to exchange views on subjects of immediate concern or to resolve urgent problems. At the global level, the numerous G7, G8, and G20 summits clearly testify to this trend, but it is also manifest both at the regional and sub-regional levels. In short, summitry has become an indispensable and ubiquitous component of contemporary world affairs. Although summits all have their own idiosyncratic properties, it is certainly useful to look at them as the expression of a generic, institutionalized form of international behavior.

The growth of summitry raises a number of questions as to the reasons for this development and its impact on governance. Why have summits become a central instrument of multilateralism worldwide?[2] As highlighted below, the literature places particular emphasis on the consequences of the growing pressures of globalization and modern interdependence. Regarding regional summits, an additional factor involves the declining legitimacy of global institutions, which are seen as enmeshed in bureaucratic politics and inefficient in managing public goods.

As for the impact of summitry on governance, this issue is both important and complex. The analytical complexity results, in most cases, from the difficulty of isolating the effects of summits from those of the institution with which they are associated. Those effects are closely linked to the notion of legitimacy underlying the whole study of summitry. A further problem is that of distinguishing the outcomes of summits from the process itself, as discussed by Emmanuel Mourlon-Druol in Chapter 10. Finally, there is the problem of establishing causality when analyzing the relationship between summit outputs and policy choices at the regional and/or national levels. These factors can explain the ambivalence and the sometimes contradictory views about the impact of summitry on regional and international governance.

To clarify the nature of summitry, the balance of this introduction summarizes the main findings of the literature on the subject. It goes on to present the key themes of the volume as well as the essential points discussed in each part.

What we know about summitry

The literature on summitry is relatively limited in comparison with research on other topics of world affairs. It is a literature dominated almost exclusively by international relations and political science scholars, although one finds notable contributions by historians.[3] The literature is mostly in English, with a few publications in French[4] and some heterogeneous contributions in Spanish.[5]

Over the years, the literature on summitry has focused on a fairly limited number of subjects. One of the top questions confronting scholars has been the definition of the term itself. Summits have generally been defined as meetings of heads of state, but early approaches insisted on power as a central criterion for participation.[6] For some authors, a summit could be held only among great powers and deal only with matters of high politics. However, high politics became less important as a defining feature of summitry in the 1970s as other issues took center stage in international affairs. This evolution led former US diplomat George Ball to write that the term summit had "become so vague in meaning as to be not only useless but downright misleading."[7] David Dunn offered a more pared-down definition of summitry, specifically that a summit was a meeting between two or more heads of state or government.[8] Others have proposed typologies of summitry—ad hoc/serial, bilateral/multilateral, regional/global[9]—but, as is true of most social science concepts, a universally accepted definition of the term remains elusive.

A second strand of literature concentrates on the causes of the rise of modern-day summitry, which are identified as a combination of factors all related to the changes affecting the international system as of the 1960s. Technological progress, particularly in the transportation and information sectors, an expanded international society as a result of decolonization, the rise of multilateralism, and the centralization of foreign policy decision making at the highest level were certainly

Introduction 3

contributing factors.[10] The principal reason, however, has to do with interdependence and the need collectively to manage problems of an increasingly supranational nature.[11] Globalization and interdependence meant that summitry must complement international organizations as the primary instrument of multilateralism.[12]

A third dimension covered by the literature is the impact and usefulness of summitry. With regard to impact, the literature is somewhat scarce[13] and centers mostly on the G7/8/20. The greatest impact of these summits is in the area of agenda setting, because summitry highlights important topics in international affairs, guides the work of international organizations, and provides direction for foreign policymaking.[14] In the particular case of the G20, summitry has enabled emerging economies to advance reforms of the Bretton Woods system.[15] More generally, summitry has significantly affected the role of ambassadors, who are circumvented more and more often as political leaders feel the need to intervene directly in global and regional matters.[16]

Concerning the usefulness of summitry, it seems clear that there is a direct relationship between the degree of institutionalization of summits and their utility.[17] The more summitry is institutionalized, the more likely it is to fulfill its objectives and produce concrete outcomes. Institutionalization can contribute to governance in various ways, particularly through socialization, agenda setting, coordination, legitimation, and other such functions.[18] However, both scholars and practitioners agree that summits are much more successful with regard to the exchange of information than to the effective coordination of policies.[19] The next section of the introduction expands on the functions of summits, which are a key component of this book's analytical framework.

A fourth strand in the literature analyzes the dysfunctional aspects of summitry, such as the saturation of presidential or prime ministerial agendas, the pressure on diplomatic and bureaucratic resources, and the potential neglect of the management of national affairs.[20] Summits may also become dysfunctional when leaders do not share the same values or worldviews,[21] when they use summits to advance national agendas to the detriment of collective management,[22] or when they lack preparation or expertise relating to the issues under discussion.[23] Finally, serial summits risk becoming dysfunctional if decisions are not acted upon and implementation fails.[24]

All in all, there exists a broad consensus in the literature on the inability of the scholarship on summitry to keep up with the phenomenon's growing importance. Summitry remains neglected and "understudied."[25] Jan Melissen's observation that "research on summitry is still patchy" holds true today.[26] There is evidently a need for more theoretically as well as empirically grounded research, and it is imperative to move from single case studies to comparative analysis so as to generate more robust conclusions.

What is this book about?

This volume fills a large gap in our knowledge of summits. It provides the first systematic comparative analysis of contemporary regional summits. While the book maintains a strong focus on the Americas, the comparative dimension is enhanced by discussions of other regional and multilateral experiences. Our focus on the Americas is justified by our belief that, among the different regions of the world, the Americas provide an especially fascinating laboratory for a study of the role that summits play. It has been estimated, for example, that from 2007 to the first half of 2012, Latin American presidents participated in 109 summits.[27] In the Americas as a whole, 303 summits of heads of state or government were held between 1990 and 2012, compared with only 31 between 1947 and 1989.[28] Clearly, the Americas is a region where summitry has become a standard tool of foreign policy. What is more, beyond their rise in numbers, summits in the Americas are very diversified because each sub-region has its own summit process. While keeping an eye on summits that take place in a variety of international contexts, the book thus seeks to take advantage of the richness of the Americas experiment to offer a wide-ranging reflection on summitry.

The book centers on the relationship between summitry and regional governance. Consequently, the emphasis is, first, on the actual practice of summitry as distinct from the workings of the institution to which it belongs and as separate from the more encompassing analysis of regional geopolitics. Second, we zero in on the design and the evolution of summits conceived as particular mechanisms of regional interaction. In other words, we are mainly concerned with the analysis of the kind of contribution that summitry makes to regional governance.

It is true that after more than 60 years of research on the subject, there is still no universally accepted definition of the concept of region. From our perspective, a region is a political construct in the sense that it is designed by political actors and structured by institutions. Given the social nature of regions, it should come as no surprise that in a given geographical space one finds various levels of regional groupings that may or may not interact. Regional governance, meanwhile, has to do with the management of regional public goods. As a process, it produces norms and/or initiates practices aimed at addressing regional problems in various issue areas. It is, in sum, the management of regional interdependence as opposed to institutionalized government. When assessing the contribution of summitry to regional governance, we are looking specifically for the adoption of regional norms and/or the initiation of regional practices. These norms and practices may bear on various spheres of activity including security, trade and finance, democracy, development, and infrastructure.

From a theoretical point of view, the study of summitry can be examined through various lenses. Thomas Legler, for example, identifies four theoretical perspectives on multilateralism that can be useful in studying summits: realism, constructivism, the political economy approach, and neoliberal institutionalism.[29] Realism involves looking at summitry through the lens of power relationships. Summits thus become sites characterized by asymmetrical power relations,[30] where states seek to advance their interests through strategies such as soft balancing, mediation or group action. Constructivism proposes to analyze summitry in terms of concepts of community and collective identity.[31] Accordingly, the success of cooperation, generally and in the context of summits, depends on high levels of "we" feelings. Identity determines how an actor plays his or her cards in summit meetings, while the sense of community belonging affects the degree of success or failure of summitry.

The third perspective on summitry is that of political economy, whereby multilateralism is seen as subject to the evolution of major trends in the capitalist world order. The dominant feature of the contemporary world economy is globalization, which affects not just the actors but also the architecture of regional and global governance.[32] According to this view, summitry, like other components of the governance apparatus, simply cannot escape the pressures of globalization. Finally, there is the perspective of neoliberal institutionalism, which regards summits as sites for policy coordination and cooperation among states.[33] Typically, institutionalism looks at summits as institutional arrangements based on states' calculations of costs and benefits in an uncertain environment.

To complete Legler's useful overview, however, one should also take into account that the institutionalist approach to summits assumes a variety of forms. Alongside the mainstream, rationalist version, there is, for instance, another, more historical version that views summitry as an international practice fulfilling a number of functions. Because the notion of summit functions is at the core of our comparative analysis, the latter approach most closely coincides with the one we have adopted here. A focus on functions, in addition to lending narrative unity to the book, enables us to more precisely characterize the contribution of summits to regional governance. In sum, the general analysis presented here may be situated within an institutionalist perspective, but readers will note that references to other points of view enrich specific case studies.

As suggested above, the functions of summits are a recurrent discussion topic among experts. These functions may be seen along a scale describing the extent to which summitry impacts governance. Summit functions can be summarized as follows. Summits contribute to governance, first, through *dialogue* and *socialization*. They do this by providing occasions for leaders to exchange views directly and to get to know each other. A personal understanding may help each leader to grasp more fully the domestic constraints faced by other leaders and to assess their intentions more accurately.[34] A second function has to do with *agenda setting* and *orientation*. Summits offer a space for leaders to identify central issues, and set a course of action for national bureaucracies and international organizations. To this end, decision makers may adopt programs of action and engage resources to deal with perceived problems.[35]

Third, summits can fulfill a function of *negotiation* and *coordination*. Summits may provide a political mechanism allowing leaders to discuss options, arrive at decisions, and mobilize regional and national bureaucracies to implement them. Indeed, summits have become an important institution of international relations because they provide a space where leaders can agree on ways to deal with the problems affecting a specific group of countries, adopt common positions, and decide on a collective course of action.[36]

Finally, summits serve a function of legitimation.[37] They legitimize regional norms and practices, and are used by leaders to reinforce their status or to justify domestic measures. As the media frequently remind us, summits provide photo ops through which leaders can project an image of solidarity and community, particularly when regional cohesion is being challenged. Not surprisingly, the legitimation function of summits is strengthened when leaders succeed in associating civil society groups and other non-state actors to the decision-making process. In short, summits can be a powerful diplomatic means of support for regional or international policies.

Functions offer a useful tool not only for assessing the contribution of summitry to regional governance but also for drawing comparisons. Comparative analysis of summits is a major contribution that this book makes to the study of summitry. However, our comparative method does not follow the strict rules of most research designs;[38] a looser type of comparison is in order here, given the exploratory nature of our investigation, the lack of previous comparative work on summitry, and the very different contexts in which each serial summit evolves. We nevertheless believe that our objectives are specific enough to generate useful conclusions.

The structure of the book

The aim of Part I of the volume is to locate summitry in its context. Two specific themes are developed. The first concerns summitry's relationship to globalization and democracy. In catalyzing a change from a state-centric to a polycentric form of world governance, and in raising new concerns of democratic control and legitimacy, globalization has had a major effect on summits. Second, we look at the phenomena of multi-layered summitry and multiple memberships, which impact on the functioning and efficiency of summits. Although such phenomena are particularly frequent in the Americas, they are in no way exclusive to that region.

Parts II and III are concerned with the comparative analysis of summitry. A distinction is drawn between the Americas, the main focus of the book, and the "world." In the Americas, the selected cases are a diversified mix in terms of membership, history, scope, and degree of institutionalization. The "world" section examines regional and multilateral summits and provides additional insights for analysis. The comparative method used for the case studies in Parts II and III is based on the framework described above.

In Part IV, the practitioner's point of view is presented as a complement to the scholarly examination found in the first three sections. This is an innovative approach offering a distinctive vision of what summitry is and what it means in the context of modern-day diplomacy. Building on their vast experience as summit "sherpas," Marc Lortie and Carlos Portales reflect on the usefulness of summits for managing regional affairs.

Overall, the book suggests that summitry is an international practice that will remain a key feature of diplomacy in the foreseeable future. Summits play a key social role as they provide a unique space for dialogue among political leaders. Because they encourage dialogue, summits can become catalysts for increased trust and peaceful change. Yet our analysis also shows that, so far, the actual contribution of summits to regional governance has remained mixed. Indeed, with few exceptions, the implementation of summit decisions has rarely been a success. Many chapters in the book concur to emphasize the gap between the lofty rhetoric of summits' final communiqués and summits' disappointing results. For things to change, larger states and originators of summits bear a special responsibility to provide leadership and articulate an inclusive vision that can appeal to all summit partners.

Taken together, the chapters that make up this book represent a rich and original contribution to the study of summitry. They fill a gap with regard to the comparative analysis of regional summits, and the contribution is further enriched by the juxtaposition of academics' and practitioners' conceptions of summitry. Our aim is for this collective effort to expand our comprehension of summitry in general and regional summits in particular.

Notes

1 We thank Hugo Lavoie-Deslongchamps for helpful research assistance.
2 Enrique V. Iglesias, "La Diplomacia de Cumbres y el Multilateralismo," in *La Diplomacia de las Cumbres: Retos y Oportunidades de los Nuevos Regionalismos*, ed. Maria Salvadora Ortiz (San José, Costa Rica: FLACSO, 2013), 15.
3 Kenneth L. Adelman, "Summitry: The Historical Perspective," *Presidential Studies Quarterly* 16, no. 3 (1986): 435–441; Keith Eubank, *The Summit Conferences, 1919–1960* (Norman, Okla.: University of Oklahoma Press, 1966); and Emmanuel Mourlon-Druol, "'Managing from the Top': Globalisation and the Rise of Regular Summitry, Mid-1970s–early 1980s," *Diplomacy & Statecraft* 23, no. 4 (2012): 679–703. See also Emmanuel Mourlon-Druol and Federico Romero, eds, *International Summitry and Global Governance: The Rise of the G7 and the European Council, 1974–1991* (London: Routledge, 2014); and David Reynolds, *Summits: Six Meetings that Shaped the Twentieth Century* (New York: Basic Books, 2007).
4 Philippe Chrestia, "Les Sommets Internationaux," *Études Internationales* 31, no. 3 (2000): 443–474; Marie-Claude Smouts, "Les Sommets des Pays Industrialisés," *Annuaire Français de Droit International* 25 (1979): 668–685; and Michel Virally, "La Conférence au Sommet," *Annuaire Français de Droit International* 5 (1959): 7–36.
5 See Carlos M. Jarque, Maria Salvadora Ortiz, and Carlos Quenan, eds, *América Latina y la Diplomacia de Cumbres* (Madrid: Secretaría General Iberoamericana, 2009); Francisco Rojas Aravena and Paz V. Milet, *Diplomacia de Cumbres: El Multilateralismo Emergente del Siglo XXI* (Santiago de Chile: FLACSO-Chile, 1998); and Ortiz, ed., *La Diplomacia de las Cumbres*.
6 Johan Galtung, "Summit Meetings and International Relations," *Journal of Peace Research* 1, no. 1 (1964): 36; and Virally, "La Conférence au Sommet," 13.
7 George W. Ball, *Diplomacy for a Crowded World: An American Foreign Policy* (Boston, Mass.: Little, Brown & Company, 1976), 34.
8 David H. Dunn, "What is Summitry?," in *Diplomacy at the Highest Level: The Evolution of International Summitry*, ed. David H. Dunn (New York: Palgrave Macmillan, 1996), 18.

9 Geoff R. Berridge, *Diplomacy: Theory and Practice*, 4th ed. (Basingstoke: Palgrave Macmillan, 2010), 161–178; Dusan Bojcev, "Summit Diplomacy," *The Macedonian Foreign Policy Journal* 3, no. 2 (2012): 109–117; and John W. Young, "A Case Study in Summitry: The Experience of Britain's Edward Heath, 1970–74," *The Hague Journal of Diplomacy* 1, no. 3 (2006): 261–293.
10 Jan Melissen, "Summit Diplomacy Coming of Age," Discussion Papers in Diplomacy No. 86, Netherlands Institute of International Relations Clingendael, 2003, 10–14; Dunn, "What is Summitry?," 5–13; Richard E. Feinberg, "Institutionalized Summitry," in *The Oxford Handbook of Modern Diplomacy*, ed. Andrew F. Cooper, Jorge Heine, and Ramesh Thakur (Oxford: Oxford University Press, 2013), 305–306; and Jean-Robert Leguey-Feilleux, *The Dynamics of Diplomacy* (Boulder, Colo.: Lynne Rienner Publishers, 2009), 300.
11 Chrestia, "Les Sommets Internationaux," 454; Melissen, "Summit Diplomacy Coming of Age," 8; Robert D. Putnam and Nicholas Bayne, *Hanging Together: Cooperation and Conflict in the Seven-Power Summits* (London: Sage, 1987), 14–16; Bojcev, "Summit Diplomacy," 113; Peter R. Weilemann, "The Summit Meeting: The Role and Agenda of Diplomacy at the Highest Level," *Nira Review* 7, no. 2 (2000): 19; and Feinberg, "Institutionalized Summitry," 305–306.
12 Chrestia, "Les Sommets Internationaux," 446–451; and Rojas and Milet, *Diplomacia de Cumbres*, 10–14.
13 See Richard E. Feinberg, "Presidential Mandates and Ministerial Institutions: Summitry of the Americas, the Organization of American States (OAS) and the Inter-American Development Bank," *Review of International Organizations* 1, no. 1 (2006): 72.
14 Putnam and Bayne, *Hanging Together*, 158–160; and Weilemann, "The Summit Meeting," 19.
15 Fen Osler Hampson and Paul Heinbecker, "The 'New' Multilateralism of the Twenty-First Century," *Global Governance* 17, no. 3 (2011): 301.
16 Abba Eban, *Diplomacy for the Next Century* (New Haven, Conn.: Yale University Press, 1998), 92–99.
17 Feinberg, "Institutionalized Summitry," 311–315.
18 See Melissen, "Summit Diplomacy Coming of Age"; Rojas and Milet, *Diplomacia de Cumbres*; Berridge, *Diplomacy*; and Weilemann, "The Summit Meeting."
19 John Hein, "From Summit to Summit: Policymaking in an Interdependent World," Conference Board report, no. 774 (New York: Conference Board, 1980), 36–42; and Nicholas Bayne, "Western Economic Summits: Can They Do Better?," *The World Today* 40, no. 1 (1984): 12.
20 Melissen, "Summit Diplomacy Coming of Age," 16; Rojas and Milet, *Diplomacia de Cumbres*, 72; Leguey-Feilleux, *The Dynamics of Diplomacy*, 300; and Elmer Plischke, "Summit Diplomacy-Diplomat in Chief," in *Modern Diplomacy: The Art and the Artisans*, ed. Elmer Plischke (Washington, DC: American Enterprise Institute for Public Policy Research, 1979), 179.
21 Berridge, *Diplomacy*, 165; Leguey-Feilleux, *The Dynamics of Diplomacy*, 302–303; and Melissen, "Summit Diplomacy Coming of Age," 2–3.
22 Feinberg, "Institutionalized Summitry," 310.

23 Berridge, *Diplomacy*, 25.
24 Chrestia, "Les Sommets Internationaux," 471; Dunn, "What is Summitry?," 16; Feinberg, "Institutionalized Summitry," 311; and Francisco Rojas Aravena, "Rol y Evaluación de la Diplomacia de Cumbres. Construyendo el Multilateralismo Cooperativo," in *Multilateralismo: Perspectivas Latinoamericanas*, ed. Francisco Rojas Aravena (Santiago de Chile: FLACSO-Chile, 2000), 27–53.
25 Feinberg, "Institutionalized Summitry," 72 and 306; Reynolds, *Summits*, 115–116; Stuart Murray, "Reordering Diplomatic Theory for the Twenty-First Century: A Tripartite Approach," Doctoral Thesis, Department of International Relations and Diplomacy, Faculty of Humanities & Social Sciences, Bond University, Robina, Australia, 2006, 296–301; and Paul Sharp, "Diplomacy in International Relations Theory and Other Disciplinary Perspectives," in *Diplomacy in a Globalizing World: Theories and Practices*, ed. Pauline Kerr and Geoffrey Wiseman (New York: Oxford University Press, 2013), 54–66.
26 Jan Melissen, "Pre-summit Diplomacy: Britain, the United States and the Nassau Conference, December 1962," *Diplomacy & Statecraft* 7, no. 3 (1996): 678.
27 Francisco Rojas Aravena, "Las Cumbres y las Relaciones Biregionales," in *La Diplomacia de las Cumbres*, ed. Ortiz, 138.
28 Chapter 13 in this volume.
29 Thomas Legler, "The Rise and Decline of the Summit of the Americas," *Journal of Iberian and Latin American Research* 19, no. 2 (2013): 180–183.
30 John J. Mearsheimer, "The False Promise of International Institutions," *International Security* 19, no. 3 (1995): 5–49; and Chapter 8 in this volume.
31 Emanuel Adler and Michael Barnett, "Security Communities in Theoretical Perspective," in *Security Communities*, ed. Emanuel Adler and Michael Barnett (Cambridge: Cambridge University Press, 1998), 9–15; and Amitav Acharya and Alastair I. Johnston, eds, *Crafting Cooperation: Regional International Institutions in Comparative Perspective* (Cambridge: Cambridge University Press, 2007).
32 Jan Aart Scholte, *Globalization: A Critical Introduction*, 2nd edn (Basingstoke: Palgrave Macmillan, 2005), 202–214; and Chapter 1 in this volume.
33 John Gerard Ruggie, "Multilateralism: The Anatomy of an Institution," in *International Institutions in the New Global Economy*, ed. Lisa L. Martin (Cheltenham, UK: Edward Elgar Publishing, 2005), 89–126.
34 Berridge, *Diplomacy*, 161–178; Melissen, "Summit Diplomacy Coming of Age"; Rojas and Milet, *Diplomacia de Cumbres*; Weilemann, "The Summit Meeting"; and Young, "A Case Study in Summitry," 266.
35 Rojas and Milet, *Diplomacia de Cumbres*; and Ulrich Schneckener, "The Opportunities and Limits of Global Governance by Clubs,"*SWP Comments*, 22 September 2009, 1–8.
36 Berridge, *Diplomacy*; Rojas and Milet, *Diplomacia de Cumbres*; and Chrestia, "Les Sommets Internationaux."
37 Weilemann, "The Summit Meeting," 19.
38 Peter Burnham, Karin Gilland Lutz, Wyn Grant, and Zig Layton-Henry, *Research Methods in Politics*, 2nd edn (Basingstoke: Palgrave Macmillan, 2008), 73–87.

Part I
Summitry in context

1 Summitry, governance, and democracy

Jan Aart Scholte

- **Summits in a transformed world politics**
- **Summits and (un)democracy within polycentric governance**
- **Democratizing summits: Various suggested avenues**
- **Conclusion**

Governance today has become suffused with summits. Most weeks bring yet another face-to-face encounter of government leaders in some bilateral, regional, or global configuration. The sheer magnitude and rapid growth of summitry in contemporary world politics call for close examination. What has prompted this trend, and what is its significance?

This chapter considers the contemporary rise of summitry in broad terms, including in particular the implications of this development for democracy. The first part of the discussion below situates the recent proliferation of government leader conferences in the context of several ongoing shifts in the deeper structures of world politics. Summitry, this analysis suggests, can be regarded as an attempt to bring coordination and control in circumstances of more complex governance. The second part of the chapter shows that contemporary structural transformations raise major questions about democracy in relation to summits. The third part reviews six general propositions for the enhancement of democracy in respect of contemporary summitry. The conclusion proposes that the democratization of summits could be pursued with a blend of approaches, including conventional parliamentary scrutiny, newer stakeholder mechanisms, expanded public deliberation, and significant counter-hegemonic resistance.

Summits in a transformed world politics

Society and its governance are not what they used to be. Fifty years ago the collective lives of people were organized well-nigh exclusively in relation to country-nation-state units.[1] Geographically, societies at this time were constructed above all as bounded territorial entities: Afghanistan, Albania, Algeria, etc. Culturally, each such country-society had a population defined primarily (if often problematically) in terms of a national identity and solidarity: Barbadian, Brazilian, Burundian, etc. Politically, governance of every country-nation-society lay almost entirely with a state apparatus: a formal, centralized, comprehensive, public, sovereign authority (whose reach in some cases extended also to colonial domains). World politics in this so-called "Westphalian" era consisted predominantly of relations between states. Within Westphalian diplomacy face-to-face meetings among state leaders ("summits") were fairly rare.

This territorialist-nationalist-statist organization of society no longer prevails. To be sure, countries, nations, and states still very significantly shape social relations today; however, these frameworks lack their previous comprehensive overriding primacy. Geographically, societal space has become less centered on countries, given the advances over recent decades of globalization, regionalization, and localization. Circumstances today tend to be "trans-scalar," operating across interlinked spaces of different extents. Culturally, identity and community have become less centered on nations through the rise of plural affiliations, where people construct their being and belonging also in terms of age, class, (dis)ability, faith, gender, race, sexuality, vocation, and more. Solidarities tend to be "intersectional," involving interplays of diverse lines of collective identity. Politically, governance has become decentered from the state, with a proliferation of trans-state, substate, suprastate, and nonstate institutions of societal regulation. Policymaking tends to be "polycentric," encompassing multiple sites across different scales and across private as well as public sectors.

These features of trans-scalar (as against country-centered) geography, intersectional (as against nation-centered) solidarities, and polycentric (as against state-centered) governance are evident across all major societal issues today. The transformations make for messy politics. As is elaborated later below, the rise of summitry might be interpreted as an attempt (albeit with generally mixed results) to gain overall control of such political disarray.

So the proposition advanced here is to situate the contemporary expansion of summitry within the wider emergence of polycentric governance, which in turn relates to altered geographies and altered political identities. What is here termed "polycentrism"[2] has been called by a host of other names elsewhere, including "networked governance," "new medievalism," "mobius-web governance," "complex sovereignty," and "multi-scalar meta-governance."[3] Under these various labels numerous analysts have identified a major ongoing transformation in the way that societal regulation is institutionalized.

In ideal-type fashion, a polycentric mode of governance can be distinguished from its statist predecessor on seven main points. First, whereas statist rule focused on country-level institutions and policies, today's polycentric governance is marked by transcalarity, where regulation transpires through interplays of agencies and initiatives with local, country, regional, and global remits. Second, whereas statist governance occurred more or less entirely through public channels, polycentric regulation has a trans-sectoral quality that combines public, commercial, civil society, and hybrid institutions. Third, whereas statism entailed considerable centralization of regulation (namely, in a state apparatus for each country unit), governance under polycentrism is highly diffuse, spread across multiple entities which are sometimes only loosely connected to one another. Fourth, whereas statist regulation involved relative institutional stability, polycentrism exhibits considerable fluidity, with the continual appearance of new regulatory bodies and frequent adjustments of organizational mandates. Fifth, whereas statist governance was organized in terms of discrete jurisdictions, with each national government ruling a separate territorial domain, polycentric governance involves many overlapping jurisdictions, where multiple agencies claim competence over a given regulatory circumstance. Sixth, whereas statist regulation followed vertical lines of command, with formally clear hierarchies of authority, polycentric governance tends towards horizontal organization with ambiguous and readily contested command structures. Seventh, whereas statism designated the state as the "sovereign" point of decision taking, with polycentrism there is no such final arbiter. To be sure, some sites (e.g. the United States Federal Reserve) clearly have more impact on regulation than others (e.g. the Bankers Association of Malawi), but in spite of such power inequalities no one exercises overall control.

Amidst these complexities and confusions of polycentric governance, it is not surprising to witness a flurry of leader summits that try to bring greater consistency and coordination to policy. Thus the Conference of the Parties (COP) for the United Nations Framework Convention on Climate Change (UNFCCC) has met annually since 1995 in hopes of establishing a single integrated policy direction on climate change. Meanwhile leader summits of the Group of 7 (from 1975) and the expanded Group of 20 (from 2008) have attempted to provide an overall steer for financial regulation. Other intergovernmental summits have sought to consolidate public policy on every issue from energy to racism.

Thus the contemporary growth of summitry might be seen as an effort to gain increased governance control in a mode of regulation, polycentrism, that has stubbornly resisted integrated direction. Summits have often been promoted as a way "to get things done": to inject executive momentum, to accelerate decisions, and to increase resolution in policy processes that are otherwise readily bogged down in muddles and squabbles among multiple agencies. It is hoped that face-to-face consultation among heads of government could bring greater simplicity, efficiency, consistency, hierarchy, compliance, accountability, and legitimacy to public policy under polycentric conditions.

As other chapters in this volume detail, in practice summits have frequently fallen short of delivering on such a purpose. Indeed, few politicians and citizens regard a summit resolution as the last word on a particular policy debate. If anything, the proliferation of summits, both globally and regionally, has compounded the messiness of polycentrism, introducing yet more policy initiatives and directions, rather than consolidating single overarching programs for key societal challenges.

Nevertheless, summits still have considerable influence in contemporary polycentric governance. Many of these leader meetings have substantially shaped agendas, affecting which issues are addressed in world politics and with what relative priority. In addition, summits can be key venues (alongside others) for policy formulation and execution. More broadly, top-level conferences are important moments for the socialization of politicians into the evolving world order. Also, as a public performance of power, summits can play a notable role in legitimating government leaders and their policies. So summits can be highly significant even if they are far from holding a sovereign final say in contemporary polycentric governance.

Summits and (un)democracy within polycentric governance

Along with their record on policy efficacy, summits might also be evaluated in terms of their implications for democracy. This issue is important inasmuch as the rise of polycentric governance has raised major questions about the fate of "people's power" in contemporary politics. It is widely commented that trends such as globalization and regionalization have put severe strains on the capacities of affected publics to participate in and control the policy processes that shape their lives. Does summitry exacerbate these shortfalls in democracy, or can leader conferences on the contrary help to alleviate this problem?

Democracy—*demos-kratos* or "people's power"—is broadly embraced as a core feature of human flourishing. Prevailing norms hold that an affected population should collectively determine the decisions that shape its joint circumstances and shared fates. In addition, democracy can often (though not necessarily always) bolster other aspects of living well. That is, a democratic society is generally more likely to embrace diversity, share resources fairly, enjoy social cohesion, etc. Thus democracy can be promoted both for its own sake and for its potential positive spill-over effects on other core values of a good society. For policy practice, too, democracy can lend significant legitimacy to governance, thereby greatly facilitating the effective implementation of decisions. Given these major stakes, a key question arises whether summits advance or undermine people's power in contemporary politics.

In times of statist governance, ideas and practices of democracy were understandably developed mainly in relation to territorial-national government. Core institutions of modern people's rule—such as bills of rights, citizenship, civil society, a nonpartisan judiciary, multiparty elections, and representative legislatures—were all elaborated with respect to the country, the nation, and the state. In other words, modern democracy has assumed that the relevant jurisdiction is the country, the relevant constituency is the nation, and the relevant instrument is the state. Critics of modern liberal democracy, too, have largely sought alternative formulas of popular power through the country-nation-state, for example, with "people's democracies" and "African socialism."

However, the territorialist-nationalist-statist assumptions that underpin modern democracy are no longer viable. With the rise of trans-scalar geography the relevant jurisdiction for most major policy issues is not the country per se. For example, the affected public in relation to infectious diseases, energy supplies, and so on is today not delimited by territorial-political borders. Moreover, variations in the ways that people are affected by the Internet, labor conditions, and so on often bear little correspondence to country boundaries. Thus to organize democratic action on the basis of country domains often poorly matches the actual map of the affected public, which nowadays tends to lie within, across, or beyond formal territorial frontiers.

As for collective identities, in contemporary politics "the people" often do not identify themselves in terms of a nation. For example, many indigenous peoples do not define their demos as the national grouping that links to the modern country in which they, the aboriginals, happen to reside. Meanwhile many sexual minorities may identify with non-territorial queer solidarity as much as, or even more than, their officially designated national affiliation. Likewise, depending on the issue at hand, many persons today may construct their political affinity less in terms of a national grouping, and more in terms of class, disability, faith, gender, and/or race.

Institutionally, meanwhile, channeling democratic action solely through the state apparatus can neglect many other influential sites within polycentric governance. For one thing, interstate organizations (such as the European Union regionally and the United Nations globally) often exert impacts of their own, with a certain autonomy from the participating governments. Hence state-based democratic processes are not always sufficient to make these suprastate institutions accountable to affected publics, especially when it comes to citizens of smaller and weaker states. For instance, how far can a democratically elected national legislature in, say, Paraguay give effective voice and influence to residents of that country as they are affected by the International Monetary Fund (IMF) or the Southern Common Market (Mercosur)?

Moreover, in today's polycentric governance much regulation occurs through trans-state networks of bureaucrats which tend to function at considerable distance from elected politicians. The Group of Eight (G8) and the Group of 20 (G20) are more prominent examples of this largely informal governance. Countless other instances of transgovernmental regulation include the Global Counter-Terrorism Forum and the International Competition Network. In all such cases, unelected officials from multiple states come together to make policy with little if any oversight from their respective judiciaries and legislatures.

Meanwhile, substantial other parts of contemporary polycentric regulation have been "outsourced" to private governance arrangements in which state-based democracy has little if any direct role. Prominent examples of nonstate regulation include the International Accounting Standards Board (IASB) and the Internet Corporation for Assigned Names and Numbers (ICANN). Then there are credit-rating agencies, corporate social responsibility schemes, and a proliferation of private security firms. Like intergovernmental and transgovernmental regimes, this greatly expanded field of nongovernmental regulation lies substantially outside the purview of democratic processes of the territorial nation-state.

In sum, a far-reaching disconnect prevails today between a polycentric character of governance and a statist model of democracy. Even if one could perfect the workings of people's power through territorial nation-states—correcting various shortcomings that have often marred modern democracy in practice—truly effective participation and control by affected publics would still not prevail. A more far-reaching overhaul of democracy is required to meet an altered mode of governance.[4]

What part could summitry play in this regard? Although democracy enhancement is not usually named among the principal purposes of summits, could these top-level conferences contribute to a reinvention of people's power to meet the conditions of contemporary polycentric governance? Could summits—particularly when they involve democratically elected leaders—provide channels for popular voice and accountability that are generally deficient in the largely technocratic suprastate, transgovernmental, and private mechanisms that have become so influential in contemporary societal regulation?

Certainly summits have on occasion advanced liberal democracy in one or the other territorial nation-state. In the Americas, for example, presidential summits of the Union of South American Nations (UNASUR) have bolstered democratically elected regimes in Bolivia and Ecuador, while the UNASUR Democratic Protocol of 2010 prescribes the imposition of sanctions on any member country that attempts to subvert national democracy.[5] Similarly, summits of the Central American Integration System (SICA) in 2002 and 2004 proclaimed support for democracy and struggles against corruption in Nicaragua.[6] The summit of the Caribbean Community (CARICOM) has taken initiatives in respect of disputed elections in Guyana and Trinidad. In addition, CARICOM's Charter for Civil Society (1997) set benchmarks for state-civil society relations in the region.[7]

Yet contributions of these kinds relate to old-style state-centered democracy and at best only indirectly advance people's power in other parts of polycentric governance. In terms of that wider democratization, summits can have the positive effect of bringing elected politicians into global and regional regulatory processes that are otherwise left to unelected bureaucrats. Moreover, although many summit proceedings are held in camera, these leader conferences tend to be more publicly visible than suprastate, transgovernmental, and private governance. Many summit decisions take the form of publicly declared commitments, and the meetings are often accompanied by a media spotlight that raises public awareness of ongoing extra-parliamentary governance. Indeed, the open display of concentrated power at summits can invite democratic resistance, as witnessed by popular demonstrations at numerous meetings of the G8, G20, Summits of the Americas, European Union Council, etc. In addition, conferences among leaders of weaker states can strengthen their collective position in world politics. CARICOM summits could in this sense be seen to have democratizing effects for small island states within polycentric governance.

This positive potential having been noted, summits can also have significant undemocratic implications. After all, these meetings involve top-down governance *par excellence*. Summits are executive clubs that convene within quite closed (and sometimes also deliberately remote) venues. Many summits are more concerned with building executive rapport than with developing democratic mandate: forging trust among leaders takes precedence over forging legitimacy with publics. Summitry can also be a way to marginalize democratically based parliamentary legislation and scrutiny. Indeed, summits to date have normally given no access for opposition politicians. (Their inclusion in certain CARICOM summits is the exception that highlights this rule.) Many summits also deal with crisis situations in which democratic procedures can be compromised with arguments that the "emergency" allows no time for public consultation, and summit decisions often have far-reaching effects on parts of the world whose governments are not included in the gathering.

This said, summits are not intrinsically democratic or anti-democratic. Their implications for people's power in a geographically trans-scalar, culturally intersectional, and politically polycentric world can be positive and/or negative: it depends very much on how the specific summit is conducted. The remainder of this chapter considers different possible ways to enhance the democratic qualities of summits and, through them, to further popular voice and public accountability in polycentric governance more generally.

Democratizing summits: Various suggested avenues

Considerable academic work has accumulated since the 1990s on constructing democracy beyond the country-nation-state, under labels such as "global," "planetary," "world," "cosmopolitan," and "transnational" democracy. This literature has offered broadly six designs for people's power in a post-statist world: i.e., communitarianism, multilateralism, cosmopolitan federalism, stakeholder democracy, deliberative democracy, and counter-hegemonic resistance. The following survey briefly describes each of these perspectives and considers what they would suggest for a democratization of summitry. Since the different prescriptions are in some respects potentially complementary, the way forward could well—as elaborated in the conclusion to this chapter—lie in a combination of several approaches.

Communitarianism

Communitarian arguments hold that democracy beyond country-state-nation units is impossible.[8] This skeptical approach holds that: (1) spaces beyond countries are too large for popular control; (2) global and regional governance institutions cannot adequately connect with constituents on the ground; and (3) no demos beyond the nation is possible. From a communitarian perspective, globalization and regionalization inherently contradict people's power, and the way to reaffirm democracy in contemporary society is to roll back these trends and reinvigorate sovereign nation-states.[9] For communitarians a redefinition of democracy for polycentric governance is not available.

When applied to summitry, communitarian ideas on democracy would urge to restrict governance beyond internal state processes to a minimum. Thus to protect democracy the number and consequence of intergovernmental conferences should be limited, and any decisions taken at summits should be unanimous, so as not to infringe upon any participating state's sovereignty. Communitarianism would moreover welcome close scrutiny of summits by democratically elected national parliaments. In this light communitarians could applaud initiatives such as the Joint Parliamentary Committee in Mercosur, the Assembly of CARICOM Parliamentarians, and the Parliamentary Confederation of the Americas.

Communitarian arguments suitably underscore that individual states can still take considerable initiative to govern a trans-scalar, intersectional, polycentric world. Active oversight of summits by country-based parliaments can also be democratically welcome. However, communitarianism overestimates the capacities of state sovereignty and national parliamentary scrutiny in contemporary politics, particularly when it comes to smaller countries. Even for the largest countries, effective governance of many major policy challenges today is simply not possible through independent state action. Meanwhile domestic parliaments everywhere have generally had a disappointing record in attending to the global and regional aspects of problems. Moreover, nation-states tend to cater inadequately to the nonterritorial peoples whose interests might be implicated in summit outcomes. Thus traditional state sovereignty is by itself not sufficient to secure participation and accountability for all affected publics in summitry—and polycentric governance more generally.

Multilateralism

A second perspective, multilateralism, is more sanguine about the possibilities of democracy beyond the country-nation-state. Theorists such as Andrew Moravcsik maintain that people's power can be secured in relation to summits (and polycentric regulation more broadly) through collaboration among democratic nation-states.[10] On the multilateralist formula, the way to democracy in contemporary politics is a universalization of modern liberal democracy at the country level. These democratic states can then together exercise "joint," "pooled," or "shared" sovereignty in regional and global governance institutions.

For multilateralists, summits can be democratic to the extent that the participating states have secure liberal-democratic regimes. On this view, summits in Latin America could become more democratic since the 1990s, as more states in the region have shifted from military rule. In contrast, summits of the Concert of Europe in the nineteenth century and the League of Arab States in the twentieth century would in multilateralist theory be democratically weak, inasmuch as the participating states were democratically weak.

In principle, a summit among liberal states would have greater democratic possibilities than a summit among authoritarian states. However, it is another thing to suggest that joint action by liberal-democratic states is by itself sufficient to secure adequate participation and control for all people who are impacted by the summit. For one thing, large political distance separates leaders at a summit meeting from affected constituents on the ground. In addition, summits can impact on many people whose elected state leaders are absent from the meeting: for example, some decisions of the G20 can significantly affect all of humanity. Moreover, various critical theories suggest that liberal states have inherent democratic limitations: e.g. in relation to gender hierarchies (according to feminists), the power of capital (according to Marxists), or disciplining surveillance (according to poststructuralists). Thus a more encompassing and deeper democracy in summitry requires more than liberal-democratic states.

Cosmopolitan federalism

A third approach, cosmopolitan federalism, offers one alternative to state-based democracy. This model suggests that fuller people's power in contemporary governance can be realized by replicating modern liberal-democratic institutions at regional and global levels. In other words, democracy in polycentric regimes would be achieved with the enactment of suprastate human rights, suprastate citizenship, suprastate civil society, and suprastate representative bodies populated by suprastate political parties.[11] In this vein cosmopolitan federalists embrace the development of United Nations human rights machinery, the growth of civil society engagement of suprastate governance agencies, and initiatives to build regional and global parliamentary assemblies.

Certain recent developments in respect of summits broadly conform to cosmopolitan-federalist designs. For example, the European Union has formalized a regional human rights apparatus, a regional citizenship, and a directly elected regional assembly with regional political parties. Indeed, the European Parliament provides a permanently institutionalized check on the summitry of the European Council. In the Americas similar democratizing functions could be nurtured by the Central American Parliament (Parlacen) vis-à-vis SICA summits, by the Mercosur Parliament (Parlasur) in relation to that regional grouping's leader conferences, and by a future South American Parliament with respect to UNASUR summits. The Latin American Parliament (Parlatino) has similar potentials, although this assembly has not engaged concertedly with summit processes.

Cosmopolitan federalism has the distinct merit of exploring new institutions of democracy, outside the inherited country-nation-state frame. However, this approach also has practical and philosophical shortfalls. Practically, it has proven very difficult to advance regional and (even more so) global institutionalizations of liberal democracy. Moreover, on those few occasions when some progress has been achieved, suprastate human rights and suprastate parliaments have usually provided only shallow if any democratic checks on summits. Philosophically, liberal democracy at regional and global levels faces the same principled objections from critical theorists as confront liberal democracy at a national level. Moreover, Western-modern constructions of cosmopolitan federalism arguably find limited cultural resonance in various non-Western contexts across the world. Tellingly, many decades of advocacy for "world government" have failed to capture a large public imagination.

Stakeholderism

Recognition of the inadequacy of state-based democracy and the current impracticability of cosmopolitan federalism has encouraged the emergence of a fourth approach, stakeholder democracy. This model promotes an alternative to electoral politics as the way to achieve democratic representation beyond the country-nation-state.[12] In so-called "multistakeholder initiatives," policymaking bodies in polycentric governance include positions not only for states, but also for sectors such as business, labor, consumers, and other groups that "hold a stake" in the issue area concerned. Concrete examples of multistakeholder agencies include the International Labour Organization (ILO) and the Global Fund to Fight AIDS, Tuberculosis and Malaria

(GFATM). Stakeholder democracy can also be enacted through external consultations by regulatory institutions of civil society associations which represent various affected groups.[13]

Summits have not become multistakeholder forums in the sense that representatives of various nonstate constituencies take formal seats at the decision-taking table. However, it has become quite common for government leaders to consult with business, labor, and other interest groups at some point in a summit process. In the case of Mercosur, such discussions are permanently institutionalized through an Economic-Social Consultative Forum, which sends a report and an emissary to each Mercosur summit. Similar inputs to assembled government leaders can come from the Consultative Committee of SICA. More ad hoc civil society consultation has occurred around CARICOM Heads of Government Conferences, Summits of the Americas, and UNASUR Summits.[14] Stakeholder consultations are now also regularly observed around summits outside the Americas: for example, in respect of Asia-Europe Meetings, Association of Southeast Asian Nations (ASEAN) Summits, Commonwealth Heads of Government Meetings, the European Union (EU) Council, and G8 Summits.[15]

Stakeholder democracy brings some decided advantages for people's power in respect of summits and overall polycentric governance. Unlike the previous three approaches, stakeholderism proposes more direct access for citizens to interstate, trans-state, and nonstate regulation, thereby bringing affected people into closer contact with post-Westphalian policy processes. Moreover, stakeholderism does not privilege national identities, allowing affected people also to organize themselves in terms of age, class, gender, or whatever other grouping they should deem relevant for their political participation. Likewise, stakeholder communities need not be defined by territorial boundaries, which opens greater possibilities for trans-scalar solidarities and strategies.

However, stakeholderism is no panacea for democracy in polycentric governance. To date relatively few regulatory bodies (and no leader summit meetings at all) have incorporated stakeholder representatives as full voting members of their committees and executive boards. Some summits have lacked any exchanges with civil society organizations. Moreover, many of the "consultations" that do occur are irregular and superficial, with little if any significance for the substance of policy. Indeed, officials can readily marginalize or exclude more troublesome critical voices from informal stakeholder dialogues. In addition, stakeholder representation around summits has tended to be biased in favor of better-resourced and more powerful circles of society: namely those who can afford air travel, speak English, etc. In such circumstances so-called "stakeholder democracy" can easily become a mechanism of elite privilege which confirms hegemonic power.

Deliberation

A fifth avenue of people's power, deliberative democracy, seeks to sustain larger, more diverse and more critical policy debates of a kind that can be lost in the context of formally institutionalized stakeholder involvement. Deliberative approaches are concerned less with interest representation and more with the quality of public discussion. This conception suggests that people's power is furthered in relation to summits and overall polycentric governance when policy decisions are informed by open, inclusive, rational debate among implicated citizens.[16] Deliberative democracy is especially distinguished from the four preceding perspectives by the explicit priority placed on encompassing diverse positions, respecting dissent, prizing argumentation above interest lobbying, and (in principle at least) making space for people who are marginalized in formal political processes.

Deliberative democracy has figured in contemporary summitry through popular gatherings that assemble alongside the official meetings. Regional examples include the ASEAN Civil Society Conference/ ASEAN People's Forum and the Asia-Europe People's Forum. Globally, civil society forums have convened alongside G8 Summits, Ministerial Conferences of the World Trade Organization, and various top-level meetings under United Nations auspices. In addition, summits can figure among the topics discussed at deliberative venues such as the World Social Forum and Occupy which do not convene in relation to a specific governance event. Further public deliberation about summits can be pursued through academic conferences, press outlets, religious gatherings, new social media, and other ad hoc exchanges.

Deliberative exercises can certainly enhance contemporary democracy by raising public awareness of summits and polycentric governance more widely. In addition, deliberative processes can help to articulate views and proposals from various affected circles, including voices that generally find less hearing in political parties and stakeholder mechanisms. Moreover, participation in political debate can in itself be an empowering experience for the people involved.

That said, deliberation can in practice involve class, gender, race, and other hierarchies that skew voice in favor of the strong: not everyone has equal access to the more influential deliberative arenas. In addition, deliberation may have limited democratizing impact on actual policy if discussion is not linked with political mobilization. However open, creative, and inclusive a debate might be, it does little to advance public accountability if the voices are not brought to bear on sites of governance power. Deliberation without strategic action yields limited substantive democracy.

Resistance

In contrast, political mobilization lies very much at the heart of a sixth approach that might be applied to the democratization of summits, namely, counter-hegemonic resistance. Drawing upon ideas of agonistic politics,[17] this perspective maintains that deeper democracy only occurs when grassroots social movements struggle to subvert prevailing structures of domination. For these critical theorists, any established order is marked by oppression, and the heart of democracy lies in continual uncompromising resistance to whatever arbitrary power rules the day.

Different variants of resistance politics conceive of hegemony differently. For example, feminists stress that undemocratic arbitrary power lies primarily in gender hierarchies. Historical materialists instead put foremost focus on capitalist exploitation. Eco-centrists highlight modernity's repression of "nature" as the deepest hegemony of contemporary society. Poststructuralists emphasize the hegemonic power of disciplining discourses such as present-day neoliberalism. Religious revivalists target hegemonic secularist silencing of the divine. Whatever the diagnosis of the character of hegemony, however, these various critical approaches all agree that the main way to public participation and control lies in grassroots mobilization against structural oppression.

Counter-hegemonic resistance has acquired high visibility in large street demonstrations around certain summits. Indeed, already in the nineteenth century the revolutions of 1848 considerably undermined the elite-centered Concert of Europe process. In contemporary history considerable mass protests have gathered around various G8 and G20 summits, as well as ministerial meetings of major global economic institutions. Regionally, large street mobilizations have unsettled EU summits in 1997 and 2001, Summits of the Americas in 2001 and 2005, and the ASEAN Summit in 2009.

Democratization of summitry through resistance can also occur through other actions besides street demonstrations. Counter-hegemonic alternatives to prevailing forms of globalization and regionalization can be promoted *inter alia* through subversive writings, consumer activism, teach-ins, occupations, radical artistic performances, humor, and private conversations. In this way much resistance to summitry can happen off radar.

Counter-hegemonic activism offers notable potential for greater people's power in contemporary governance. Street protests have arguably done more than any other form of action to draw public attention to the dubious democratic credentials of much contemporary summitry. In addition, subversive action has generally put a more insistent spotlight on structural inequalities than mainstream political channels. The inbuilt critical posture of resistance has likewise challenged the authoritarian power of "common sense" discourses which readily suppress democratically supported alternative visions to, say, capitalism or ecological anthropocentrism.

However, like the other prescriptions for a democratization of summits covered here, resistance also has important shortcomings. For example, some counter-hegemonic initiatives around summits have mainly opposed the status quo, without proposing clear and convincing alternatives and how they could be realized. Moreover, direct actions against neoliberal policies have tended in practice disproportionately to involve disaffected elements in the global North and elite classes, rather than the more deeply subordinated circles in contemporary society.[18] This sociological profile of protests can raise questions about democratic participation and accountability in the resistance itself.

In sum, then, the six-fold typology above covers a wide range of notions of people's power vis-à-vis contemporary governance. The categorization presented here is obviously a simplification, since in practice many concrete initiatives straddle and blend several of the six approaches. One point emerges very clearly, however, which is that people's power in a trans-scalar-intersectional-polycentric society cannot be achieved solely or even principally through the country-nation-state. As the conclusion that follows suggests, the way forward in democratizing summits may lie in combining possibilities from these various perspectives.

Conclusion

This chapter has situated summitry within (a particular understanding of) contemporary governance as a whole. In this perspective the rise of summitry over the past half-century has not "just happened," but has been intertwined with certain transformations in underlying structures of geography, identity, and regulation. Three parallel macro shifts—namely, from country-centered to trans-scalar social space, from nation-centered to intersectional affinities, and from state-centered to polycentric governance—have together generated qualitatively more complex and messy politics. The growth of summitry in the context of these changes can be interpreted as an attempt (largely unsuccessful) to reintroduce a kind of sovereignty—a point of final say and direction—into the policy muddles of postmodern society.

The chapter has more specifically explored the implications of summitry for democracy. Most analysts have tended to evaluate regional and global leader conferences principally in terms of their effectiveness at policy problem solving; however, it is important also to assess summit politics from the angle of democratic legitimacy. Yet summit processes tend currently to be quite deficient when it comes to involvement by and accountability to affected publics. To this extent regional and global leader conferences can exacerbate the considerable democratic deficits of polycentric governance. The concluding issue for this chapter is then what could be done to raise the democratic qualities of summitry.

Several of the perspectives covered earlier may have something to contribute in this regard. For one thing greater democratization of summits could be pursued at least partly through old-style modern-liberal formulas. Electorates, political parties, and parliaments in the participating countries could increase and sharpen their attention to the formulation, implementation, and review of summit decisions. In addition, democratization of summits could be nurtured through increased and upgraded stakeholder inputs. However, stakeholderism would need to attract more than lip service, and concerted care would be needed to involve all affected people, and not just elite "civil society." Deliberation could play into a democracy-enhancement package for summits as well, with more discussion of leader conferences in civil society forums, mass media, and other public spaces. As with stakeholder inputs, though, it is vital that deliberative exercises offer equivalent opportunities of participation for all relevant circles, rather than falling into familiar hierarchies of class, gender, race, etc. Indeed, opening summits to the full range of affected publics probably also requires large-scale, sustained, and effectively executed resistance, in which subaltern forces in particular play a leading role.

The precise combination of propositions for a democratization of summitry will largely reflect the politics of the proposer. Thus observers with less ambitious visions may give greater weight to communitarian and multilateralist mechanisms. In contrast, subaltern circles who identify existing governance arrangements as prime sources of their oppression may give greater weight to deliberation and resistance. Thus the nature and expression of democracy vis-à-vis summits will itself remain a subject of ongoing politics.

Notes

1 The integrity of the present analysis requires that a strict distinction of vocabulary be maintained between "country" to refer to a geographical entity, "nation" to refer to a cultural construction, and "state" to refer to a governance apparatus.
2 Jan Aart Scholte, *Globalization: A Critical Introduction* (Basingstoke: Palgrave, 2005), 187.
3 Wolfgang Reinicke, *Global Public Policy: Governing without Government?* (Washington, DC: Brookings Institution Press, 1998); Jörg Friedrichs, "The Meaning of New Medievalism," *European Journal of International Relations* 7, no. 4 (2000): 475–502; James N. Rosenau, *Distant Proximities: Dynamics beyond Globalization* (Princeton, N.J.: Princeton University Press, 2003); Edgar Grande and Louis W. Pauly, eds, *Complex Sovereignty: Reconstituting Political Authority in the Twenty-First Century* (Toronto: University of Toronto Press, 2005); and Bob Jessop, "From Governance via Governance Failure and from Multilevel Governance to Multi-Scalar Meta-Governance," in *The Disoriented State: Shifts in Governmentality, Territoriality and Governance*, ed. Bas Arts, Arnoud Lagendijk, and Henk J. van Houtum (Heidelberg: Springer, 2009), 79–98.
4 Jan Aart Scholte, "Reinventing Global Democracy," *European Journal of International Relations* 20, no. 1 (2014): 3–28.
5 Chapter 4 in this volume.
6 Chapter 7 in this volume.
7 Chapter 5 in this volume.
8 David Miller, *On Nationality* (Oxford: Oxford University Press, 1995).
9 Walden Bello, *Deglobalization: Ideas for a New World Economy* (London: Zed, 2004).
10 Andrew Moravcsik, "Is There a 'Democratic Deficit' in World Politics? A Framework for Analysis," *Government and Opposition* 39, no. 2 (2004): 336–363.
11 Torbjörn Tännsjö, *Global Democracy: The Case for a World Government* (Edinburgh: Edinburgh University Press, 2008).
12 Terry Macdonald, *Global Stakeholder Democracy: Power and Representation beyond Liberal States* (Oxford: Oxford University Press, 2008).
13 Jonas Tallberg, Thomas Sommerer, Theresa Squatrito, and Christer Jönsson, *The Opening Up of International Organizations: Transnational Access in Global Governance* (Cambridge: Cambridge University Press, 2013).
14 Chapters 3–5 in this volume.
15 Jan Aart Scholte, ed., *Building Global Democracy? Civil Society and Accountable Global Governance* (Cambridge: Cambridge University Press, 2011); and Chapter 9 in this volume.
16 John S. Dryzek, *Foundations and Frontiers of Deliberative Governance* (Oxford: Oxford University Press, 2010).
17 Chantal Mouffe, *On the Political* (London: Routledge, 2005).
18 Isabelle Sommier, *Le renouveau des mouvements contestataires à l'heure de la mondialisation* (Paris: Flammarion, Champs, 2003).

2 Multilayered summitry and agenda interaction in South America

Olivier Dabène

- Types of interaction among agendas
- Empirical evidence (South America, 2000–13)
- Explaining agenda interactions
- Conclusion

Around the globe, the anarchic development of multilateralism has resulted in a growing number of regime complexes[1] and institutional overlaps.[2] However, the effects of this development are not entirely negative. A special issue of *Global Governance*,[3] edited by Amandine Orsini, Jean-Frédéric Morin, and Oran Young, reviews various instances in areas such as piracy, taxation, energy, food security, emissions reduction, carbon sinks, biosafety, and refugee governance, where regime complexes tend to create both barriers and opportunities at the same time. According to the editors, institutional interplay can "generate conflicts ... but can also lead to mutual adjustments and even generate collaboration that is beneficial to all institutions involved."[4] Similarly, it has been shown that forum shopping can offer certain advantages, for example in the realm of environmental governance.[5]

Although a significant body of scholarship exists in the field of international relations, relatively little attention has been paid to the proliferation of summit meetings that tends to accompany the development of regime complexes. Common sense suggests that regional governance would grow more complicated as summit meetings proliferate, with interdependence becoming more difficult to manage,[6] but can this increase in summitry also have positive outcomes?

The presence of nested groupings and multi-layered summitry in South America makes it an ideal region to study for an analysis of regional governance. In recent years, the Americas have experienced a fourth wave of regionalism in a context of crises and political swings.[7] Beginning with the 2000 South American summit, an unusually high number of ordinary summits have been held in order to create and consolidate new regional arrangements. A multitude of extraordinary summit meetings were also called to address regional crises. Each new summit has overlapped with the meetings of pre-existing, older regional groups. The same countries tend to gather at ever more numerous summits, hence the possibility of seeing the same issues addressed in separate arenas, with the attendant risk of yielding contradictory norms. It is likely, therefore, that the Union of South American Nations (UNASUR),[8] which overlaps with older existing sub-groups such as the Southern Common Market (Mercosur)[9] and the Andean Community (CAN),[10] will influence South American governance.

The aim of the present study is to assess such influence, proposing a preliminary exploration of the agenda-setting function of summit meetings.[11] A summit represents a moment and space in which certain issues are given prominence and an agenda is established. My analysis focuses on the ways in which multilayered summitry can generate interactions among agendas that potentially involve duplications or redundancies.

Do the different South American summits interact with or adapt to each other? This study's findings indicate that there are different types of interactions, but, counterintuitively, there are few clear-cut indications of agenda overlap. To understand better the surprisingly scarce evidence of overlap, I have combined two analytical approaches: international relations (IR) and linkage politics. The conclusion arrived at is rather optimistic: South America's regional governance is not as incoherent as might be expected, given the prevailing spaghetti-bowl type of regionalism. The presidents of the various member states have been keen to avoid duplication, although there are variations among topics.

Section one of this chapter offers a typology of interactions among agendas, while section two presents empirical evidence from South America. Section three explains variations in interactions among agendas, and the final section offers concluding remarks and suggestions for further research.

Types of interaction among agendas

This chapter considers nested groupings and explores interactions between a new regional integration process (NRIP) and existing subgroups (ESG). During an NRIP summit, the agenda that is set can either overlap with the agendas of ESGs or not. In both situations there can be several different types of interaction.

If the agendas do not overlap, the reason could be that the NRIP has placed on its agenda a new topic, one never tackled at a previous

ESG summit and which therefore would represent an innovation. Another reason could be that an NRIP summit has taken into account the norms adopted by previous ESG summits. Thus, the NRIP may simply rely on the outcomes of a specific ESG policy and suggest expanding that policy's field of application to a wider group of countries. I call this strategy subsidiarity.[12]

In the event the agendas do overlap, different kinds of interaction are also possible. A simple interaction in the form of duplication occurs when the NRIP includes in its agenda a topic (or part of a topic) that has already been dealt with by an ESG. The degree of duplication can vary. In some instances, the NRIP may duplicate an issue that has not been properly addressed in an ESG, as when the ESG agencies concerned have not been active; this interaction is known as "soft duplication." For example, the UNASUR council on energy appears to overlap with the Mercosur working group on energy, but because the Mercosur group has not met regularly in recent years, UNASUR has enjoyed greater latitude. By contrast, "hard duplication" refers to situations where existing organs in an ESG have actively addressed a given issue. The UNASUR council on social development, for instance, clearly overlaps with the Mercosur ministerial meeting on social development, which has been highly active over the years. The agency of institutions is crucial to distinguishing between different types of duplication.

On occasion, ESGs are encouraged to re-examine their norms and policies and merge those that overlap, an interaction I describe as aggregation. Last, the NRIP can offer to take action and add value to existing norms and policies, a strategy that one can identify as synergy.

The different interaction types are shown in Table 2.1, and a range of examples will be examined later in the chapter. It is important to note that these types of agenda interactions are not fixed. Because of multiple variables, strategies can change during a summit, so that the differences among them may become blurred. The boundary between aggregation and subsidiarity, for instance, can easily be crossed. By the same token, the added value generated by a synergy strategy may be such that it can be considered an innovation.

In the next section, I further explore these categories as they have evolved in response to historical and political realities.

Empirical evidence (South America, 2000–13)

The fourth wave of regionalism has generated multilayered summitry. Indeed, between 2000 and 2013, South American presidents have had

Table 2.1 Existing sub-groups (ESG) embedded in a new regional integration process (NRIP): Types of agenda interaction

No overlap	Innovation	Different agendas (NRIP $\neq$ ESG)
	Subsidiarity	NRIP's agenda as a subset of ESG's agendas (NRIP $\subset$ ESG)
Overlap	Duplication	Same or more or less the same agendas (NRIP = or $\simeq$ ESG)
	"Hard" or "soft"	Depending on ESG institutions' agency
	Aggregation	NRIP's agenda as the sum of ESG's agendas (NRIP = $\sum$ ESG)
	Synergy	NRIP adding value to the sum of ESG's agendas (NRIP = $\sum$ ESG + added value)

138 occasions to meet in 11 different kinds of summits,[13] including meetings involving one or more of the following: the United States, Arab countries, African states, Europe, Central America, and the Caribbean. As far as South American regionalism alone is concerned, the summits came in various forms during the 2000s, from the earliest South American (SA) Summit (2000–04), to the Community of South American Nations (CSN) (2005–07), to the Union of South American Nations (UNASUR) (as of 2008). For our present purposes, I will refer to this entire sequence as SA-CSN-UNASUR summits.

This section will focus primarily on South American ordinary summits (n=12), which I view as agenda-setting summits. In addition, I will look at three other summits types: South American extraordinary summits (n=12), CAN (n=12), and Mercosur (n=39) ordinary and extraordinary summits. The database used for the study consists of the final declarations of all the Mercosur, CAN, and SA-CSN-UNASUR summits. The discussion will center on three empirical questions: (1) Does SA-CSN-UNASUR take Mercosur and CAN into account? (2) Given that UNASUR's extraordinary summits are often crisis-solving efforts, does the issue addressed affect the agenda and, if so, how? (3) Regarding CAN and Mercosur, is it possible that member states decide to adjust to the ESG rather than to the NRIP?

Does SA-CSN-UNASUR take Mercosur and CAN into account?

During the first South American summit (SA1)[14] in 2000, the member state presidents clearly wanted to coordinate (*articular*) South America by building on the existing sub-regional blocs, and thereby help to strengthen the Latin American and Caribbean region. They confirmed this goal at the SA3 in 2004, stating that they wanted to avoid duplications and additional costs. Coordination (*articulación*) and convergence were the magic words, but there was little detail as to how to proceed. CSN1, held in September 2005, was no more specific regarding the pursuit of coordination and convergence efforts; it merely mentioned that the dual association of Mercosur and CAN members would help to build the South American union.

The presidents essentially had three methodologies in mind with regard to their agenda: synergy, innovation, and subsidiarity. Synergy was applied to a wide range of issues. SA-CSN-UNASUR adopted some measures already enforced within Mercosur and CAN with the intention of adding some value. SA1's final declaration, for instance, made democratic stability a condition for attendance at subsequent South American summits, and this came in addition to existing clauses on democracy in CAN and Mercosur, thus strengthening the overall defense of democracy in the region. On the subject of trade, SA1 offered to build on a future CAN-Mercosur agreement in order to add value. A South American Free Trade Agreement (SAFTA) would result from Chile, Guyana, and Suriname joining CAN-Mercosur negotiations.

During SA2, the presidents addressed two new issues using the same synergy method. They adopted a declaration on South America as a zone of peace. Mercosur had made a similar declaration in 1999, and CAN would also issue several declarations on the matter. In 2004, in order to "deepen" the South American initiative, CAN formally adopted a declaration on the Andean peace zone. Moreover, following earlier initiatives taken within the framework of the Regional Conference on migrations, first convened in 1996, SA2 adopted a plan concerning international migration. Furthermore, Mercosur and CAN also extensively addressed this topic.

In 2005, CSN1 listed a range of sectoral policies, based on existing Mercosur and CAN mechanisms, for which they envisioned collaboration. During the same 2005 summit, the presidents approved a declaration on the convergence of South American integration processes, and an extraordinary summit organized a few months later created a "Strategic commission to reflect on South American regional integration," whose mission was to design a "new model of integration."[15] This new model, endorsed by the presidents during CSN2, clearly entailed a convergence of agendas.

Second, SA1 publicly discussed issues that constituted genuine innovations, infrastructure being the most important. The Initiative for the Integration of the Regional Infrastructure in South America (IIRSA) has been widely praised as an important step towards regional integration in the realm of communication, energy, and transport.[16] Drug control was another subject addressed by the presidents, who decided to develop a strategy to reduce supply, combat money laundering, and implement arms control. Their plan was not to pool resources but rather to harmonize their efforts in this area.

Third, on some issues the South American presidents relied on existing Mercosur and CAN norms and invited both groups to examine the feasibility of extending them to the entire region. Here, the method used by SA-CSN-UNASUR was subsidiarity: no further action was deemed necessary. During CSN1, for instance, the final declaration invited all member countries to take up Mercosur's strategy to eliminate aphthous fever.

Since the signing of the UNASUR treaty in 2008, South American summits have no longer referred to a strategy of articulation or convergence. The 2008 treaty did not mention Mercosur or CAN. However, in 2012, during UNASUR6, the theme resurfaced with Decision 6 on "Guidelines for relations with third parties" (*Lineamientos políticos de UNASUR para las relaciones con terceros*). The presidents reiterated that "coordination and convergence with other regional integration processes will be based on complementarity and cooperation, and will try to avoid duplication, adding values to pre-existing policies and agreements." Article 4.7 added: "UNASUR will identify opportunities for collaboration with extra-regional integration processes, while preserving the principles of the Union."[17]

As to the question of how to meet these objectives, UNASUR6 provided no additional details, but during the same summit, the presidents launched an initiative called "Toward a network of South American cities" that appeared not to take MERCOCIUDADES[18] into account. This blatant example of duplication indicates that, despite the rhetoric to the contrary, UNASUR was no longer trying to build on existing dynamics but, instead, was working independently. In fact, the issue of convergence was not mentioned even once during UNASUR7.

Since 2008, UNASUR institutions have grown rapidly, but the resultant changes to the agenda are not necessarily discussed during summit meetings. It is beyond the scope of this study to assess those changes, but it is worth noting that a total of 12 councils were created and the General Secretariat gradually asserted its agency, albeit with a certain unevenness. Spillover effects and unplanned agenda overlaps with ESG are possible in the future.[19] Agenda interactions between UNASUR and Mercosur-CAN are summarized in Table 2.2.

Table 2.2 SA-CSN-UNASUR strategy regarding Mercosur and CAN agendas, 2000–13

Period	Agenda interaction	Issue areas
2000–08	Synergy	Democracy, trade, peace, migrations
	Innovations	Infrastructure, drug control, energy
	Subsidiarity	Sanitary
2008–13	Subsidiarity	Trade
	Possible hard and soft duplications	Cities, other sectoral policies

Does Mercosur react or adjust to SA-CSN-UNASUR?

No issue area more effectively epitomizes the ambiguity of agenda interaction associated with multilayered summitry in South America than the issue of trade. Brazil has pushed for a South American Free Trade Agreement ever since the United States first proposed the Free Trade Area of the Americas (FTAA) in 1994. At the same time, Brazil developed Mercosur with the participation of Argentina, Paraguay, and Uruguay. On 16 April 1998, CAN and Mercosur members signed a framework agreement for the creation of SAFTA. Two rounds of negotiations followed, one involving tariff preferences, the other focusing on a free trade area (FTA). Discussions of tariff preferences were split into two separate negotiations; the first involved Brazil/CAN, and the second, the other member states of Mercosur/CAN. Brazil signed a "complementary economic agreement" (known in Spanish as ACE 39) with CAN in 1999, and a year later the remaining countries signed ACE 48. A framework agreement for the FTA was reached in 2002 (ACE 56), followed by a full agreement in 2004 (ACE 59). As a Mercosur associate member, Bolivia already had an agreement, and Peru signed separately in 2005 (ACE 58).

During this intense sequence of trade-related events, no mention of the nascent South American dynamics was made in the final declarations of Mercosur summits, except in February 2002, at a Mercosur extraordinary meeting held six months prior to SA2. The meeting focused on infrastructure, the flagship initiative of SA1. The first reference to SA appeared in 2004. The final declaration of Mercosur27, held nine days after SA3, stated that SAFTA would contribute to CSN. During subsequent summits, Mercosur endorsed and supported South American summits but its endorsement and support were for the most part discursive. This second sequence lasted until 2008, when the UNASUR treaty was signed.

The 2008 UNASUR treaty referred to the necessary convergence of sub-regional processes. Mercosur did not sidestep this issue in its final declaration. It reiterated its wish to collaborate in a "gradual coordination, complementation, and convergence" of all institutions and forums. In 2012 it made a decision (CMC 24/12) that required it to work on coordinating its policies in order to "optimize resources, avoid task overlaps, and strengthen the efforts deployed in the different integration schemes." In order to facilitate the convergence, Mercosur members all became CAN associate members in 2005. Mercosur later included every other South American country as associate members, including Guyana and Suriname.[20]

When Mercosur's declarations have referred to the agenda, they have tended to focus on infrastructure, energy, finance, and democracy. Infrastructure was addressed from the very beginning, in 2000, under the influence of Brazil and the Inter-American Development Bank. Energy and finance were introduced by Venezuela. Once it became a full member of Mercosur, Venezuela managed to persuade the other member states to give these issues a prominent position on the agenda. Following the Ecuadorian crisis in 2010, Mercosur40 acknowledged the UNASUR democratic clause.

Mercosur's declarations also applauded the growing capacity of UNASUR to steer its way through crises, expressing Mercosur's apparent eagerness to delegate this responsibility. Since its inception, UNASUR has been forced to confront two important crises: the threat of civil war in Bolivia in 2008, and Colombia's entrance into a defense agreement with the United States in 2009. In both cases, UNASUR successfully managed to cool tensions among its members.

In sum, Mercosur's response to South American summits has been varied. On a general, "systemic" level, Mercosur has supported the creation and institutionalization of CSN/UNASUR and has proven favorable to collaboration. Once UNASUR was firmly established, Mercosur endorsed the convergence process, although jump-starting the process took little initiative beyond the matter of risk prevention, for which Mercosur launched a coordination between existing regional agencies.

Concerning the issue-areas on the UNASUR agenda, Mercosur seemed to contemplate a division of labor. Issues fell into several categories. (1) Trade: Mercosur was able to conclude and sign an agreement with CAN. Mercosur did not react when SA/CSN/UNASUR's synergy strategy failed. Nor did it appear to be affected by the development of the Pacific Alliance. (2) Infrastructure: Mercosur welcomed IIRSA and considered it an enhancement with respect to its own policy (Mercosur's Structural Convergence Fund, or FOCEM)[21]. However,

Mercosur never mentioned coordination between IIRSA and FOCEM. (3) Democracy: Mercosur praised UNASUR's democratic clause and viewed it as a reinforcement of its own clause. (4) Energy and finance: Mercosur considered UNASUR's initiatives (Petrosur, Bancosur) to be valuable innovations. (5) Drugs, social development, and health: Mercosur has been silent on these issues, the implication being that there could be gray zones subject to overlap.

Table 2.3 summarizes the different findings. Except for the issue areas referred to above, Mercosur has been instrumental in developing a convergence process in the region.

Table 2.3 Mercosur strategy regarding the SA-CSN-UNASUR agenda

Issue area on SA-CSN-UNASUR agenda	Mercosur's reaction	Agenda interaction
Trade	Agreement with CAN as a contribution to the dynamics of convergence	Aggregation
Infrastructure (IIRSA)	Considers it an enhancement	Synergy
Finance (Bancosur)	Considers it an innovation	Innovation
Energy (Petrosur)	Considers it an innovation	Innovation
Defense	Considers it an enhancement	Synergy
Democracy	Considers it an enhancement	Synergy
Drugs, social development, health	No reaction	Possible hard and soft duplications

Does CAN react/adjust to SA-CSN-UNASUR?

CAN summits are far less frequent than those of Mercosur, a fact that clearly indicates a profound crisis. Between 2000 and 2013, CAN members met only 12 times, whereas Mercosur met 39 times during the same period. CAN held only one ordinary summit and one extraordinary meeting, in 2011, after UNASUR was created in 2008. As a consequence, CAN's responses to SA-CSN-UNASUR have been far from prolific. Still, CAN has shown greater interest in the SA agenda than in Mercosur's, particularly with regard to infrastructure. Understandably, CAN is in a position to benefit from IIRSA. During its first summit after SA1, CAN13 welcomed this new initiative and announced its intention to collaborate and to focus on trade.

The next summit did not take place until two years later. CAN members showed support for IIRSA. During the 2004–07 period, CAN verbally endorsed SA3 and the convergence process involving CAN, Mercosur, and Chile. In 2011, CAN emphatically called for a greater convergence of the "three processes": CAN, Mercosur, and UNASUR. At the 2011 extraordinary summit, the Andean presidents decided to reactivate the integration process on the basis of a Colombian proposition to downscale its institutional framework (*reingeniería*). It remains to be seen whether this institutional restructuring will take UNASUR into account. With reference to its agenda, CAN appears willing to focus on trade, infrastructure, citizenship, and culture. At the same time, trade and infrastructure are areas where the agendas of CAN and UNASUR councils clearly overlap.

In this section we have demonstrated that South American presidents have manifested their willingness to avoid duplication during summits, an objective they have met with a reasonable degree of success. In fact, the occasional instances of agenda overlap have come in the shape of synergy, and the resulting added value can be seen as a form of innovation. This finding is dealt with in greater detail in the next section.

Explaining agenda interactions

This section proposes two complementary explanations for the apparent absence of overlaps between the various agendas existing in the region. The first approach is based on a classical "international relations" explanation that assumes that state actors defend their interests and ideas during summits. The second can be described as "linkage politics"[22] because it emphasizes the impact of domestic politics on coalition formation and agenda setting during summits.[23] Because it is less commonly applied in studies of summits, I will emphasize the second approach.

Interests and ideas

Trade is the most significant issue area addressed during the SA-CSN-UNASUR summits. The presidents pursued a strategy of synergy concerning Mercosur and CAN. Some analysts have characterized UNASUR as a "post-trade" agreement,[24] suggesting this new orientation was due to the leadership of Brazil and its challenger, Venezuela.[25] The impact of the context has also been investigated.[26] In addition, basic statistics on the attendance of the region's presidents at the various summits provide further insight into the evolution of the way trade issues were addressed during the summits.[27]

Figure 2.1 shows a sharp decline in the pro-free trade[28] group of presidents, which has not represented a majority since 2005–06, compared with the group promoting the leftist "new model of integration." The decline is not surprising, given the "left turn" that South American politics has seen and the leftist conception of regional integration that has prevailed ever since.[29] Note that because of low attendance, the 30 November 2012 UNASUR summit represented an exception.

As mentioned earlier, SAFTA was conceived to produce synergy between existing agreements (Mercosur and CAN). However, trade was no longer on the summit agendas after 2005, which was about the moment when the free traders lost the majority. Since then, final declarations have made no reference to SAFTA.

However, from 2004, free-trade supporters had launched an alternative plan: bilateral negotiations involving the United States and Ecuador, Colombia, and Peru, which got underway a few months after the United States–Chile FTA came into effect.[30] In addition, the Pacific Alliance offers interesting prospects for Chile, Peru, Colombia, and Mexico, as it provides new perspectives to expand trade relations with Asia. Thus, having lost their majority, free-traders entered into an alternative coalition and no longer fought to have trade included in the UNASUR agenda. As for UNASUR, after 2008 it adopted a new course of action that ignored Mercosur and CAN. As a result, discussions on trade moved to other arenas, such as the Pacific Alliance.

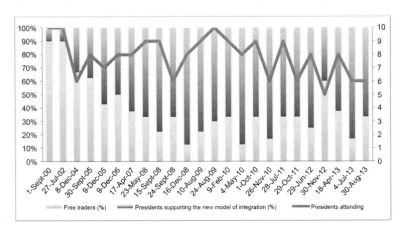

Figure 2.1 SA-CSN-UNASUR summits: Participation and model of integration, 2000–13
(Author's summitry database, based on information collected from official websites and media.)

In addition to trade-related initiatives, there have been notable innovations and synergies stemming primarily from a paradigm shift driven by a renewal in regional leadership. At CSN1, which took place in September 2005, the South American heads of state identified a wide array of issue areas. Then, in December of the same year, an extraordinary CSN summit commissioned a strategic study that would be delivered and examined a year later, at CSN2. The resulting "New Model of South America's Regional Integration" discarded the notion that trade was the sole objective of integration and proposed instead a broader range of cultural, social, and political cooperation issues. This policy shift received solid support from several newly elected left-leaning presidents, who had become a majority within the group. The issue areas specified by the group did not overlap with those on the CAN or Mercosur agendas; its strategy was to innovate or suggest synergies within existing norms. At UNASUR1 in April 2007, for instance, Venezuela introduced the energy issue. The "new model" shaped the agenda of UNASUR after its treaty was signed in 2008.

The instances of agenda interaction examined thus far have resulted from strategies. IR analyses that refer to different types of leadership[31] can shed light on the way in which actors behave rationally in order to assert influence or defend particular interests or ideas. An NRIP agenda can be shaped or influenced by advocacy groups, epistemic communities, or recently elected presidents with fresh ideas displaying idea-based leadership at the summits.[32]

However, unintended agenda interactions are also possible. Political instability at the regional level due to frequent political turnovers in member states can lead to improvisation on the part of new presidents having incomplete knowledge of the achievements of previous summits. On the other hand, political stability allows presidents to acquire experience and become progressively socialized into their roles; summits are thus protected from unexpected outcomes.[33] Unintended agenda interactions can also be caused by unforeseen domestic or international political events requiring urgent collective action and inevitably affecting the agenda-setting process. The next section looks more closely at these possible impacts of political instability and crises.

Domestic politics and summitry

This section's aim is to trace political shifts, and to that end the database employed here distinguishes between changes caused simply by the participation of newly elected presidents in a summit and those caused by the participation of new presidents whose electoral victories represent political swings in their countries or regions. A qualitative approach supplements quantitative analysis, because political permanence in a country is no guarantee of diplomatic continuity and, conversely, diplomacy can potentially remain unaffected by political changes.[34]

As Figure 2.2 shows,[35] the initial SA-CSN sequence was punctuated by frequent political changes. The summits held between 2000 and 2008 were repeatedly forced to cope with new, inexperienced presidents. The second South American summit in 2002 was attended by four new presidents—Duhalde (Argentina), Quiroga (Bolivia), Uribe (Colombia), and Toledo (Peru)—as was the first CSN summit, held in September 2005, where fully half of the participants were neophytes, including Kirchner (Argentina), Rodríguez (Bolivia), Palacio (Ecuador), and Duarte (Paraguay). After 2008, however, political stability prevailed.

With the exception of Chile and Venezuela, every country in the region experienced significant political shifts between 2002 and 2008. Conversely, between 2008 and 2013, major political changes took place only in Chile, Peru, and Paraguay. The elections of Piñera and Humala in Chile and Peru did not entail significant changes with regard to those countries' approaches to defending their national interests. Cartes' election as president of Paraguay made possible the country's reinstatement in UNASUR and Mercosur, after its suspension in 2012 on account of the coup against Lugo.

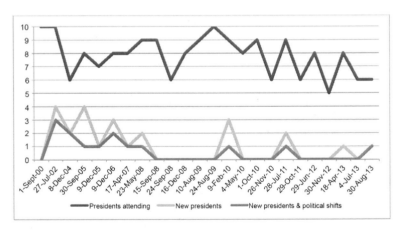

Figure 2.2 SA-CSN-UNASUR summits: Participation and political shifts, 2000–13
(Author's summitry database, based on information collected from official websites and media.)

As Figure 2.2 and Table 2.4 clearly indicate, UNASUR developed during a period of exceptional political stability, under the influence of a committed core group of five presidents: Néstor Kirchner (Argentina), Evo Morales (Bolivia), Luiz Inácio Lula da Silva (Brazil), Rafael Correa (Ecuador), and Hugo Chávez (Venezuela). These leaders had numerous opportunities to become acquainted with each other and to develop long-term working relationships. This group did not coincide with any particular ESG. With respect to agenda coordination, the implication was that UNASUR, as an NRIP, could not rely on its most active members to avoid overlaps. Brazil (and Argentina) could have orchestrated a division of labor between UNASUR and Mercosur, but Mercosur was no longer a diplomatic priority for either Lula or Kirchner. The group nevertheless epitomized the "left turn." Despite certain differences, all the presidents embraced the "new model of South America's regional integration," thus enabling a coherent defense of innovative issue areas. It must be acknowledged, however, that their bid to build something new on the rubble of former "neoliberal" groupings such as Mercosur and CAN might exacerbate overlaps in the future.

Starting in 2008, UNASUR's agenda was affected by crisis-resolution efforts. Between 2000 and 2013, no fewer that 12 out of 24 SA-CSN-UNASUR summits were "extraordinary,"[36] and 11 of them took place after 2008. During the first half of the decade, SA-CSN did not constitute a legitimate forum for addressing crises, as evidenced by an informal meeting convened in Quito to discuss the Venezuelan crisis on 15 January 2003, the day of Ecuadorian President Gutiérrez's inauguration. The meeting included Organization of American States (OAS) General Secretary César Gaviria and the presidents of Brazil (Lula), Colombia (Uribe), Chile (Lagos), Bolivia (Sánchez de Lozada), and Peru (Toledo). Brazil, Chile, the United States, Mexico, Spain, and Portugal created a "Group of Friends." Two years later, the impact of the 2005 CSN extraordinary summit was such that a paradigm shift was set in motion.

UNASUR stands in stark contrast to this record of South American diplomatic weakness. Wholly in keeping with the tradition of the Rio Group,[37] the organization rapidly transformed itself into a crisis resolution system. This pattern began a few months after UNASUR's treaty was signed in 2008; for three consecutive extraordinary meetings the member state presidents' attention was focused on the Bolivian crisis. Then, in 2009, a summit dealt with the diplomatic tensions generated by news reports about a United States–Colombia defense agreement. The following year saw the eruption of the "30S" crisis,

Table 2.4 SA-CSN-UNASUR ordinary and extraordinary summit attendance, 2000–13

Summits	Place	Date	Argentina	Bolivia	Brazil	Chile	Colombia	Ecuador	Paraguay	Peru	Uruguay	Venezuela
SA1	Brasilia	1/9/2000	De la Rua	Banzer	Cardoso	Lagos	Pastrana	Noboa	Gonzalez	Fujimori	Battle	Chávez
SA2	Guayaquil	27/7/2002	Duhalde	Quiroga	Cardoso	Lagos	Uribe	Noboa	Gonzalez	Toledo	Battle	Chávez
SA3	Cusco	8/12/2004		Mesa	Lula	Lagos	Uribe			Toledo		Chávez
CSN1	Brasilia	30/9/2005	N. Kirchner	Rodriguez	Lula	Lagos		Palacio	Duarte	Toledo		Chávez
CSNex	Montevideo	9/12/2005	N. Kirchner	Rodriguez	Lula	Lagos			Duarte		Vazquez	Chávez
CSN2	Cochabamba	9/12/2006		Morales	Lula	Bachelet		Palacio	Duarte	Garcia	Vazquez	Chávez
UNASUR1	Margarita	17/4/2007	N. Kirchner	Morales	Lula	Bachelet	Uribe	Correa	Duarte			Chávez
UNASUR2	Brasilia	23/5/2008	C. Kirchner	Morales	Lula	Bachelet	Uribe	Correa	Lugo	Garcia		Chávez
UNASURex	Santiago	15/9/2008	C. Kirchner	Morales	Lula	Bachelet	Uribe	Correa	Lugo		Vazquez	Chávez
UNASURex	New York	24/9/2008	C. Kirchner	Morales	Lula	Bachelet	Uribe		Lugo			
UNASURex	Salvador	16/12/2008	C. Kirchner	Morales	Lula	Bachelet		Correa	Lugo		Vazquez	Chávez
UNASUR3	Quito	10/8/2009	C. Kirchner	Morales	Lula	Bachelet		Correa	Lugo	Garcia	Vazquez	Chávez
UNASURex	Bariloche	24/8/2009	C. Kirchner	Morales	Lula	Bachelet	Uribe	Correa	Lugo	Garcia	Vazquez	Chávez
UNASURex	Quito	9/2/2010	C. Kirchner	Morales		Piñera	Santos	Correa	Lugo	Garcia	Mujica	Chávez
UNASURex	Las Cardales	4/5/2010	C. Kirchner	Morales	Lula	Piñera		Correa	Lugo		Mujica	Chávez

Summits	Place	Date	Argentina	Bolivia	Brazil	Chile	Colombia	Ecuador	Paraguay	Peru	Uruguay	Venezuela
UNASURex	Buenos Aires	1/10/2010	C. Kirchner	Morales		Piñera	Santos	Correa	Lugo	García	Mujica	Chávez
UNASUR4	Georgetown	26/1/2010	C. Kirchner		Lula		Santos	Correa	Lugo			Chávez
UNASURex	Lima	28/7/2011	C. Kirchner	Morales	Rousseff	Piñera	Santos	Correa		Humala	Mujica	Maduro*
UNASUR5	Asunción	29/10/2011		Morales		Piñera		Correa		Humala		Maduro*
UNASURex	Mendoza	29/6/2012	C. Kirchner	Morales	Rousseff	Piñera		Correa		Humala	Mujica	Maduro*
UNASUR6	Lima	30/11/2012				Piñera	Santos	Correa		Humala		Maduro*
UNASURex	Lima	18/4/2013	C. Kirchner	Morales	Rousseff	Piñera	Santos			Humala		Maduro
UNASURex	Cochabamba	4/7/2013	C. Kirchner	Morales				Correa		Humala	Mujica	Maduro
UNASUR7	Paramaribo	30/8/2013		Morales	Rousseff			Correa	Cartes	Humala		Maduro
Number of ordinary/extraordinary summits attended			7/12	10/12	10/9	10/11	7/7	11/9	10/8	10/7	4/11	12/11
Total			19	22	19	21	14	20	18	17	15	23

* Standing in for Chávez during his illness.
(Author's summitry database, based on information collected from official websites and media.)

which the Ecuadorian president described as an attempted coup against him, and an extra-regional crisis (Haiti) prompted the holding of a summit. Another summit, convened in 2010 to appoint a new general secretary, can also be placed under the heading of crisis resolution because of the tensions engendered by the rivalry between Uruguay and Argentina. In 2012 a summit was organized in reaction to a coup successfully carried out against President Lugo of Paraguay. In 2013, Maduro's controversial election after the death of Chávez, as well as the forced grounding of Morales's plane in Europe, occasioned two additional extraordinary summits. Finally, only a single extraordinary summit, in Lima in 2013, focused on a particular issue—reducing inequalities—which was discussed on the day Peru's new president, Ollanta Humala, was inaugurated.

The question arises as to whether these extraordinary summits influenced the UNASUR agenda and eventually gave rise to overlaps with the agendas of the Mercosur and CAN summits. Once again, a look at the participants and their political orientations proves instructive. Indeed, the attendance record for extraordinary summits follows a slightly different pattern from that of regularly scheduled meetings.

Venezuela is the uncontested champion of summit attendance, with or without Chávez.[38] This is a clear indication of Venezuela's wish to challenge the hegemony of Brazil and to influence the agenda, while helping to resolve crises. Venezuela's efforts have paid off: UNASUR's name was a Venezuelan idea, and certain Venezuelan proposals, such as Petrosur[39] or Bancosur,[40] were integrated into the UNASUR agenda. Venezuela played an instrumental role in urging support for democracy when faced in the region with a threat of being destabilized. Brazil, despite its ambition to assert leadership, is not always present and prefers to opt out whenever there is a risk that the discussion will become excessively politicized. For example, Brazil was absent from the Quito summit in February 2010, despite the fact that the meeting was intended to examine Lula's aid proposal for Haiti.[41] Again, in 2013, Brazil was absent from an extraordinary meeting whose purpose was to support Morales's bid to obtain apologies from France, Spain, Italy, and Portugal. Moreover, like other countries, Brazil's domestic political agenda takes precedence over its international commitments. In October 2010, Lula did not attend an extraordinary UNASUR meeting because he was too busy campaigning in support of his chosen successor, Dilma Rousseff.

Aside from Venezuela, other countries such as Argentina, Bolivia, Chile, and Uruguay also have a high rate of attendance at extraordinary summits, whereas Colombia and Peru are rarely in attendance.

Turning to the impact of crises on UNASUR's agenda, the Colombian and Ecuadorian crises played a key role in having defense and democracy, two major issues, placed on it. Defense represents an innovation if we consider the history of regional integration in Latin America. As for the issue of democracy, there is an overlap vis-à-vis Mercosur and CAN clauses. However, UNASUR's democratic clause provides an added value as compared with Mercosur and CAN's ones. More countries are covered, the scope of application is larger, and potential sanctions are more severe.[42] The inclusion of these two issues can be seen as an important example of a synergy type of agenda interaction. It was the case of the Brazilian initiative to prompt other member states to join in offering humanitarian aid to Haiti in 2010. With respect to regional integration, the Brazilian move was highly innovative as it resulted in the first case of collective humanitarian relief being directed towards a non-member country.

This section has reviewed a number of approaches and demonstrated how they can contribute to an understanding of the agenda interactions associated with multilayered summitry. In the end, it can be argued that the UNASUR agenda as defined during the summits did not overlap significantly with CAN and Mercosur, primarily because of the region's exceptional political stability.

Conclusion

This chapter makes a twofold contribution to the scholarly literature on summitry. First, my examination of multilayered South American summits from 2000 to 2013 has discovered few clear-cut cases of duplication between agendas. Given the history of regional integration, the low level of ESG institutionalization, the high rate of political turnover, and the proliferation of summit meetings, this is an unexpected finding—one that can be attributed to a paradigm shift leading to post-trade integration, which has in turn paved the way for the introduction of innovative issues at summit meetings. The group that promoted the "new integration model" was far from homogeneous, but they shared an aversion to trade-centered integration and proved able over time to collaborate on behalf of a common cause. The free-traders deemed the renewed agenda acceptable because they also benefited from the Pacific Alliance as an alternative coalition.

Less duplication can potentially lead to more efficient regional governance, provided that institutions do not overstep their mandates. Indeed, close examination of multilayered South America summitry confirms earlier, counterintuitive findings in IR studies on regime complexes,[43] to the effect that the agenda-setting and orientation functions of summits are not excessively constrained by the proliferation of meetings.

Second, on a more theoretical note, this study has demonstrated the value of factoring in domestic politics to usefully complement more conventional approaches to international relations analysis. Debates during any given summit are ultimately influenced by domestic political factors.[44] Political evolution inside attendee countries—along with even more significant parallel evolutions among several attendees (Latin America's left turn)—is a key element for the formation of coalitions that can propel agenda innovations during summits. The ability of some presidents to win several elections in a row has also proven essential for a degree of stability that tends to enhance consistency within and between summit meetings. Clearly, instability has the potential to make unplanned meetings necessary and to upset the agenda-setting process.

Further research along three lines is needed to verify our findings. First, the analysis could be broadened so as to shed light on how regional institutions implement decisions that are made at summits and how this process consolidates regional governance. Second, the scope of comparison could be expanded to contrast Latin American and Caribbean summits with UNASUR and ESG (Mercosur, CAN, the Central American Integration System—SICA, and the Caribbean Community—CARICOM). Even a superficial examination of the five Latin American summits held since 2008 shows that presidents have been willing to nurture synergies and aggregation. This may be a healthy sign for regional governance. Finally, a research program based on interregional comparisons would enable a more effective delineation of the specificities of Latin America, while also allowing greater insights into the ways in which multilayered summitry fosters global governance.

Notes

1 Kal Raustiala and David G. Victor, "The Regime Complex for Plant Genetic Resources," *International Organization* 55 (2004): 277–309.
2 Karen Alter and Sophie Meunier, "The Politics of International Regime Complexity," *Perspectives on Politics* 7, no. 1 (2009): 13–24.
3 Amandine Orsini, Jean-Frédéric Morin, and Oran Young, "Regime Complexes: A Buzz, a Boom or a Boost for Global Governance," *Global Governance* 19 (2013): 27–39.
4 Orsini et al., "Regime Complexes," 28.
5 Aynsley Kellow, "Multi-level and Multi-arena Governance: The Limits of Integration and Possibilities of Forum Shopping," *International Environment Agreements* 12 (2012): 327–342.
6 See the Introduction to this volume.

7. Olivier Dabène, "Explaining Latin America's Fourth Wave of Regionalism: Regional Integration of the Third Kind," 30th LASA Congress, San Francisco, 25 May 2012.
8. Created in 2008. Members include all 12 South American countries.
9. Created in 1991. Members include Argentina, Brazil, Paraguay, Uruguay, and Venezuela.
10. Created in 1969. Members include Bolivia, Colombia, Ecuador, and Peru.
11. See the Introduction to this volume.
12. I use the term "subsidiarity" here in a simple "non-European" sense. No regional integration process in Latin America has an equivalent to Article 5 of the Treaty of the European Union, and there is no verification that action at the regional level is justified compared with lower levels.
13. This includes the following summits: Andean Community (CAN), Common Market of the South (Mercosur), South American/Community of South American Nations/Union of South American Nations (SA/CSN/UNASUR), Rio Group/Latin America and the Caribbean Summits/Community of Latin American and Caribbean States (RG/CALC/CELAC), Pacific Alliance (AP), Africa and South America Summits/Summits of South American and Arab countries (ASA/ASPA), Latin America, the Caribbean and the European Union Summits (ALC/UE), Organization of American States (OAS), Summits of the Americas, Ibero-American Summits.
14. In the remainder of the chapter, I use the acronym of the regional bloc followed by the number of the summit. See Table 2.4 for a full list of summits and their attendees.
15. "Un nuevo modelo de integración de América del sur. Hacia la Unión sudamericana de naciones," Strategic Commission final report, 2006.
16. See Chapter 4 in this volume.
17. UNASUR, *Lineamientos políticos de UNASUR para las relaciones con terceros*, 2012.
18. MERCOCIUDADES is a network of Mercosur cities launched in 1995.
19. UNASUR has a total of 12 councils: elections; infrastructure and planning; drugs; education; culture; science, technology, and innovation; energy; social development; economy and finance; defense; health; and security and justice (Mercosur's FCCP, LXXIV meeting, Montevideo, 22–23 May 2013). According to Mercosur's Policy consultation and consensus forum (FCCP, 2013), there are cases of hard duplication in which active Mercosur ministerial meetings address the same issue areas (health, education, and culture).
20. See Chapter 6 in this volume.
21. FOCEM is Mercosur's policy of structural funds designed to reduce asymmetries between member countries.
22. James Rosenau, ed., *Linkage Politics: Essays on the Convergence of National and International Systems* (New York: The Free Press, 1969).
23. See Laura Gómez-Mera, *Power and Regionalism in Latin America: The Politics of Mercosur* (Notre Dame, Ind.: University of Notre Dame Press, 2013), 30–34, for a discussion on domestic politics approaches.
24. Pia Riggirozzi and Diana Tussie, eds, *The Rise of Post-Hegemonic Regionalism* (New York: Springer-United Nations University Press, 2012).
25. José Briceño-Ruiz, "From the South America Free Trade Area to the Union of South American Nations: The Transformations of a Rising Regional Process," *Latin American Policy* 1, no. 2 (2010): 208–229.

50 Olivier Dabène

26 See Olivier Dabène, "The Contingency of Agenda Setting in the Union of South American Nations (UNASUR)," 7th European Consortium for Political Research (ECPR) Conference, Bordeaux, 5 September 2013 for a discussion.
27 The database used in this section covers only ten South American countries and does not include Guyana and Suriname. Because they are not familiar with Mercosur and CAN, Guyana and Suriname could be responsible for unexpected overlaps, but they are not actively pushing issues. This study interprets presidents' participation as a display of interest in the processes and of their motivation to influence the agenda.
28 In the database, "free-traders" are countries governed by rightist presidents and/or that have signed free trade agreements with the United States, including Argentina before Kirchner, Bolivia before Morales, Brazil before Lula, Chile with Lagos and Bachelet, Colombia, Ecuador before Correa, Paraguay before and after Lugo, Peru with Humala, and Uruguay before Vazquez.
29 Olivier Dabène, "Au-delà du régionalisme ouvert. La gauche latino-américaine face au piège de la souveraineté et de la flexibilité," in *La gauche en Amérique latine, 1998–2012*, ed. Olivier Dabène (Paris: Presses de Sciences Po, 2012), 369–399.
30 Dabène, "The Contingency of Agenda Setting in the Union of South American Nations (UNASUR)."
31 Oran Young, "Political Leadership and Regime Formation: On the Development of Institutions in International Society," *International Organization* 45, no. 3 (1991): 281–308.
32 Young, "Political Leadership and Regime Formation."
33 See Chapter 9 in this volume.
34 Chilean rightist President Piñera did not differ much from his leftist predecessor Bachelet regarding foreign policy, and particularly the promotion of trade.
35 For a full list of summit participants, see also Table 2.4.
36 See Chapter 4 in this volume.
37 Created in 1986, the Rio Group included all Latin American countries and served as a permanent mechanism of political consultation. It has been instrumental in easing tensions between Colombia and Ecuador after the 2008 bombing of a Colombian guerrilla camp in Ecuadorian territory. In 2010, the Latin American and Caribbean Community (CELAC) replaced the Rio Group.
38 In the database, Vice-President Nicolas Maduro standing in for Chávez during his illness has not been counted as an "absence" of Venezuela. Chávez missed only one summit—the extraordinary meeting held in parallel to the UN General Assembly in New York (24 September 2008). Maduro has not yet missed a single meeting.
39 Petrosur is a 2005 agreement to coordinate regional energy policy.
40 Launched in 2009, Bancosur (Bank of the South) was designed to become an alternative to the International Monetary Fund and the World Bank.
41 Chávez criticized the United Nations mission in Haiti (MINUSTAH), and Correa feared that humanitarian aid might entail a loss of sovereignty. In the end, UNASUR did sign on to the proposal.

42 Dabène, "The Contingency of Agenda Setting in the Union of South American Nations (UNASUR)."
43 Orsini et al., "Regime Complexes."
44 Peter Evans, Harold Jacobson and Robert Putnam, eds, *Double-edged Diplomacy: International Bargaining and Domestic Politics* (Berkeley, Calif.: University of California Press, 1993).

Part II
Case studies—Americas

3 The Summits of the Americas process
Unfulfilled expectations[1]

Gordon Mace and Jean-Philippe Thérien

- **Genesis of the Summits of the Americas process**
- **Years of consensus (1994–2003)**
- **The confrontational years (2003–15)**
- **Conclusion**

Over the 20 years that followed the establishment of the Organization of American States (OAS) in 1948, there were two Meetings of American Heads of State. The first took place in Panama in 1956 and has been nearly forgotten; the other, held in Punta del Este in 1967, is remembered for its failure to restart hemispheric cooperation in a context of strained inter-American relations.[2] It should be recalled that in the wake of the Cuban Revolution, the 1960s was a confrontational period in the history of United States–Latin American relations. Strong nationalist winds swept across the region and guerrilla movements spread throughout several countries. The tendency of US foreign policy to counter the perceived communist threat by supporting dictatorships and right-wing governments was epitomized by the 1965 US intervention in the Dominican Republic. That episode, just like the US-supported coup in Guatemala in 1954, further eroded the OAS's already diminished legitimacy and threatened the very existence of the inter-American system.

One of the goals of the Punta del Este summit was to rebuild bridges and to put inter-American relations on a sounder basis, particularly through economic integration understood in the broad sense. Unfortunately, the goal was not achieved. Twenty years later, hemispheric cooperation remained difficult and the OAS was barely surviving. Until the end of the Cold War, inter-American summits never occupied a central position in the diplomatic ballet of the Americas, in contrast to summitry at the sub-regional level.

The 1990s, however, was a period of renaissance for hemispheric regionalism, a renaissance that started with an offer of economic cooperation made by president George H.W. Bush in June 1990. His Enterprise for the Americas Initiative (EAI) comprised a set of measures that demonstrated the willingness of the US Administration to support economic development in Latin America and the Caribbean that followed a free market model. The ensuing rejuvenation of the OAS was best illustrated by the adoption of the Santiago Commitment to Democracy and the Renewal of the Inter-American System in 1991, and of the Washington Protocol in 1992. The new environment paved the way for a resumption of inter-American summitry as of 1994 in Miami. The Miami summit was followed by those in Santiago (1998), Quebec City (2001), Mar del Plata (2005), Port-of-Spain (2009), Cartagena (2012), and Panama City (2015). In addition to the seven regular meetings, a special hemispheric summit on sustainable development was held in Santa Cruz in 1996, and another took place in Monterrey in 2004 on the topic of poverty and inequality.

How does one explain the revival of hemispheric summitry and what assessment can be made of its evolution? To answer these questions, this chapter proposes to demonstrate how the capacity of summitry to fulfill the functions ascribed to it in the literature has evolved in conjunction with the changing political context in the Americas.[3] Our demonstration is divided into three parts. The first part explains the resurgence of hemispheric summitry and describes the new institutional design of inter-American cooperation that was put in place in 1994. The second part examines the objectives, agenda and achievements of the first ten years of the Summits of the Americas (SOA) process and shows how this initial period was marked by a relatively high degree of consensus. By contrast, the more recent phase of hemispheric summitry—from the Summit of Mar del Plata to the Summit of Cartagena—has been dominated by a climate of confrontation, and that is the subject of the third part. Overall, the chapter suggests that the contribution of hemispheric summits to the regional governance of the Americas has varied according not just to material forces but to ideational factors as well.

Genesis of the Summits of the Americas process

In the 1980s the world system underwent a profound change, which was manifested at both the international and regional levels. The end of communism, in tandem with the improvement of East–West relations, dramatically changed the global order that had been in place since 1945, offering new prospects for state and non-state actors. The difficult progress of the Uruguay Round of multilateral trade negotiations heralded a significant transformation of the world economy as large Third World countries began using the General Agreement on Tariffs and Trade (GATT) to advance their trade agendas, which often conflicted with the one pursued by the industrialized countries. All these changes, occurring in the context of expanding globalization, affected the political environment in the Americas and around the world.

However, the greatest impact on the evolution of inter-American relations resulted from transformations happening in the Americas themselves—namely, the passage from dictatorships to democracy and the replacement of import-substitution strategies by liberalization policies and open regionalism. Democratization started in Bolivia in 1979, spread throughout South America during the 1980s, and culminated in the fall of the Pinochet regime in 1988. The transformation of the political scene in Latin America was accompanied by a no less significant change in the economic sphere, as national governments experimented to varying degrees with market-friendly measures.[4] Furthermore, when Canada (1990), Belize (1991), and Guyana (1991) joined the OAS, the inter-American system became more inclusive than ever.

For a time, the Central American crises obscured the social changes occurring in the region, but by the time George Bush moved into the White House in 1989, the diplomatic initiative known as the Esquipulas Peace Process had borne fruit, and a new era of cooperation in the hemisphere was in the offing. Along with the political and economic transformation of Latin America, this diplomatic success prepared the way for a renewal in inter-American affairs. The renewal, however, would be based on misperceptions, in particular those of US decision makers, who were right in taking notice of the important transformation occurring in Latin America but wrong in believing that the transformation represented a real "convergence of values"[5] between Latin America and the United States. A "window of opportunity" indeed had opened, but the convergence was certainly not as profound as the US Administration liked to believe.

There were also misperceptions, or at least silences, on the part of many Latin American governments concerning the "new" commonality of interests between Latin America and the United States and the likelihood of Washington being more open to demands emanating from the South, especially with regard to trade issues. Together, these misperceptions largely explain the break-down of negotiations on the Free Trade Area of the Americas project (FTAA) as well as the malaise that has persisted in inter-American relations ever since.

Nevertheless, the context in 1990 was quite favorable for a fresh start in hemispheric diplomacy. As mentioned above, President Bush's EAI provided a significant impetus. At the time, Latin American economies were struggling to emerge from a "lost decade" of development. The per capita domestic product in the region had dropped 8 percent below its 1981 level, and inflation rates had averaged more than 700 percent.[6] Intended for governments embracing neoliberal policies, the EAI received a generally enthusiastic welcome in Latin America and the Caribbean.[7] It thus provided a political catalyst for the strengthening of inter-American cooperation.

In sum, the 1990s witnessed momentous changes in the Americas as well as other parts of the world. By modifying perceptions and reorienting policies, those changes led to a redefinition of hemispheric regionalism. The institutionalization of the Summits of the Americas was a crucial element of this process.

Years of consensus (1994–2003)

As is the case for the world system since the end of the Cold War,[8] it is useful to distinguish two phases in the evolution of modern inter-American summitry. During the first phase, US hegemony and unipolarity played a major role in the successes of the process; in the second phase, the diffusion of power and conflicting interests made consensus impossible to reach.

The first period lasted from 1994 to 2003. It started against a backdrop of widespread intergovernmental convergence around the Washington Consensus[9] and with high expectations among the interested parties for a new era in inter-American relations. That said, many Latin American countries were apprehensive about the impact of the upcoming North American Free Trade Agreement (NAFTA) on United States–Latin American economic relations, and their anxiety goes some way to explaining their involvement in shaping the first summit's agenda and in putting free trade at the center of discussions. The period of consensus ended when FTAA negotiations broke off abruptly in November 2003, after the United States and Brazil concluded that it was impossible to reconcile their fundamental differences over the trade agenda.

Spurred by the revival of the OAS, the optimism that characterized inter-American relations in the 1990s largely explains the Clinton Administration's decision to convene the Miami Summit and, in so doing, to relaunch a high-level dialogue that had been interrupted 27 years earlier. Even though the road to Miami was a bumpy[10] one and there was no clear, ready-made blueprint for hemispheric cooperation, the meeting nevertheless redesigned hemispheric regionalism and gave birth to a renewed inter-American system.

In the wake of the summit, President Bill Clinton predicted that it would give rise to "a whole new architecture" for hemispheric relations. The new architecture, as we shall see, would ultimately be short on resources, but Miami did generate a new institutional design composed of two structures.[11] The first one was political in nature and revolved around the summits of heads of state; its tasks were to set the agenda for hemispheric cooperation and to oversee the implementation of the mandates adopted at the summits. Leaders' summits were to be complemented by regular ministerial meetings on defense, trade, transport, health, justice, the environment, and other areas. Between summits, the implementation of mandates was to be supervised by a Summit Implementation Review Group (SIRG) created in 1995.[12] The second structure had a more operational function. It was made up of a host of partner organizations—most importantly the OAS and the Inter-American Development Bank (IDB)—and was responsible for implementing the mandates assigned to them by the summits. After the Quebec City Summit, this second structure was given a higher profile through a Joint Summit Working Group (JSWG), which was established to coordinate the work among the various organizations.[13]

Thus, the initial purpose of hemispheric summits was quite ambitious with respect to functions usually associated with summitry. The new architecture went far beyond merely promoting dialogue and socialization, as it attempted to manage agenda setting and coordination. On paper, the new institutional architecture seemed sufficiently well designed to serve as a strong basis for the renewed hemispheric project. It gave the impression that the SOA had the capacity to meet its objectives not just by facilitating interactions between leaders but also by defining regional policies and regulating hemispheric cooperation.

Yet it soon became clear that the institutional foundation was not as solid as it appeared. Despite the creation of the SIRG and the JSWG, coordination remained difficult for political and bureaucratic reasons. At the regional level, the OAS and the IDB had very different agendas, while at the national level there were constant rivalries between foreign ministries on one hand and financial and technical ministries on the other.[14] Other factors linked to reporting and lack of political will—most obviously on the part of Mercosur countries[15]—also hindered agenda setting and implementation of summit decisions.

When it began, the SOA process was extremely ambitious with regard to agenda. Table 3.1 presents the scope of the agenda and the extent of the themes covered. For the period 1994–2003, institutions were the most important theme in regular summits, followed closely by democracy/governance. Other important subjects included, in order of

Table 3.1 Frequency of key terms in Summits of the Americas documents (1994–2012)

Main themes of discussion	Miami 1994	Santiago 1998	Québec 2001	Mar del Plata 2005	Port-of-Spain 2009	Cartagena 2012
1) Democracy/governance						
Democracy	25	17	17	11	6	0
Human rights	18	26	39	15	16	7
Civil society	3	13	31	6	6	2
Good governance	0	0	5	1	3	0
Globalization	0	1	6	2	0	0
Dialogue	3	10	17	13	5	0
Cooperation between institutions	28	33	62	29	37	7
Democratic governance/order	0	0	0	16	2	1
Total	*77*	*100*	*177*	*93*	*75*	*17*
2) Institutions						
OAS	37	40	45	63	17	0
UN	18	14	21	4	7	0
FTAA	5	18	9	5	0	0
ECLAC	2	11	9	3	2	0
PAHO	7	5	8	4	7	0
SIRG	0	6	12	1	1	0
IACHR	1	2	10	2	1	0
IDB	15	24	22	2	3	0
SOA	4	10	17	2	7	0
JSWG	0	0	0	2	4	0
Total	*89*	*130*	*153*	*88*	*49*	*0*
3) Trade, labor, and economy						
Economic integration	11	6	3	3	0	0
Free trade	18	12	2	1	0	0
Liberalization	8	2	1	1	0	0
Labor	7	35	24	44	0	5
Trade	30	15	11	15	3	1
Labor standards/decent work	0	5	1	25	5	0
Energy security/energy cooperation	1	2	0	0	7	2
Prosperity/human prosperity	13	1	11	6	6	0
Physical integration/infrastructure	15	11	11	5	4	6
Poverty/inequality	10	7	13	55	17	11

Main themes of discussion	Miami 1994	Santiago 1998	Québec 2001	Mar del Plata 2005	Port-of-Spain 2009	Cartagena 2012
Information and communication technologies (ICT)	0	1	0	3	2	7
Total	113	97	77	158	44	32
4) Security						
Corruption	13	12	9	7	6	2
Drugs	20	20	17	5	7	0
Terrorism	8	7	3	3	6	0
Crime	5	5	4	2	9	4
Hemispheric security	0	2	3	0	0	0
Public security	0	0	0	0	6	1
Organized crime	1	2	6	0	0	3
Citizen security	0	0	0	0	0	6
Disaster risk	0	0	0	0	1	5
Total	47	48	42	17	35	21
5) Education, society, and culture						
Education	20	75	33	29	32	14
Cultural values and diversity	8	1	5	8	15	2
Indigenous people	0	10	1	6	4	0
Women and role of women	29	18	31	8	6	2
Total	57	104	70	51	57	18
6) Environment						
Sustainable development/sustainability	20	7	16	12	15	3
Environment	41	10	29	12	24	1
Biodiversity	10	0	2	0	4	0
Climate change	2	4	4	3	7	1
Food security	0	0	0	1	2	1
Total	73	21	51	28	52	6
Grand total	456	500	570	435	312	94

(Authors' compilation using official documents available at www.summit-americas.org/pub_en.html.)

Note: The documents analyzed are the Declarations and Plans of Action of the Miami, Santiago, Quebec City, and Mar del Plata Summits; the Declaration of Engagement of Port-of-Spain; and the Cartagena List of Mandates. It should be noted that the documents of the last two summits differ from the preceding ones. In spite of obvious limitations, comparative analysis of the documents produced by the six regular summits remains useful in order to identify general trends. The analysis was made from the English version of the documents.

importance, trade/labor/economy, education/society/culture, and security and environment. The Miami Summit had a broader focus, while education was particularly important at the Santiago Summit. The Quebec City Summit, with its special emphasis on cooperation, human rights, and civil society, was labeled the democracy summit.[16] The diversity of themes and mandates amply reflects how ambitious the SOA process was at the outset with regard to functions such as agenda setting and coordination. In reality, however, the picture is a sobering one. Evaluations of the implementation of the Miami Summit mandates show limited progress for all mandates except health care, civil society, and liberalization of financial markets. Lack of financial resources for regional institutions, limited capacity and expertise of the smaller member countries, and the absence of effective implementation mechanisms have been identified as the most significant reasons for the modest results.[17]

Regional summits are generally not expected to provide immediate and substantial responses to fundamental problems.[18] Yet the first phase of the SOA process indicates that summits can produce positive results. In considering the 1994–2003 period as a whole, historians will probably point out that the implementation of summit mandates was far from optimal and that the FTAA project ended in failure; nevertheless, they will also note that the idea of free trade made significant progress in many parts of the hemisphere. They will highlight the progress of the democratic idea, as evidenced by the adoption of the Inter-American Democratic Charter,[19] and they will certainly mention the important shift from a traditional security framework to a new paradigm based on multidimensional security, a concept geared to the security of the individual more than that of the state.

These ideational elements represent major achievements of the SOA process, especially if one takes into account the high level of tension that had characterized the inter-American system in previous decades. Notwithstanding the egregious lack of implementation of many summit mandates during the 1994–2003 period, hemispheric summits did fulfill most of the functions assigned to summitry. During its first decade, inter-American summitry undoubtedly succeeded in fostering dialogue and socialization and in setting an agenda for regional affairs. In addition, the SOA process was relatively successful in legitimating a number of basic norms such as the desirability of free trade, the need to protect democracy as a public good, the necessary participation of civil society in hemispheric politics, and the multidimensional nature of security. Clearly, however, inter-American summitry failed to develop efficient coordination and implementation mechanisms.

The confrontational years (2003–15)

The failure of the FTAA negotiations in 2003 was a major stumbling block for the SOA process, first, because several governments of the region regarded the FTAA project as central to their efforts to renew hemispheric cooperation. Without this foundational element, hemispheric regionalism lost much of its appeal for them. In addition, the sudden ending of the FTAA negotiations occurred soon after Washington had shifted its attention to the "war on terror," thus diminishing Latin America's importance for US foreign policy. At the same time, opposition to the hemispheric project was on the rise in the region, as indicated above all by the creation of the Bolivarian Alliance for the Peoples of Our America (ALBA) and the Community of South American Nations, later to become the Union of South American Nations (UNASUR).

If there was any doubt that inter-American summitry and hemispheric cooperation had entered a conflictual period, the doubt was dispelled at the Summit of Mar del Plata in 2005. On that occasion, it became clear that the consensus achieved at the Miami Summit had largely been replaced by confrontation and polarization, particularly as to the future of hemispheric trade negotiations.[20] The Port-of-Spain Summit was much more constructive, at least with regard to dialogue and socialization, due to the presence of the newly elected president of the United States, Barack Obama; nevertheless, the summit's final declaration was signed only by the host, Prime Minister Patrick Manning of Trinidad. This odd conclusion resulted from the rejection of the request made by ALBA governments to insert a statement on the reintegration of Cuba in the inter-American system.[21] Even more oddly, the 2012 Cartagena Summit ended without any final declaration and in the absence of three ALBA members, primarily because no consensus was reached on the question of Cuba and on the approach to the drug problem.

The overview of summit mandates provided in Table 3.1 indicates that between the first and second phases of modern inter-American summitry, leaders' interest in the issue of hemispheric regionalism declined significantly. The most notable change affected institutions, particularly the OAS, still an important theme at Mar del Plata, less so at Port-of-Spain, and then completely ignored at Cartagena. There was also a considerable loss of interest in democracy/governance, an issue that most Latin American and Caribbean leaders have increasingly preferred to deal with within the framework of UNASUR.

It is worth noting that the theme of trade/labor/economy has remained relatively important from one period to the next. This situation, which may seem intriguing at first, results from a significant change of focus. Indeed, trade and economic integration were replaced by labor standards, poverty, and inequality as the highest priorities. The main reason for this shift has to do with the Mar del Plata Summit, where Argentine President Néstor Kirchner imposed his country's views about the importance of social policies. Interestingly, the theme of poverty/inequality remained an important issue in all subsequent summits.

There has, lastly, been a notable reduction of mandates for the other themes. In the education/society/culture category, education has remained a major concern but the issue of gender has not. In the area of security, corruption and drugs are still in the spotlight, but as of the Port-of-Spain Summit there appears to be a new emphasis on crime and citizen security. Finally, sustainable development and the environment are still considered key issues, but to a lesser degree than during the first period of hemispheric summitry.

The marked reduction in the number of mandates between the first and second periods of the SOA process suggests a gradual narrowing of the hemispheric agenda. It can be hypothesized that this narrowing stems more from leaders' skepticism about the capacity of summitry to help resolve inter-American problems than from their collective will to manage regional affairs more efficiently. In any case, the reduced number of mandates is not the only sign of disaffection toward the SOA process. Further indications include the growing disinterest of member countries in the implementation of summit mandates as well as the increasingly divergent visions of governments regarding the very legitimacy of the inter-American framework. It should be noted, more positively, that the diplomatic fiasco of Mar del Plata was avoided in later meetings. Compared with the meeting held in Argentina, the Port-of-Spain and Cartagena summits were more convivial and enabled the leaders at least to present their positions and discuss their differences. Still, the fact remains that the results of recent summits were far from impressive.[22]

What explains the transformation of the SOA from an institution fulfilling a wide range of functions to one confined to dialogue and socialization? Some authors have suggested that the sub-regions of the Americas have become so diversified that the SOA process cannot frame policies applicable to the whole hemisphere.[23] Others have argued that the region has entered a period of post-hegemony,[24] with Latin American economies "going global" and "shifting the global balance."[25] While such explanations certainly capture key aspects of the situation, our own analysis of the recent decline of hemispheric summitry zeros in on a combination of factors.

The first factor is a legacy of the first phase of the SOA process: insufficient resources, failed coordination, and lack of compliance.[26] To give just one example concerning the funding of the OAS, the contribution of member countries declined by 12 percent for the period 2003–13.[27] This legacy has produced a major credibility gap for hemispheric summitry. A second factor is the turning of US foreign policy away from the Americas. This shift came in the aftermath of the terrorist attacks on 11 September 2001 and the failure of the FTAA negotiations, and it was later reinforced by the rise of China and the financial crisis. In the regional context, hemispheric summitry can only succeed if constantly supported by the United States. The absence of that support goes a long way to explaining the difficulties of the SOA process after 2004. The opposing views and interests on regional affairs of a number of Latin American governments constitute another factor. Rooted to a great extent in the commodities boom that boosted Latin American confidence in the 2000s, these opposing views were expressed most forcefully, though not exclusively, by the member states of ALBA. ALBA governments have been the most vocal opponents to market-oriented policies, free trade, and liberal democracy. The most consequential resistance, however, has come from Brazil, which considerably weakened the SOA process by being lukewarm about the FTAA negotiations and by fostering competing institutions such as UNASUR and the Community of Latin American and Caribbean Nations (CELAC). Certainly, the US Trade Act and Farm Bill of 2002 lent legitimacy to the Brazilian government's position of preferring multilateral to regional trade negotiations, but Brazil's strategy has indeed hampered the evolution of hemispheric regionalism.

In sum, the second phase of modern inter-American summitry unfolded in a context of indifference and confrontation that prevented it from performing most of the functions generally assigned to summits. In fact, in recent years, the most inter-American summitry could do was to keep a political space open for dialogue.

Conclusion

The history of modern inter-American summitry enables us to draw a few lessons concerning the relationship between summits and regional governance. A first lesson is the absolute necessity of consensus between participating governments with regard to the basic principles and fundamental orientations of the summit process. When most member governments share a common vision of where a region should be headed, summitry can play an important role in setting the agenda and facilitating policy coordination.[28] This is all the more true when the leaders' position reflects robust domestic support.

Such a convergence of views was particularly strong during the first phase of inter-American summitry, from 1994 to 2003, when summits not only provided a space for dialogue but were instrumental in allowing leaders to influence regional governance through agenda setting and the conception of an institutional architecture that would support the new hemispheric agenda. Inter-American summits then also provided a forum for the re-engineering of hemispheric cooperation with the ambitious aim of coordinating policies in select areas. In addition, during its first decade, inter-American summitry fulfilled an important legitimating function by promoting values such as free trade and representative democracy, and by helping to replace the Cold War security paradigm in the region with the more nuanced concept of multidimensional security.

A second lesson is that summits will succeed only if there is a continual commitment on the part of participating states. This commitment must take the form of political will exercised by national governments as well as the use of domestic resources to implement leaders' decisions. Half-hearted commitment has been a major drawback for the SOA almost from the start, as many governments were reluctant to follow up on summit plans of action. Lack of resources was an important factor for smaller countries but not for the larger ones, some of which simply refused to become fully engaged in hemispheric cooperation.

When consensus and commitment disappear, as was the case in the second phase of inter-American summitry, which began in 2004, it is difficult for summits to go beyond providing a mechanism for political dialogue, where leaders can do no more than discuss and perhaps better understand opposing points of view. The fact is that the evolution of hemispheric summitry since 1994 has been a story of consensus giving way to confrontation. The last hemispheric summits have shown that leaders can exchange views in a civil manner but it is not certain that the opposing points of view have been understood.

A third lesson concerns the need for larger countries to remain constantly engaged on behalf of summitry with the various means at their disposal. In each regional experience of summitry, regional powers act as paymasters by providing substantial support for the process or by shouldering a larger portion of the costs associated with leaders' decisions. In the case of inter-American summitry, that role falls quite naturally to the United States. However, with the failure of the FTAA project, the new centrality of the "war on terror" in US foreign relations, and the growing skepticism on the part of many Latin American countries, Washington suddenly became disengaged from hemispheric cooperation. Thereafter, inter-American summitry lost its initial political momentum.

What, then, lies ahead for hemispheric summitry? It has been suggested that the Cartagena Summit of 2012 may have signaled not just the end of summitry but also the non-viability of the inter-American system itself.[29] If the impasse that this scenario implies is to be avoided, the time may have come to rethink hemispheric summitry, taking into account the changing political landscape in the Americas over the past 15 years. The SOA process certainly remains valuable as a space for socialization.[30] Nevertheless, with the creation of UNASUR and CELAC, it may be opportune to envisage a new division of labor among regional institutions, such that each forum would focus on managing the problems that it can address most efficiently.[31] Inter-American summitry could then concentrate on issues that affect all the countries of the hemisphere, such as democracy, drugs, migration, and climate change, leaving to other institutions issues best dealt with at the sub-regional level. Whatever happens in this connection, it seems clear that hemispheric cooperation, particularly the SOA process, will need to be profoundly rethought if the inter-American system is to remain politically relevant. In this sense, the historic shift in US policy toward Cuba at the end of 2014, paving the way for the participation of Cuba in the SOA process, is certainly a step in the right direction.

As for the study of summitry in general, a close examination of inter-American summitry leads to one overall finding: the success of summits is in no way guaranteed. The creation of the SOA process in 1994 was a substantial improvement over the limited dialogue that existed in inter-American affairs from the mid-1960s to the end of the 1980s, yet the results of that political initiative have fallen considerably short of initial expectations. For summits to contribute effectively to hemispheric governance, all the functions of summitry must be fulfilled. In particular, the process needs to be open so as to gain public support. Indeed, without a democratic foundation, summitry can hardly become the diplomatic engine that it aspires to be.

Notes

1 We would like to thank Hugo Lavoie-Deslongchamps for his excellent research assistance. We are also grateful to Daniel Navarro for updating information on summit mandates. Finally, we thank the Social Sciences and Humanities Research Council of Canada and the Ministère des

Relations Internationales et de la Francophonie du Québec for their financial support.
2 Gordon Connell-Smith, *The United States & Latin America, An Historical Analysis of Inter-American Relations* (London: Heinemann Educational Books, 1974), 226–266; and Henry Raymont, *Troubled Neighbors: The Story of US-Latin American Relations from FDR to the Present* (Boulder, Colo.: Westview Press/The Century Foundation, 2005), 157–175.
3 See the Introduction in this volume.
4 Gordon Mace, "The Origins, Nature & Scope of the Hemispheric Project," in *The Americas in Transition: The Contours of Regionalism*, ed. Gordon Mace, Louis Bélanger, and contributors (Boulder, Colo.: Lynne Rienner Publishers, 1999), 28–32; and Peter H. Smith, *Talons of the Eagle: Dynamics of US-Latin American Relations* (New York: Oxford University Press, 1996), 241–243.
5 Bernard W. Aronson, "Our Vision of the Hemisphere," *US Department of State Dispatch*, 15 October 1996: 184; and George H.W. Bush, "Remarks to the Council of the Americas," *Public Papers of the President of the United States*, vol. 1 (Washington, DC: US Government Printing Office, 1989), 505.
6 Robert A. Pastor, *Exiting the Whirlpool: US Foreign Policy Toward Latin America and the Caribbean* (Boulder, Colo.: Westview Press, 2001), 88–89.
7 Raymont, *Troubled Neighbors*, 265.
8 Steen Fryba Christensen, "Brazil's Foreign Policy Priorities," *Third World Quarterly* 34, no. 2 (2013): 271.
9 Jorge E. Taina, "América Latina y la Diplomacia de Cumbres," in *América Latina y la Diplomacia de Cumbres*, ed. Carlos M. Jarque, Maria Salvadora Ortiz, and Carlos Quenan (Madrid: Secretaria General Iberoamericana, 2009), 84; and Thomas Legler, "The Rise and Decline of the Summit of the Americas," *Journal of Iberian and Latin American Research* 19, no. 2 (2013): 184.
10 Raymont, *Troubled Neighbors*, 286–287.
11 Gordon Mace and Hugo Loiseau, "Cooperative Hegemony and Summitry in the Americas," *Latin American Politics and Society* 47, no. 4 (2005): 124–129.
12 Ronald L. Scheman, "The Inter-American System: An Overview," in *Governing the Americas: Assessing Multilateral Institutions*, ed. Gordon Mace, Jean-Philippe Thérien and Paul Haslam (Boulder, Colo.: Lynne Rienner Publishers, 2007), 21–22; and Gordon Mace and Jean-Philippe Thérien, "Inter-American Governance: A Sisyphean Endeavor?," in *Governing the Americas: Assessing Multilateral Institutions*, ed. Gordon Mace, Jean-Philippe Thérien, and Paul Haslam (Boulder, Colo.: Lynne Rienner Publishers, 2007), 40–42.
13 Richard E. Feinberg, "Commentary by Richard E. Feinberg," in *The Road to Hemispheric Cooperation: Beyond the Cartagena Summit of the Americas*, ed. Consuelo Amat (Washington, DC: The Brookings Institution, 2012), 102; and Joint Summit Working Group, *From Mar del Plata to Port-of-Spain* (Washington, DC: Summits of the Americas Secretariat, 2009).
14 Richard E. Feinberg, "Presidential Mandates and Ministerial Institutions: Summitry of the Americas, the Organization of American States (OAS) and the Inter-American Development Bank (IDB)," *Review of*

International Organizations 1, no. 1 (2006): 81–89; and Robin L. Rosenberg, "The OAS and the Summit of the Americas: Coexistence, or Integration of Forces of Multilateralism?," *Latin American Politics and Society* 43, no. 1 (2001): 96.
15 Chapter 6, this volume.
16 As discussed in Chapter 12.
17 Leadership Council for Inter-American Summitry, "From Talk to Action: How Summits Can Help Forge a Western Hemisphere Community of Prosperous Democracies," in *Civil Society and the Summit of the Americas: The 1998 Santiago Summit*, ed. Richard E. Feinberg and Robin L. Rosenberg (Coral Gables, Fla.: North-South Center Press, University of Miami, 1998), 139–140; and Richard E. Feinberg, *Summitry in the Americas: A Progress Report* (Washington, DC: Institute for International Economics, 1997), 182–183.
18 Abraham F. Lowenthal, "De la Hegemonia Regional a las Relaciones Bilaterales Complejas: Estados Unidos y América Latina a Principios del Siglo XXI," *Nueva Sociedad* 206 (November–December, 2006): 74.
19 Legler, "The Rise and Decline of the Summit of the Americas," 184.
20 See Peter Hakim, "Why we are Together," *FOCAL Point* 7, no. 6 (2008); and Günther Maihold, "Las Cumbres Hemisfericas y su Impacto Regional—un Balance," in *América Latina y la Diplomacia de Cumbres*, ed. Carlos M. Jarque, Maria Salvadora Ortiz, and Carlos Quenan (Madrid: Secretaría General Iberoamericana, 2009), 66.
21 Olivia D. Howe, "Summit of the Americas," *Law and Business Review of the Americas*, no. 15 (2009): 927; and Jorge Salaverry, *Cumbre de las Américas o Cumbre sobre Cuba?* (Madrid: Fundación Ciudadania y Valores, 2009), 5–6.
22 See Peter Hakim, "A Consequential Summit?," 12 April 2012, www.thedialogue.org/page.cfm?pageID=32&pubID=2939; and Jorge Heine, "A Tale of Two Very Different Summits," *The Hindu Times*, 24 April 2012, www.thehindu.com/opinion/lead/a-tale-of-two-very-different-summits/article3346328.ece.
23 Lowenthal, "De la Hegemonia Regional a las Relaciones Bilaterales Complejas," 74.
24 See Pia Riggirozzi and Diana Tussie, eds, *The Rise of Post-Hegemonic Regionalism*, United Nations University Series on Regionalism (London: Springer, 2012); Thomas Legler, "Multilateralism and Regional Governance in the Americas," in *Latin American Multilateralism: New Directions* (Ottawa: FOCAL, 2010), 12; and Legler, "The Rise and Decline of the Summit of the Americas," 183.
25 Jorge Heine, "Latin America Goes Global," *Americas Quarterly* 7, no. 2 (2013): 28–29.
26 Leadership Council for Inter-American Summitry, *Advancing Toward Quebec City and Beyond: Policy Report III* (Coral Gables, Fl.: North-South Center, University of Miami, 2001), 2; and Carlo Dade, "Will There Be Another Summit of the Americas? A Case for Reform," *FOCAL* (January 2009): 2.
27 OAS, Secretariat for Administration and Finance, "Presentation to CAAP January 17, 2013: Gap Between Income & Expenditures" (2013): 5, scm.oas.org/pdfs/2013/CP30058.ppt.
28 On this, see Chapters 4 and 6 in this volume.

29 Jaime Aparicio-Otero, "The Summit of the Americas and the Inter-American System," in *The Road to Hemispheric Cooperation: Beyond the Cartagena Summit of the Americas*, ed. Consuelo Amat (Washington, DC: The Brookings Institution, 2012), 93–94. See also Heine, "A Tale of Two Very Different Summits"; and Peter J. Meyer, *Fifth Summit of the Americas, Port of Spain, Trinidad and Tobago, April 2009: Background, Agenda and Expectations* (Washington, DC: Congressional Research Service, 2008), 5.
30 Legler, "The Rise and Decline of the Summit of the Americas," 190.
31 Adrián Bonilla, "Las Estrategias de Inserción Internacional en el Espacio Iberoamericano," in *De Cádiz a Panamá: La Renovación en el Espacio Iberoamericano*, ed. Adrián Bonilla and Isabel Álvarez (San José, Costa Rica: FLACSO Secretaría General, 2014), 130–131.

4 Presidential diplomacy in UNASUR

Coming together for crisis management or marking turfs?

Diana Tussie

- **Workings, challenges, and expectations**
- **Emergency calling: Rising to the occasion**
- **Presidential solidarity: Going further afield**
- **Less urgency, some evasion?**
- **Conclusion**

The plan to create the Free Trade Area of the Americas (FTAA) ushered in both summits and active presidential diplomacy to the forefront in the Americas.[1] In the comparatively short time period after the demise of the FTAA a large number of initiatives have sprung up. In contrast to the virtual lack of summitry in North America,[2] South America has experienced a proliferation of summits. The Union of South American Nations (UNASUR) became part of this ambitious policy agenda of transformative regionalism. Building on the stepping stones of trade agreements, it emerges from an effort to broaden the scope of institutions beyond trade preferences. The spirit of UNASUR, in other words, diverged from the US-dominated hemispheric mold that informed the Organization of American States (OAS) and the Inter-American Treaty of Reciprocal Assistance during the Cold War, as well as from post-Cold War initiatives such as the Southern Common Market (Mercosur) or the North American Free Trade Agreement (NAFTA). UNASUR comes as part of the new cycle of regionalism,[3] as an emergent illustration of the new South American regionalism[4] or post-hegemonic regionalism.[5]

The emergence of UNASUR is an interesting case study of the evolution of regional governance. Very quickly it acquired a high profile, though certainly not an uncontested one. One of the central motivations behind the creation of UNASUR was to provide forums in which leaders could explore their differences in a structured framework with the gentle support and tutelage of member nations when needed—a process that has enabled ties and a dimension of socialization. It is naturally a process fraught with complexities. The leaders' aim was to carve out niches for flexible and pragmatic cooperation focusing on infrastructure, energy, health, security, and natural resources. These issues have a certain life of their own and move on at the technical level.[6] In the meantime, other processes march on. Some of the member countries are more active in the Pacific Alliance (clearly anchored on trade)[7] and all are engaged in the Community of Caribbean and Latin American Countries (CELAC).

UNASUR is in fact rather more than a standalone summit process, although as an institution it is still a work in progress. It is an international organization with legal personality established by the UNASUR Constitutive Treaty, which was signed in Brasília in 2008. Twelve countries are involved in UNASUR: Argentina, Bolivia, Brazil, Chile, Colombia, Ecuador, Guyana, Paraguay, Peru, Suriname, Uruguay, and Venezuela. Its headquarters have been established in Quito. Ordinary summits are held annually while extraordinary ones may be summoned by the Pro Tempore Presidency (PTP), which represents leaders in international meetings. It is held by each member state in alphabetical order for a period of one year. In the early years extraordinary summits tended to be quite frequent due to the new mindset the presidents were bent on shaping, coupled with resistances they faced and the geopolitical tensions that flared up. In those circumstances the summitry process was called in as a crisis management committee and having lived up to its calling, it gained credibility. A golden age followed from 2008 to 2010 with a series of extraordinary summits convened to resolve crises. Since then UNASUR has lost momentum as it finesses the need to live up to expectations while facing a more slippery political environment.

The chapter proceeds in four sections. I first revise the workings and challenges of UNASUR summits. In sections two and three I then go on to look at how summits have so far laid the ground for regime stability and regime maintenance by contributing to defusing conflicts between members with different and at times quite opposing views of their respective national interests. For this I flesh out its rapid rise as a collective safety net among leaders, hand in hand with tight solidarity mechanisms for presidents in distress. The last section delineates how presidents grab elements of a minimalist solidarity agenda abroad while the conclusion brings together the threads and weaves them with the impending challenges posed by the outburst of violent clashes in Venezuela. The chapter suggests that the diplomatic success and hence the continued contribution of these summits to regional governance varies not only in relation to ideational factors but also to changing material interests.

Workings, challenges, and expectations

The UNASUR treaty was signed in 2008 but the process started much earlier at the behest of Brazil, when President Cardoso took the lead to convene a South American summit in Brasília in 2000. At that point, against the backdrop of Argentina's soon to implode crisis, Mercosur was being torn apart. By gathering South America (but not Mexico and Central America) Cardoso intended to create a South American agenda to offset that of the FTAA. If the latter was biased to trade, the former would center on articulating a regional space as such, by virtue of infrastructure and border connections. In an economic reading, regionalism came to be seen not so much as a space to attract extra regional foreign direct investment, but as a space for the internationalization of Brazilian business.[8] The 2000 summit was the first ever South American summit. It was a difficult act so long as many countries were not keen to detour from their priority track with the United States. In fact, Peru and Colombia later signed free trade agreements with the United States in 2005 and 2006, respectively. In 2004, another summit was held in Cusco, Peru. During this event, at the height of Venezuela's sponsored Bolivarian Alliance for the Peoples of Our America (ALBA), the Community of South American Nations was mooted. After the subsequent summits in 2005 in Brasília and 2006 in Cochabamba the leaders decided at the South American Energy Summit held in 2007 in Venezuela to change the community's name to the Union of South American Nations and to establish a general secretariat based in Ecuador. While President Chávez did not waste the opportunity to refer to Mercosur and the Community of Andean Nations (CAN) as pointless, Argentina, Brazil, and Bolivia tried to smooth all rough edges. To avoid quasi-religious squabbles on trade, the UNASUR treaty includes only some lip service on CAN and Mercosur, but not much else.

UNASUR became a clever way of defusing geopolitical rivalry between Venezuela and Brazil, with their especially active leaders, Chávez and Lula da Silva, both struggling to gain ascendancy in the region. The contrast between Brazil's well documented, relatively passive role in Mercosur to a more vigorous provider in UNASUR is evidence of the influence of Hugo Chávez's activism as well as the concern of some leaders with such a display.[9] Polycentrism faces a daunting array of challenges. The product of this tension became a paradoxical project grounded on contrasting motivations which at the same time was able to act as a quite effective crisis management committee. At another level, the level of would-be-followers, differences could not be swept under the carpet. Countries did not always find it easy to sit collegially around the same table. Whilst some leaders were quite committed to the idea of creating a South American turf, others made clear that their main interest lay in integration with the United States. Some weeks before Brazil's call to the First Summit in 2005, the leaders of three countries (Colombia, Chile, and Uruguay) expressed skepticism. Chile and Colombia had substantive political differences with the Lula-Chávez twosome and Uruguay was seriously at odds with Argentina over the establishment of pulp factories in the shared river basin. These differences dwindled as new presidents were subsequently sworn in, but they show the number of hurdles that are bound to rise time and again as presidential cycles change gear and preferences mutate along the way.

UNASUR is a clear outcome of the turn to "presidentialization" of regional policy.[10] Presidential diplomacy in Latin America picked up promptly in the late 1980s as democratically elected governments inaugurated forms of mutually supportive safety nets, such as the coordination of debtors[11] or the peace process in Central America, the latter led by President Arias of Costa Rica, for which he won a Nobel Prize. Presidential diplomacy involves not only the multiplication of presidents' trips abroad but also a qualitative increase related to the presidents' ambition to project their personal ideas on the international screen and their capability to alter diplomatic outcomes.[12] It can also be seen as part of the move away from the old guard in control of the ministries of foreign affairs inclined to secretive five o'clock tea diplomacy. Such intense presidential empowerment tries to find some legitimacy in the pluralization of the actors involved. Although the Council of Heads of States is preeminent in the building of the institution as such, it relies on a number of bodies to support decision making from meeting to meeting and provide some institutional density. A welfare component has developed around specialized councils for social issues.[13] A security dimension, in turn, took shape with the creation of the South American Defense Council (SADC) and a separate council devoted to the issue of illegal drugs. In 2010, UNASUR adopted a democracy clause that sought to deter the overthrow of incumbents and called for sanctions on member governments that came to power by *coups d'état*; subsequently an Electoral Council was established to monitor elections. No president in the region is immune to destabilization, a fact that explains the closing of ranks among them on these otherwise historically hyper-sensitive issues.

A special place in the structure of UNASUR is held by the SADC. This body was pushed forward mainly by Brazil in 2008 after

Colombian troops chased and killed operatives belonging to the Revolutionary Armed Forces of Colombia (FARC) in Ecuador with evident US logistical and intelligence support. The offensive, which resulted in the killing of Raul Reyes (FARC's spokesman and second in command), put President Chávez on guard. He quickly mobilized troops to the Colombian frontier. Before full escalation could get out of control, Brazilian minister Nelson Jobim promoted the idea of sponsoring collective security under what became the SADC—now an integral part of the UNASUR initiative. Brazil had originally wanted the SADC to be a North Atlantic Treaty Organization (NATO)-like mechanism based on the principle of collective defense, but this time it was confronted with resistance, particularly from Colombia. The 12 members of UNASUR ultimately agreed to the establishment of a mechanism for conflict prevention on the basis of mutual consultation.[14]

In fact, one of the greatest challenges for UNASUR still lies in the divergence of security interests, especially in the volatile Andean region. For one thing, in a bold challenge to Washington, Bolivian President Evo Morales expelled the US ambassador and agents of the Drug Enforcement Agency in 2008 for allegedly inciting the opposition and encouraging secession in Santa Cruz. He also ended an agreement with the United States Agency for International Development (USAID) for reducing coca leaf plantations in the Chaparre region. Five years later he expelled USAID on the grounds that the agency was undermining his government. At the other end of the spectrum we find Colombia, whose cooperation with the United States has been a fundamental pillar in its struggle against armed groups such as the FARC, the National Liberation Army (ELN), paramilitaries and groups of drug traffickers.

Despite the improvement in bilateral relations, with understandably apprehensive neighboring countries and the opening of peace talks with armed groups initiated by President Santos, Plan Colombia and the risk of spiraling militarization continues to be a tense and delicate subject with the existence of quite contrasting views in Peru, Ecuador, and Venezuela. On a more positive note, however, UNASUR was able to ensure good behavior among neighbors and to overcome one of its first difficulties by successfully incorporating Colombia in its framework despite the reservations of some members, and despite Colombia's own serious reservations. In fact, Colombia managed to reinforce its image as a committed state, putting forward a candidate to secure the position of secretary-general (SG) after the death of Néstor Kirchner.

While for some leaders the UNASUR process generates opportunities for neutralizing the traditional role of the United States, for all it allows a platform for cooperation and dialogue, and for Brazil, in particular, it enables a way to consolidate its role as a regional power trying to put together elements of common thought. For the Andean countries, the success of the South American initiatives acts as an anchor for their hopes of continued cooperation free of risky flare ups.[15] The summits work within these ideational limits and institutional idiosyncrasies. Despite festering differences and potential fractures among leaders, the marking of turfs and rapid reaction to crisis have been the most publicized strengths of presidential diplomacy, as we shall see below. Only 18 months after signing the treaty they were drawn to make good on a serious institutional crisis in Bolivia that risked turning into civil strife.

Emergency calling: Rising to the occasion

UNASUR summits took on an unintended urgency as leaders were confronted with the fallout from a string of crises over 2008–10. Conflicts in South America over the last decade can be grouped into two sources. On one hand, security crises have flared up around the combustible mix of internal conflict and transnational illicit activities in Colombia, which have spilled over to neighboring Ecuador and Venezuela.[16] On the other, there have been clashes between neoliberal governments and anti-neoliberal social movements (Chile) and the reverse dynamic between reformist governments and the pro-status quo opposition (Argentina, Venezuela, Ecuador, Bolivia, and Paraguay). The ascension and indeed long reign of left-leaning governments with distinctly transformational politics[17] have engendered hostile reactions from entrenched elites and often endangered the peaceful termination of presidential terms. The leaders acquired standing and an impressive track record in conflict resolution following rampant political violence in Bolivia in 2008, Colombia's military incursion in Ecuador the same year, and the attempt to destabilize Ecuador in 2010. The crisis in Venezuela has yet to prove that there is no fallback on this track record.

The value of the arrangement as a collective safety net was first put to the test by the Bolivian crisis in 2008. The right-wing governments of the Media Luna Eastern departments (rich in energy and mineral resources) revolted in order to shield themselves from egalitarian reforms. Accompanied by strikes and protests, they held a referendum, calling for autonomy from La Paz, drafting their own separate

Table 4.1 Milestones in the evolution of summits in UNASUR, 2000–14

Date	Place	Milestone
		Ordinary summits
2000	Brasília, Brazil	First South American Summit
2004	Cusco, Peru	Second South American Summit (Cusco Declaration)
2005	Brasília, Brazil	I UNASUR Summit
2006	Cochabamba, Bolivia	II Summit
2007	Margarita, Venezuela	First South American Energy Summit (oil vs. ethanol)
2009	Quito, Ecuador	III Summit, financial architecture
2010	Georgetown, Guyana	IV Summit, adoption of democratic clause
March 2011		*UNASUR comes into legal force*
2011	Asunción, Paraguay	V Summit
2012	Lima, Peru	VI Summit
2013	Paramaribo, Suriname	VII: Civil society forum created; Paraguay reenters UNASUR
July 2014		*Former Colombian President Samper elected SG*
2014	Guayaquil and Quito, Ecuador	President Correa flags regional financial architecture. Inaugurates building to house UNASUR
		Extraordinary summits
2008	Santiago, Chile	Pando killings
2008	Costa do Sauípe, Brazil	SADC and Health Council set
2009	Quito, Ecuador	Colombia/Venezuela tension
2009	Bariloche, Argentina	US bases in Colombia
2010	Los Cardales, Argentina	Kirchner election as SG

Date	Place	Milestone
		Ordinary summits
2010	Buenos Aires, Argentina	Ecuador crisis, November. Democratic clause introduced
2012	Cartagena, Colombia	SG Maria Emma Mejia departs
2012	Mendoza, Argentina	Paraguay suspended
2013	Lima, Peru	Monitoring Venezuelan election
2013	Cochabamba, Bolivia	Grounding of Evo Morales's plane in France (Colombia, Chile, and Peru absent)

constitution. The OAS flew in to settle the contention, supported Morales and called for respect of democracy and the constitution. However, the OAS stopped short of condemning the referendum and the impending possibility of unilateral declaration of independence. Nevertheless, opposition groups took to disrupting gas exports and occupying public buildings in a series of violent moves that escalated to a peak on 11 September 2008, when a bloody clash took place between groups supporting and opposing President Morales in the province of Pando. Over a dozen were wounded or killed, others disappeared and hundreds of survivors sought refuge in neighboring Brazil. Morales declared a state of emergency and things escalated out of control with the very real risk of civil conflict. Only three days after the "Pando killings" Michele Bachelet (at the time UNASUR's PTP), under the pressure of events (and after various appeals from Venezuela) called an extraordinary summit in Santiago. There were stark differences of opinion over what needed to be done. Venezuela wanted full backing for Morales, who faced the twin anathemas of secession and US interference. Chile, Argentina, and Brazil thought that urgent de-escalation was needed (not least to ensure their own continued gas supplies). In their eyes, UNASUR should strive for Bolivian stability while avoiding the risk of secession and either direct or indirect US involvement via the OAS.

The presidents' reaction introduced standing practices over intervention in domestic disputes. Such attempts were not altogether new; they built on the precedents of the Contadora Support Group which had tried to contribute to the peace process in Central America between 1983 and 1986. If this time round, free of the Cold War straightjacket, the intervention resonated in a different way, it was not easy to tone down Bolivia and Venezuela's anti-US rhetoric while avoiding direct or indirect US involvement, alone or through the OAS. Nonetheless, as a non-confrontational sign, the OAS's secretary-general was invited to Santiago as an observer to an effective *fait accompli*. All 12 presidents closed ranks in support of Evo Morales without inviting opposition or civil society to the debate. On that backing Morales arrested Governor Fernandez, urged the opposition to demobilize and a special commission for investigating the Pando massacre was created (later on stating the act was a crime against humanity). Other than a mere declaration, the summit issued a full-fledged plan of action. UNASUR's intervention was channeled through the establishment of three support groups staffed by renowned experts: one fact-finding commission to investigate the killings; a political commission to organize the dialogue between government and opposition; and a third commission designed to offer assistance to local institutions.

One week after the Pando killings, as they came to be known, a conciliation meeting between Morales and opposition leaders was organized by UNASUR leaders, together with several other facilitators and mediators invited to attend. Two months later the fact-finding commission had released its report on the Pando events. The active collaboration of the Bolivian government and opposition all through the work of the three commissions legitimized the intervention and marked an unprecedented departure from the long-standing commitment to sovereignty and non-intervention. Violence decreased sharply and political dialogue was restored. Empowered, President Correa came out saying: "Before, we used to go North to resolve our problems, but now, we go South and this time we went to Santiago de Chile."

This summit was a landmark in another, more important respect, not only for Bolivia but for the region as a whole, which had formerly been unassailably committed to a policy of non-intervention and utter respect for sovereignty. The crisis revealed the benefits of a safety net, of trust and of strength in numbers, as well as the value all leaders at the time placed on ensuring stability. That set the stage for Morales's call at the August 2009 summit where he criticized the presence of foreign military bases in South America and proposed the creation of a regional "School of Defense"[18] that could strengthen the civilian hand vis-à-vis that of the armed forces, which still exert inordinate influence in the security sector of South America.

However, Plan Colombia and the risk of spiraling militarization would continue to raise new challenges and flare up fresh controversies along the same lines. In the midst of the allegation that the United States was supporting secession in Bolivia, the US Navy announced the reactivation of its Fourth Fleet to patrol Latin American waters without consultation. The fleet, originally established to defend US oil interests in Venezuela during World War II and dismantled in 1950, would now conduct contingency operations and fight the war on drugs in aid of Plan Colombia. President Lula went on record as suspecting that American naval forces constituted a threat to Brazil's offshore oil reserves.[19]

When President Uribe in May 2009 deepened cooperation with the United States with the offer of allowing seven US military bases to operate in Colombia for the next ten years, the fear of militarization made hairs stand on end. Chávez accused Uribe of paving the way for an invasion and another coup in Venezuela. Venezuela also threatened to nationalize Colombian companies and seal the border. An extraordinary summit was convened in Quito but President Uribe failed to show up. A week later, a second extremely tense meeting was convened in Bariloche, Argentina, which Uribe attended after going on an appeasement tour of capitals and on condition that the meeting be televised. An agreement was hammered out which included the disclosure of the agreement while accepting the presence of the bases subject to verification.[20] Chávez left disgruntled, having failed to obtain outright condemnation, but Colombia was allowed to exorcise its fears that UNASUR was the mere projection of Chávez's whims. The subsequent election of Juan Manuel Santos as president of Colombia further contributed to a better climate of cooperation to the extent that in 2010 the country submitted a candidate to succeed Kirchner as secretary-general, and did so again in 2014.

All such rapid deployment summits over such a short time show troubled waters in the region but they allowed the leaders to provide an alternative of sorts to the well-oiled bureaucracies of international organizations and particularly the OAS. Presidents are attracted to such heavyweight problem-solving dynamics and enjoy the opportunity for epic struggles. Unless disagreements pose serious risks of fracture, it is hard to envisage that the leaders will surrender the benefits reaped by the high political profile of summit diplomacy and crisis management. This is the challenge they now face with the crisis that erupted in Venezuela as soon as Chávez passed away, to sustain their track record at a time when consensus has become thinner by the day.

Presidential solidarity: Going further afield

A new call for an emergency summit with a similarly vigorous message was replayed responding to the attempt to destabilize President Correa in Ecuador. At the end of September 2010, elements of the national police and military forces occupied Congress, and blocked two big international airports and important highways in response to a law reducing their benefits. After he made a speech at the police headquarters, the rebels attacked Correa with tear gas and held him hostage. While popular mobilization in support of Correa was key to averting the coup, the international condemnation and the support received by the South American nations were essential to weaken the attempt further. That same night, an emergency meeting was called in Buenos Aires by recently appointed Secretary-General Kirchner. Heads of state gave full and unqualified support to Correa. The following morning, the foreign ministers of UNASUR traveled to Quito to back the president further. Not only did the emergency meeting succeed in reacting quickly and strongly, but it also put forward the "Democratic Protocol" for the following summit: an agreement signed in November 2010 with the aim of imposing diplomatic, political, and economic sanctions on any country that might eventually break the democratic order. The "clause"—the principle of which also exists in the treaty—specifies measures to be taken against member states whose political processes are not being respected, and establishes sanctions, such as shutting down borders and the suspension of trade. Additional decisions in support of democracy have been made, such as the creation of the Electoral Council of UNASUR in 2011. This council sent its first observation mission to Guyana in November 2011 and then into the polarized climate in Venezuela in 2012, where it passed the test. UNASUR sent a 40-member technical observer mission under former Argentine Vice-President Carlos Alvarez to monitor the elections, indicating a strong commitment to overseeing stability.

Despite the precedents, a so-called parliamentary coup was hatched in Paraguay in June 2012, when Congress replaced the democratically elected president, Fernando Lugo, with Federico Franco. An impeachment process was staged against President Lugo after the shooting of 17 persons—11 farmers and six policemen—during a violent confrontation when the police tried to remove farmers charged with illegally occupying land said to be owned by large landowners. Despite the fact that Lugo dismissed his interior minister and his chief of police over this action, he was blamed for their deaths by the rightist Colorado Party, which had held power for 61 years before Lugo's election in 2008. Right away the legislative body, acting in unity, moved to file impeachment charges.

The rapidity of the impeachment plans, in fact, caught the rest of South America by surprise. On the day before the impeachment vote was held, the leaders of UNASUR, then attending the Rio+20 summit, hurriedly dispatched a delegation of foreign ministers along with the organization's secretary-general, Ali Rodríguez, to meet with the relevant parties. They met with Lugo, expressed their support for him, and stated that the impending impeachment did not respect due process. However, they could not change the congressional leaders' determination to proceed with the trial. Reacting strongly to this development, countries with embassies in Asuncion withdrew their ambassadors. Furthermore, Ecuador suggested the closing of borders while Venezuela stopped oil supplies. However, Argentina opposed following through with economic sanctions on humanitarian grounds.[21] Since Lugo held the annual rotating presidency of UNASUR at the time of his impeachment and ouster, the position was relinquished to Peruvian President Ollanta Humala on 24 June, when UNASUR foreign ministers—minus that of Paraguay—convened in Lima to discuss the situation in preparation for the Extraordinary Summit to be held in Mendoza, Argentina, five days later.

The summit announced the suspension of Paraguay's membership and stated that the government ought to comply with transparent elections for its reinstatement as a member of the organization. It described the events as "a rupture of democratic order" and the procedure to remove Lugo as a "summary trial" and a violation of due process. A year later, in August 2013, after holding elections, Paraguay was reinstated as a member at the VII Ordinary Summit in Suriname. Former President Lugo was mooted as secretary-general of UNASUR, a move that the new government, in an effort to build bridges, did not openly oppose, but which Lugo himself declined.

Less urgency, some evasion?

The repeated call to extraordinary summits seems to be petering out. Even issues that in the early years would have immediately raised hairs and triggered action are now accepted as routine differences. When Colombia announced in 2014 that it would be setting up a cooperation agreement with NATO, presidents were not called in, nor was the SADC. Even though some presidents raised serious concerns, it was not enough to summon others to an extraordinary summit and an epic struggle. With Lula not at the helm, the passing away of Chávez and serious social and financial distress in Venezuela, regional hegemonic competition has quietened considerably. The consensus reached over the election of a former president of Colombia as secretary-general for a two-year period could contribute to a summitry process with marked ideological differences. It is certainly an indication of quieter regional times.

The extensive literature on summitry has argued that one of the key elements to ensure effectiveness over and above the obvious injection of presidential empowerment over long-standing national bureaucracies is the setting up of technical bodies to carry out agreements and make the process jell. In the case of UNASUR, functional cooperation and policy coordination (as distinct from the political coordination at leaders level) has floundered in some areas such as finance,[22] whereas in health,[23] defense, and electoral oversight it has made inroads and laid stepping stones to institutional development.[24]

UNASUR joined the United Nations as an observer. Despite a chair in the General Assembly, the golden age of UNASUR summit diplomacy might have been the 2008–10 period, when a string of crises happened in rapid succession and there was enough consensus to induce the leaders to take action. When the VI UNASUR Summit met in Lima in 2012, the presidents of Argentina, Brazil, and Venezuela, who had suspended Paraguay in Mercosur (as well as in UNASUR) were all absent. The VII UNASUR Summit in Suriname in August 2013 failed to give summitry a shot in the arm. Despite grandiloquent declarations, four of the 12 UNASUR heads of state were absent. Moreover, the summit was overshadowed by the detention of the son of Suriname's president and summit host, Desi Bouterse (who himself has a checkered past) in Panama the day before the summit and extradition to the United States, where he faced drug- and arms-trafficking charges. With four leaders absent, UNASUR was unable to take on the appointment of a new secretary-general. A resolution condemning US initiatives regarding Syria was one of the few relevant and consensual results of the summit.[25]

All in all, the launching of peace talks in 2012 in Colombia has reduced pressure on the summitry process and opportunities for showcasing UNASUR. At the same time the crisis in Venezuela since the death of Chávez in 2013 showed that a routine for convening extraordinary summits is not in place. If coming together for crisis management has lost momentum, agglutination on the impacts of global issues comes naturally and opens roads for new functions, marking of turfs. When the founder of WikiLeaks, Julian Assange, requested asylum in the tiny Ecuadorian embassy in London on 19 August 2012, the British foreign office (citing the 1987 Diplomatic and Consular Premises Act) threatened to skirt the inviolability of the mission. The standoff that ensued cut through the intrigue of the "Assange Affair," and was caught in the undercurrent of the emerging geopolitical dynamics of the region. By 24 August, UNASUR—and also ALBA and the OAS—had convened ad hoc high-profile ministerial meetings and issued strong coordinated statements to protect the inviolability of Ecuador's diplomatic premises. Upholding the sovereign rights of member countries to manage their affairs independently during an extraordinary meeting of foreign ministers on 19 August 2012, UNASUR unanimously supported the Ecuadorian government's decision to provide asylum to Assange, against the wishes of the United Kingdom. The meeting also condemned Foreign Minister William Hague's threats to the Ecuadorian Embassy in London and interference in the sovereign right of a country to manage its asylum policy.

Conclusion

The summitry process has been a conflict-reduction instrument valued by presidents for different reasons. For some it allows an opportunity for neutralizing the United States. For Brazil, in particular, the creation of a region where it can feel comfortable is of the highest order. For all it allows the carving out of a platform for joining forces over pet issues and the creation of a region free of conflict. The polarization over the assessment of security threats (and the function or dysfunction of US influence) could still fragment the bloc in years to come. Such polarization is much more serious than the different outlooks on trade issues, where countries show that they are prepared to live with diversity. Amidst the string of disputes that have simmered domestically and endangered the peaceful termination of presidential terms, many policymakers fear a collapse of stability. Policy failures are bound to happen. Though leaders cannot guarantee solutions, the holding of regular summits can provide a sense of unity and a forum for consultation where none previously existed. Regular summits are certainly part of a wider phenomenon, not a prerogative of UNASUR. As such, they also tend to lose momentum, especially in competition with others springing up and taking up new directions.

For all its shortcomings, the leaders' process has enabled learning and a dimension of socialization. The outcome could be the acquisition of precedents, codes, and rules but it is too premature to say whether these are permanent. Three elements stand out: solidarity, the building of trust, and elements of cooperation despite differences. The closing of ranks in support of presidents in distress (i.e. presidential terms at risk of termination) works as a sort of "holy alliance" or even a safety net of *Présidents sans Frontières*. In an unstable region this cannot be demeaned. This crucial dimension of the interaction between regional governance and stability is, however, being put to the test in Venezuela at the moment of writing.

At the leaders' level the regular and recurrent extraordinary summits created a new way of life in South American politics for a time. Summit meetings attracted considerable media attention; they became important political events and one of the privileged forums where interconnectedness became apparent. While this of course cannot prejudge the actual impact of decisions, it showed that participants could encircle threats, tone down extremes of right and left, and agree on the need to preserve stability in times of turmoil. Although the mere existence of UNASUR and its summits will not prevent the outbreak of crises, or enable ousted presidents to be returned to power—as shown by the cases of Paraguay and Honduras (where the presidents also tried their hand at supporting President Zelaya, but to no avail)—it could contribute to the development and institutionalization of dynamics that facilitate prevention and management through political coordination. Political coordination includes rapid summons to summits when the time is ripe for confronting crises and a fast-track approval mechanism.

Crisis management in the 2008–10 period that required and allowed spaces for intervention and mediation was an outstanding achievement at a time when despite contrasting motivations, a consensus could be hammered out. Can that level of ambition endure? Or will ordinary summits carry on with less ambition and less urgency as a useful (but less epic) political space for dialogue? Was that the golden age when Lula and Chávez as trailblazers drove the agenda—with their respective styles and respective ideas in open competition but jointly ensuring followers and providing the necessary muscle and direction to the process? UNASUR's polycentrism may not allow it to sustain a steady course. Will present leaders sustain the early consensus to intervene in domestic crises as they did in Bolivia and Ecuador? Will they agree to continue in the early footsteps? How much counter-hegemony will they collectively tolerate and sustain?

The outcome of the crisis in Venezuela can give us pointers. The decision to send a delegation of foreign ministers to Venezuela places the ball firmly in UNASUR's court but not at the presidential level. The delegation, composed of the foreign ministers of Brazil, Colombia, and Ecuador, together with the papal nuncio, departed empty handed in May 2014. Addressing the Venezuelan crisis in UNASUR may have been difficult but there was an incentive to reduce the pressure of unilateral measures from outsiders. While President Maduro pushed for the crisis to be addressed by UNASUR precisely so as to avoid pressure from outside South America, for UNASUR to have left empty handed undermined its credibility as a crisis committee and surely weakened its missionary resolve. Albeit, UNASUR is in the company of the Vatican.

Notes

1. Chapter 3 in this volume.
2. Chapter 8 in this volume.
3. Chapter 2 in this volume.
4. Ernesto Vivares, *Exploring the New South American Regionalism* (Farnham: Ashgate, 2014).
5. Pia Riggirozzi and Diana Tussie, eds, *The Rise of Post-Hegemonic Regionalism* (London: Springer, 2012).
6. Marcelo Saguier, "Socioenvironmental Regionalism in South America," in *The Rise of Post-Hegemonic Regionalism*, ed. Riggirozzi and Tussie.
7. Cintia Quiliconi, "Modelos Competitivos de Integración en el Hemisferio Occidental: Liderazgo Competitivo o Negación Mutua?," *Revista CIDOB d'Afers Internacionals* 2013, nos. 102–103 (2013): 147–168.
8. Diana Tussie, "Os Imperativos do Brasil no Desafiador Espaço Regional da América do Sul: uma Visão da Economia Política internacional," *Lua Nova*, no. 90 (2013), www.scielo.br/scielo.php?script=sci_arttext&pid=S0102-64452013000300009&lng=en&nrm=iso&tlng=pt.
9. Rut Diamint, "Regionalismo y Posicionamiento Suramericano: UNASUR y ALBA," *Revista CIDOB d'Afers Internacionals*, no. 101 (2013): 55–79.
10. Francisco Rojas Aravena and Paz Milet, *Diplomacia de Cumbres: El Multilateralismo Emergente del Siglo XXI* (Santiago, Chile: FLACSO, 1998).
11. Diana Tussie, "La Coordinación de los Deudores Latinoamericanos: ¿Cuál es la Lógica de su Accionar?," *Desarrollo Económico* 28, no. 109 (1988): 67–88.
12. Jeffrey W. Cason and Timothy J. Power, "Presidentialization, Pluralization and the Rollback of Itamaraty: Explaining Change in Brazilian Foreign Policy Making in the Cardoso-Lula Era," *International Political Science Review* 30, no. 2 (2009): 117–140.
13. Pia Riggirozzi, "Acción Colectiva y Diplomacia de UNASUR SALUD: La Construcción Regional a través de Políticas Sociales," *Documentos de Trabajo-Área de Relaciones Internacionales FLACSO Argentina*, no. 63 (2012), rrii.flacso.org.ar/wp-content/uploads/2013/02/FLA_Acci%C3%B3n-colectiva-y-diplomacia-de-UNASUR-Salud_Riggirozzi-Sept-2012.pdf.
14. Daniel Flemes and Michael Radseck, "Creating Multilevel Security Governance in South America," GIGA Working Papers no. 117 (2009), www.resdal.org/producciones-miembros/art-flemes-radseck.pdf.
15. Fredy Rivera, "Trends, Strategic Tensions and Cooperation in Security and Intelligence in the Andean Region," in *Exploring the New South American Regionalism (NSAR)*, ed. Ernesto Vivares (Farnham: Ashgate, 2014).
16. Carlos Espinosa, "The Origins of the Union of South American Nations: A Multicausal Account of South American Regionalism," in *Exploring the New South American Regionalism (NSAR)*, ed. Vivares.
17. Nicolás Falomir Lockhart, "La Identidad de UNASUR: ¿Regionalismo Post-Neoliberal o Post-Hegemónico?," *Revista de Ciencias Sociales*, no. 140 (2013): 97–109, www.redalyc.org/articulo.oa?id=15329874007.
18. Paul Kellog, "Union of South American Nations," in *The Wiley-Blackwell Encyclopedia of Globalization*, ed. George Ritzer (Oxford: Blackwell Publishing, 2012).

19 Jorge Battaglino, "Defence in a Post-Hegemonic Regional Agenda: The Case of the South American Defence Council," in *The Rise of Post-Hegemonic Regionalism*, ed. Riggirozzi and Tussie.
20 Disclosure revealed that the US troops would not be operating outside of Colombia. Moreover, the establishment of the bases did not materialize, not because of UNASUR but thanks to the Colombian courts; a decision that was not appealed by President Santos.
21 One can assume that given the intimate interdependence amongst the countries of Mercosur, in terms of migration, energy, and investments, etc., sanctions, in any case, would not be feasible.
22 The agreement for Bank of the South was signed in 2009 but did not actually take off, allegedly because Brazil is keener to internationalize its BNDES and/or join forces with the BRICS Bank. The regional payments system and other elements of the financial architecture, a deeply felt issue for Ecuador, crop up time and again but do not make inroads.
23 José Antonio Sanahuja, "Post Liberal Regionalism in South America: The Case of UNASUR," EUI Working Papers, EUI RSCAS, Florence, Italy, 2012.
24 Pablo Trucco, "The Rise of Monetary Agreements in South America," in *The Rise of Post-Hegemonic Regionalism*, ed. Riggirozzi and Tussie.
25 Andrés Serbin, "UNASUR looking for Leadership and Direction," *Aula Blog*, aulablog.net/2013/11/18/unasur-looking-for-leadership-and-direction.

5 Summitry in the Caribbean Community
A fundamental feature of regional governance

Jessica Byron

- **Origins, goals, and structure of the CARICOM summit process**
- **The evolution of the summit process**
- **Dialogue and socialization**
- **Agenda setting and orientation**
- **Negotiation and coordination**
- **Legitimation**
- **Other functions**
- **Conclusion**

The Caribbean Community (CARICOM) is a multi-purpose regional grouping established in 1973. It has 15 full member territories and five associate members.[1] Although summitry has been an integral part of Commonwealth Caribbean regional cooperation, this grouping has received little attention in the global literature on summit diplomacy. CARICOM Heads of Government (CHG) meetings have, however, received critical reviews in discussions on regional governance. CARICOM summitry has made a substantial but ambiguous contribution to shaping the regional movement. It has generated the political impetus and collective identity to drive the organization. On the other hand, the CHGs are also perceived as perpetuating top-down regional governance, keeping CARICOM firmly in the confines of intergovernmentalism and slowing the development of other organs and actors in regional governance—creating an "elite rapport" rather than a "community of interests."[2]

In 1963 Trinidad Prime Minister Eric Williams initiated regular meetings of the political leadership of the newly independent and self-governing territories of the Commonwealth Caribbean. Those meetings were modeled on those of the Organization of African Unity (OAU).[3] The aim was to build a closer relationship and ultimately an economic community. Three summits were held between 1963 and

1965, involving Barbados, Guyana, Jamaica, and Trinidad and Tobago. These were the precursors to founding the Caribbean Free Trade Association (CARIFTA, 1968) and CARICOM (1973). They set the stage for substantial engagement of the region's heads in the functioning and evolution of CARICOM.

CARICOM was established for the purposes of economic integration, functional cooperation, and foreign policy coordination.[4] The Revised Treaty of Chaguaramas (2001), in the context of globalization and economic liberalization, expanded these objectives to include regional economic development, convergence and improved standards of living for Caribbean people, increased trade and economic relations with the rest of the world, increased productivity, competitiveness, and economic leverage. The revised treaty also made reference to the enhanced participation of non-state actors in the regional processes, the protection of human rights, and elaborated on a range of dispute settlement mechanisms.

The CARICOM process began in 1973–76 with irregular summits, progressing in 1982 to serial summitry and *de facto* institutionalization.[5] CARICOM summitry has passed through four evolutionary phases: the initial one of irregular meetings and severe growing pains culminating in a six-year hiatus; the second phase, which established serial meetings but "retreated into ritual"[6] buffeted by politico-ideological and security crises which polarized the region during the early 1980s; a third phase of renewed momentum and a dramatic increase in summits after 1989; and the current phase, dating from 2000, characterized by the travails of implementation and the operational challenges of a partially constituted single market underpinned by a weak system of governance.

The summits are a core feature of regional governance, institutionalized and highly structured, with the support machinery of the CARICOM Bureau, prime ministerial portfolios and sub-committees, and the CARICOM Secretariat. CARICOM's integration process has been intricately bound up with the personalities of and relations among some prominent and long-serving leaders, their periodic conflicts but also their understanding of the value of regional unity and perceptions of themselves as guardians of this process.[7] It is rooted in the political culture of the region. Over four decades, the summitry process has evolved in tandem with generational changes in leadership, the demands of external and national environments and regional institutional developments. We agree with Andrew Cooper and Timothy Shaw[8] that for these small Caribbean states, summitry is a collective diplomacy resource to be used for innovative engagements with the global community in their search for resilient development.

The chapter examines CARICOM's summitry and its role in regional governance, exploring the extent to which summitry fulfills the functions of dialogue and socialization of regional leaders, agenda setting and orientation of the organization's programs, coordination of negotiating strategies and policy alignment, legitimation of domestic policies, and leadership. The next section examines the origins, expectations, and goals when the CARICOM summits began. It also traces the institutionalization of summitry and its supporting mechanisms. This is followed by an overview of CARICOM summitry in different time frames and a discussion of its functions. We assess the extent to which CARICOM summitry has fulfilled the functions outlined in the literature and identify some additional functions that may be specific to the region's political and organizational culture. The conclusion confirms the contribution and directions for regional summitry.

Origins, goals, and structure of the CARICOM summit process

> Just as a house does not a family make, but the quality of relationships under the roof that gives it the character of a home—so a Treaty does not a Community make, but the quality of the relationships between its member States that give life and constant freshness to the formal ageing parchment ... in the busy rush for development ... we sometimes forget to pause, to inform, to consult, to reassure, to coordinate with our Community colleagues ...[9]

Soon after its inauguration, CARICOM experienced the after-shocks of the global oil crisis. The ensuing political and economic tensions resulted in a six-year suspension of CHG meetings. When the CHG Conference was reconvened in 1982, Guyana's president, Forbes Burnham, and Dominica's prime minister, Eugenia Charles, reflected on the critical need for and function of summits in the *modus operandi* of CARICOM. The former asked "Can a regional movement really survive if there is ... infrequency of meetings between the decision-makers? You cannot run this region unless those who are clothed with the power to relay their cabinet decisions meet regularly..."[10] Dame Eugenia argued that the summits were essential for the management of the region's social and economic development, they were opportunities to deepen acquaintance, cement friendships, and plan regional programs of action.[11]

The CHG Conference is described in the Treaty of Chaguaramas (1973) and the revised treaty as the principal organ of the regional grouping with primary responsibility for determining community policy. It is the final authority on most community matters, including the assumption of international treaty obligations, financial and budgetary arrangements, establishment of programs, and machinery to carry out community decisions. The revised treaty expands the functions of the conference to include, among other things, conflict management among member states. It also establishes a new entity, the Bureau of the Conference, consisting of the outgoing, current, and next chair of the conference. The bureau is supposed to broker consensus on policy matters, mobilize the implementation of conference decisions, initiate policy proposals, and provide guidance for the CARICOM Secretariat.[12] The CHG Conference and bureau work closely with the Community Council and secretariat.

Initial expectations were that the conference as final decision-making organ of CARICOM would play a major hands-on role in approving initiatives and directing the process of cooperation. This is an extension of national approaches to governance in the Commonwealth Caribbean states, which are characterized by small populations, generally limited territorial space, scarce resources, small bureaucracies with limited capacity, considerable concentration of executive power, and very personalized political systems. The past 50 years have witnessed many strong, idiosyncratic, sometimes charismatic Caribbean political leaders. They have generally had populist and nationalist orientations and powers of oratory. All these elements have influenced the style and patterns of regional summitry.

Neither Chaguaramas treaty provides for frequency of summit meetings, merely stating that the conference shall regulate its own procedures.[13] Institutionalization began in 1983 when the CHG endorsed Forbes Burnham's proposal that summits should be convened every year on 4 July, the anniversary of the signing of the Treaty of Chaguaramas. Intersessional Summits were introduced in 1990 as a tool to propel the implementation of the Single Market and Economy.[14] CHG would thenceforth meet in normal sessions twice per year, in February/March and July, with additional special meetings when required.

CARICOM summitry is supported by three other mechanisms. *Pro tempore* chairmanship of the organization rotates alphabetically among the full member states for six-month periods. The CARICOM Bureau, on which the secretary-general (SG) also sits as an *ex officio* member, provides continuity and ensures smooth transitions. In the early 1990s a "quasi-Cabinet" mechanism was established, giving CHG portfolio responsibilities for coordinating various sectors of regional integration.[15] Also, some Prime Ministerial Sub-committees evolved, either to deal with the volume of work in some portfolios, or as temporary committees to address specific issues that emerge on the regional agenda. All portfolio heads and committees report to the summits.

All member states can propose inputs for summit agendas but three entities have major responsibility for shaping them, namely the conference chair in consultation with other members of the bureau, the CARICOM SG and the Community Council. The latter gives the final approval for summit agendas. They generally include the substantive areas of CARICOM integration: CARICOM Single Market and Economy (CSME) matters, foreign policy coordination, security cooperation and functional cooperation in a wide range of development programs, and the renewal of regional governance institutions.[16] The CARICOM Secretariat prepares and circulates the working document and background papers.

CARICOM summits are divided into plenaries and a closed session. The plenaries are open to the national delegations, observers, and invited guests. The closed caucus may be restricted to the CHG and the CARICOM SG. However, for most caucuses, each head is accompanied by one government official. There is a large attendance of CARICOM functionaries and regional agencies at the summits.

The evolution of the summit process

CARICOM summits over four decades have addressed the following themes:

- economic development challenges and strategies, and ultimately the construction of the CSME;
- where possible, domestic dispute management and the management of inter-state disputes;
- international diplomatic themes and foreign policy coordination; and
- regional crises and disaster management.

1973–76

During this inaugural phase, the CHGs met five times. The dynamic of the relations among the four independent more developed countries (MDCs), Barbados, Guyana, Jamaica, and Trinidad, was crucial to the development of the embryonic group. Meetings focused on the institutional development of the organization and the expansion of functional cooperation. A central theme became the negative impact of high energy prices, the economic difficulties of leading member states, and the ensuing crisis for regional trade flows and payments.

Resumption of summitry, 1982–89

CARICOM held eight regular summit meetings and two special meetings[17] in the 1980s. The composition of the grouping changed with the advance to full sovereignty of seven member states by 1986.[18] Electoral changes and death introduced a new generation of political leadership. The 1982 summit was, moreover, the first to include a government that had not come to power through elections—the Grenadian People's Revolutionary Government. The final change to the regional landscape was the establishment of the Organization of Eastern Caribbean States in 1981. Within CARICOM, there was now a formally constituted sub-regional bloc of the Eastern Caribbean less developed countries (LDCs).

This period was possibly the most challenging in CARICOM's political history. It started out with deep regional and international ideological divisions, security concerns, and the impossibility of harmonizing many areas of foreign policy. In October 1983, the Grenadian Revolution collapsed, followed by a US military intervention that was supported by some member states, opposed by others. A chasm of recrimination and mistrust opened up in regional relations. Nonetheless, the CHGs continued to go through the motions of annual summits at which they voiced their differences, deliberated on cooperation programs, and gradually rebuilt working relationships. The most significant legacy concerned regional democratic norms. In 1981, CARICOM had adopted a norm of ideological pluralism to avoid the community's fragmentation. The demise of the Grenadian Revolution, other political crises and engagement with Haiti caused CARICOM by 1990 to evolve towards explicit emphasis on membership norms of parliamentary democracy, human rights observance, and inclusive state-civil society relations, reflected in institutional innovations and new practices.[19]

The 1980s brought continued economic challenges. Several states wrestled with structural adjustment programs, and all had economic difficulties and chronic shortages of investment capital. One outcome was the 1984 Nassau Summit's Understanding on Structural Adjustment, CARICOM's first attempt to reconcile national development strategies with international policy and with a regional framework for development cooperation.

Although CARICOM leaders failed to coordinate foreign policy in crucial areas, they found common ground on many international development questions and began coordinating approaches towards the multilateral financial institutions. Likewise, they formulated common policies on apartheid, relations between the European Union and the African, Caribbean, and Pacific Group of States within the organization (ACP-EU relations) and the territorial integrity of Guyana and Belize. They also initiated membership expansion in 1984–86 by admitting the Dominican Republic, Haiti, and Suriname as observers in functional cooperation committees. In 1988, after the fall of Jean-Claude "Baby Doc" Duvalier, "CARICOM leaders felt so disturbed by developments in Haiti that they met in extraordinary session to talk about their concerns—a procedure that has never before been used in a political crisis not directly involving a member state."[20] This meeting and Jamaican initiatives would lead to Haiti's eventual incorporation into CARICOM.[21]

Summit speeches in the 1980s evidenced leaders' concerns about the functioning of regional institutions and effective integration.[22] Heads commissioned three reports on CARICOM governance. They debated but did not adopt proposals to strengthen regional governance and institutions.[23] Finally, in the 1989 Grand Anse Declaration[24] they agreed to establish a Single Market and Economy and tackle longstanding institutional problems. They appointed a West Indian Commission to consult with Caribbean societies and report on how to advance the goals of Caribbean integration. The 1980s proposals reappeared as recommendations for a revamped CARICOM in the new era.

The long road to the CSME, 1990–2000

Driven by the agenda of renewal, the post-Cold War global environment and hemispheric developments, the 1990s witnessed a dramatic increase in CARICOM summits. There were 26 meetings for the decade. In each year there were two regular meetings and in some years there were additional ones. Summitry became more formalized. The host countries for each of the July summits were decided on two years in advance, which provided more preparatory time for organizing a large, costly regional conference. Notwithstanding the increased number of summits, agendas were heavily loaded due to the momentum of international and regional developments.

There were changes in participation at the 1990s summits. Suriname joined CARICOM in 1995 and Haiti, in preparation for accession, was often present with effect from 1996. Three associate members joined: the British Virgin Islands, and Turks and Caicos Islands in 1991, and Anguilla in 1999. There was a significant increase in the number and diversity of invited guests. The practice began of ceremonial or business visits from heads of government or foreign ministers from other hemispheric countries, Commonwealth or African countries, and senior officials from international organizations. Finally, in 1993 annual dialogues began with non-state actors, starting with the Caribbean labor movement and the private sector, and by 1996 including a wider cross-section of civil society. They were designated CARICOM's "Social Partners."

Summits addressed the CSME, security and trade issues, hemispheric diplomacy, and political crises during this phase. After the attempted coup in Trinidad in 1990, small state security and sovereignty re-emerged as a prominent theme. Narco-trafficking and the Shiprider policy response[25] ultimately resulted in more effective regional coordination of US–Caribbean relations. This gave rise to a United States-CARICOM special summit in December 1996 in which they explored mutual security concerns, calling for these to be addressed in a spirit of dialogue, respect for sovereignty, and partnership devoid of coercion.[26] In the wake of numerous destructive hurricanes and Montserrat's volcanic eruptions in 1995, disaster preparedness and management became another security focus at summits. This resulted in the establishment of the Caribbean Disaster Emergency Response Agency (CDERA) in 1991 and intergovernmental cooperation with the financial sector to expand the availability of disaster insurance facilities in the region.[27]

The 1990s summits dealt extensively with CARICOM's external trade agenda in the context of the World Trade Organization (WTO) international trade regime, EU-ACP matters, the launch of the Free Trade Area of the Americas (FTAA) initiative, and growing concerns about preserving preferential market access and "special and differential treatment" for small economies. Such concerns led to the establishment of the Regional Negotiating Machinery (RNM) in 1997.

Likewise, a Greater Caribbean/Latin American diplomatic space emerged with numerous ministerial visits from Latin American countries and the construction of joint institutions and channels for cooperation. These included the Association of Caribbean States,[28] the Cuba-CARICOM Commission and the naming of CARICOM's first representative in the Rio Group in 1991.

CARICOM summits assumed a more active political crisis management role. In 1996, they appointed a mediator in response to the threat of secession in St Kitts and Nevis. They appointed an independent commission in response to Guyana's electoral dispute in 1998. The outcome was the Herdmanston Accord and CARICOM's involvement in an electoral audit. In Haiti, CARICOM provided assistance for elections in the 1990s.

The summits had an active community agenda, seeking to implement the commitments made in the Grand Anse Declaration.[29] A special summit in October 1992 considered the West Indian Commission Report, and rejected, modified, or agreed to various recommendations. By 2000, eight protocols to establish the CSME had been signed. The Assembly of CARICOM Parliamentarians was convened twice. The CARICOM Charter of Civil Society, setting benchmarks for regional state-civil society relations, was tabled in 1997. The heads had approved the agreement to establish the Caribbean Court of Justice (CCJ).

However, despite the advances in regional integration, some policies adopted by the CHGs strengthened national sovereignty to the detriment of strong, effective regional governance,[30] thereby sowing the seeds of problems for the single market arrangements. A special summit in 1999 produced the Consensus of Chaguaramas, a long checklist of CSME tasks to be completed, commitments to civil society and to the strengthening of CARICOM institutions, but equally it distributed more portfolios to CHGs.[31]

As the 1990s drew to a close, various CHGs themselves were critical of the structures that they had approved, concluding that the governance system was unsustainable. Prime Minister Lester Bird of Antigua in 1996 highlighted CSME implementation deficits thus: "having served on the Bureau for the last few months, I am strengthened in my view that it is not an adequate substitute for the Commission ... Heads of Government simply do not have the time to give the work of the Bureau the dedicated and devoted time it deserves ... We need to return to the concept of a Caribbean Commission as proposed by the WIC [West Indian Commission]."[32] Prime Minister Kenny Anthony of Saint Lucia remarked in 1997 that "a new style of governance in CARICOM requires that we make decisions that are capable of implementation ... We will need to ... de-emphasize the idea of summitry and of conference diplomacy ... in which leaders bargain for advantages for their individual sovereign island states ... an essential part of the challenge is the need to depoliticize the regional integration process."[33]

CARICOM summitry in the twenty-first century

The twenty-first century demonstrates the possibilities and limitations of summitry as a tool of regional governance among small vulnerable states facing intensifying challenges of globalization and environmental risks. There were approximately 35 CARICOM summits between 2000 and 2014. Three new members or associates acceded. Summit agendas addressed recurrent economic crises, from the post-9/11 recession to the profound global financial crisis affecting the Caribbean since 2009. Natural disasters have loomed large—the 2010 Haitian earthquake, the ravages of hurricanes in Haiti, Grenada, the Cayman Islands, and Jamaica among others. There have been political conflicts including the complete breakdown of Haiti's political system between 2004 and 2007. Efforts to implement the CSME continued throughout, and starting in 2000 there was a new focus on human development. CHGs continued perennial discussions about regional governance deficits and the need for reform, accompanied by tentative experiments with wider societal involvement in regional integration. CARICOM increasingly became a platform for regional engagement in hemispheric and global governance initiatives.

A summit decision in July 2001 launched the construction of the "Fourth Pillar" of regional security cooperation. Trinidad, Jamaica, Barbados, and many regional and national security agencies featured prominently in its implementation by ratifying the 2006 Treaty on Regional Security Assistance, establishing the CARICOM Implementation Agency for Crime and Security and subsequent programs.[34] Likewise, the heads' Nassau Declaration in 2001[35] launched new health initiatives which emphasized the Pan-Caribbean HIV-AIDS Partnership and other areas of health cooperation, ultimately consolidating five regional agencies into the Caribbean Regional Public Health Agency in 2013. Other new initiatives included programs for climate change adaptation.

In 2001 the Revised Treaty of Chaguaramas and the CCJ Statute were signed. The court began operations in 2004, and by 2006, 12 member states had signed on fully to the CSME. There were new overtures to civil society. In 2002, CHGs met with 150 nongovernmental organization (NGO) representatives and adopted the Liliendaal Statement of Principles.[36] This reaffirmed the norms that should guide their joint participation in regional integration and committed to facilitating greater engagement of civil society with CARICOM functional organs. However, the annual consultations with CHGs were gradually discontinued.[37]

In 2004, Antiguan Prime Minister Spencer called for governments and opposition parties to collaborate more closely in regional governance:

> There is no means of preparation for a first time PM who finds himself Chair of Conference the very moment he takes his oath of office ... very regrettably, a No Admittance to Opposition Politicians sign continues to hang over the door to the councils of CARICOM ... In seeking national consensus on the CCJ, Caribbean governments might have to venture into uncharted waters in their relations with opposition leadership in the region.[38]

This led to initial consultations with the regional parliamentary opposition in 2005,[39] and a committee meeting of three heads and four opposition leaders in Jamaica in 2006. They discussed the CSME, strengthening the Assembly of Caribbean Community Parliamentarians for regional governance, and endorsed the 1997 Charter for Civil Society.[40]

The final outreach to civil society concerned appointing a commission in 2007 to make recommendations on empowering Caribbean youth and improving their quality of life. The final report was presented at a special summit, concluding with the 2010 Declaration of Paramaribo.[41]

Summits continued to address crises affecting member states. Conflict management initiatives included the appointment of a mediator in the Guyana–Suriname maritime territorial dispute in 2000[42] and a mission to Trinidad after the electoral impasse of 2002. Engagement in Haiti's governance conflicts was done in partnership with the Organization of American States (OAS) and the United Nations (UN). After President Aristide's removal in 2004, the CHGs suspended Haiti's participation in the organization.[43] Engagement resumed in 2006, intensifying after the 2010 earthquake.

Economic crisis initiatives included the 2002 special summit in Saint Lucia which produced support measures for Dominica's balance of payments crisis. Financing from Trinidad and other sources was channeled into the establishment of a Regional Development Fund in 2006. Between 2009 and 2012 CARICOM experienced a severe economic crisis, which almost paralyzed regional integration.[44] Reports abounded of national administrations reneging on their commitments to CSME labor mobility. The summits of 2009–12 focused on response measures. These included consultations with the international financial institutions, establishing a task force to contain the crisis of collapsed financial firms, putting in place regulatory systems for the region's financial sector, and the maintenance, as far as possible, of free movement across the region.

Nonetheless, regional integration experienced major strains. This was acknowledged at a special summit in Guyana in May 2011 which agreed to pause the single-economy implementation and focus on completing the single market.[45] In 2003, a summit in Trinidad had discussed the institutional malaise and appointed a prime ministerial group to make recommendations on future governance.[46] The result was the Rose Hall Declaration on Governance which endorsed recommendations for CARICOM decisions to be legally binding within member states, for a commission to replace the bureau and for automatic financial transfers to CARICOM institutions.[47] However, the recommendations were never implemented, and the secretariat became progressively more underfinanced and overburdened, unable to respond effectively to a plethora of crises in subsequent years. Regional integration discourse in the twenty-first century became imbued with frustration and pessimism about CARICOM's ability to reinvent itself. The current reform initiative concerns secretariat and agency rationalization, which may result in a scaling down of commitments in line with limited resources.[48]

Since 2000, CARICOM states' foreign policies have demonstrated growing divergence and unilateral tendencies. Paradoxically, the foreign policy coordination function of CARICOM summits has expanded during the same period. An increasing number of summits have been jointly convened with regional groups or with individual hemispheric states; likewise CARICOM has coordinated its participation in the Summits of the Americas. Consultations with third country heads of state and officials, and international organization heads increased in frequency and number throughout these years. Finally, the summits provided regular opportunities for heads to consider and approve the reports and recommendations of the CARICOM units that directed the group's involvement in the FTAA, Cotonou/Economic Partnerships Agreement, and other international trade and economic cooperation negotiations and agreements.

Dialogue and socialization

CARICOM summits provide a space for consensus building and also for acrimonious exchanges. Caucuses are periodically used for discussing major domestic challenges. The discussions give better insight into the stances, concerns, and constraints of national administrations and individuals. Heads become better acquainted with one another and expand their networking possibilities at CARICOM summits. The summits give them a greater awareness of the regional and global environments and the perspectives of other actors in the community. In some cases they succeed in formulating common positions on global and regional issues. The dialogue function is particularly significant during regional crises. While it has not prevented conflicts from occurring, it has contributed to their management, and over time the region's leadership seems to have acquired greater tolerance for disagreement than existed originally. Even if retreat into ritual remains their default mode, they have continued to meet, avoided gridlock,[49] and overall attendance of heads at the summits is high.

In terms of socialization, the summits are used to reaffirm and transmit regional norms, traditions, and values such as democracy or unity. This can be done through ceremonies and speeches. New heads are always invited to speak at their first summit. It is a welcome ritual which presents them to the regional community. New heads are not only socialized into the club, but they also introduce new attitudes and ideas to the group.

The summits have contributed to expanding women's representation in Caribbean governance in tandem with the election of four female CHGs, starting with Eugenia Charles of Dominica in 1982. The annual summits made women more visible in regional leadership to Caribbean societies. Charles, in particular, brought a very different tone to the summits with her outspoken criticism of some aspects of regional governance[50] and irreverent views on some of the region's dominant personalities and hallowed traditions: "It was not a woman that was there, it was a person with a strong personality ... things that Eugenia could tell Forbes [Burnham], nobody else could tell him ... it was a clash of ideology ... a clash of intellect, it was a clash of the sexes all combined ..."[51] As Charles herself stated, "Cricket was the most binding thing between us (CARICOM Heads). I didn't agree that cricket was an important thing—I didn't play cricket! But ... there is more unification in talking cricket than there is in talking money."[52] Other female heads have continued to exercise significant functions in the "quasi-Cabinet."

Agenda setting and orientation

The conference is the most authoritative organ in CARICOM. The summits propose or at least approve new programs, initiatives, and regional machinery. Many programs have had their genesis in proposals from individual heads while others are proposed by regional institutions. Many are derived from global/hemispheric initiatives and CARICOM is the channel for orienting national and regional bureaucracies and gaining access to development support for health, climate change, etc. Summit agendas always include consultations on international developments and appropriate regional/national responses.

While the summits identify and approve many regional programs, the decision-making process has been criticized for insufficient attention to identifying the resources for implementation. This may be symptomatic of small developing state, resource-scarce diplomacy. As national economic difficulties have intensified, increasingly the secretariat is instructed to find the resources from multilateral sources. The process has been criticized for poor prioritization and alignment with regional resources, for inadequate cost-benefit analysis, and the current trend is towards more stringent rationalization of programs.[53]

Negotiation and coordination

CARICOM summits envisage endorsing common regional policies and coordinating domestic ones, but national policies are not always successfully aligned or common courses of action followed. Summits are used by countries to explain domestic situations to other member states and justify inability to conform to a joint policy. They may be used to give blistering defenses of a country's regional commitment or critiques of member countries' compliance.[54] However, coordination and harmonization are evident in the region's preparation for international trade negotiations and global multilateral diplomacy.[55] The heads examine options prepared by technical experts and agree on regional positions before crucial international consultations. CARICOM caucuses occur even during multilateral conferences. The region seeks to maximize the leverage of having a bloc of 14 votes in such forums.

Legitimation

The summits certainly are a means of "validating member countries and regimes."[56] They validate the idea of the Caribbean Community since biannual conferences held in each full member territory offer their populations a concrete symbol of regionalism. They provide occasions for endorsing the legitimacy of domestic policies and the effectiveness of national leadership. They furnish the opportunity to defend or attribute responsibility for unpopular national policies. The summits welcome impressive arrays of distinguished international guests, and this increases the prestige value and media impact for the grouping and the host country. Nonetheless, there are communication weaknesses in regional summitry. Communication channels could be better employed to maximize the legitimation, affirmation, and mobilization effects of the summits.

Other functions

CARICOM summits provide cost-effective opportunities for member states to consult on bilateral issues not necessarily related to regional integration.[57] Associate members have been socialized into a Caribbean political space, given a voice in regional forums and some degree of access to multilateral programs despite their limited sovereignty.

The summits have become a convenient platform for third states and international organizations to engage in dialogue with CARICOM.

These encounters are mutually beneficial, providing international visitors with an effective diplomatic channel to the entire bloc. Processes of intra- and inter-regional summitry have evolved, evidenced by the CARICOM-Cuba summits, the CARICOM-SICA dialogues, meetings with the G-3 (Mexico, Colombia, and Venezuela, 1993) and Brazil (2010). Despite challenges of coordination, CARICOM summits remain essential for agreement on regional policies towards the Community of Latin American and Caribbean Nations (CELAC), the Southern Common Market (Mercosur), and the Union of South American Nations (UNASUR). CARICOM summitry offers a diplomatic tool for responding to global power shifts and new hemispheric actors.

The CARICOM experience of working with international organizations confirms Philippe Chrestia's argument that summits can be a tool for managing interdependence. CARICOM also bears out analyses about determinants of summit success,[58] including the effectiveness of the preparation process, overall quality of participation, and adequate attention to communication flows among the governmental actors themselves and with the wider regional community.[59] Geoff Berridge emphasizes the importance of logistical planning which has been significant for CHG access to technical advisors during caucuses.[60]

Conclusion

CARICOM and its summits have been great survivors for over 40 years.[61] Regular summits have helped to build a regional community and construct the norms, policies, and practices for its governance, although there are deficits in their contributions to strengthening non-state participation in regional governance. The summits are significant platforms for multilateral hemispheric and global diplomacy, increasing the international visibility of these micro-states. Despite its challenges, CARICOM continues to generate interest for non-independent territories in the Caribbean because of the functional cooperation possibilities, the regional community space and international platform afforded to their territorial leadership.[62]

Notes

1 CARICOM full members: Antigua and Barbuda, the Bahamas, Barbados, Belize, Dominica, Grenada, Guyana, Haiti, Jamaica, Montserrat, Saint Lucia, St Kitts and Nevis, St Vincent and the Grenadines, Suriname, and Trinidad and Tobago. Associate members: Anguilla, Bermuda, British Virgin Islands, Cayman Islands, and the Turks and Caicos Islands. All members and associates attend CARICOM summits.

2 Anthony Payne, *The Political History of CARICOM* (Kingston, Jamaica: Ian Randle Publishers, 2008), 216.
3 Payne, *The Political History of CARICOM*, 16.
4 CARICOM, Treaty of Chaguaramas (1973), www.caricom.org.
5 Geoff Berridge, *Diplomacy: Theory and Practice* (Basingstoke: Palgrave Macmillan, 2010), 167–171; and Philippe Chrestia, "Les Sommets Internationaux," *Etudes Internationales* 31, no. 3 (2000): 443–474.
6 Anthony Payne, "Caribbean Regional Integration," in *Charting Caribbean Development*, ed. Anthony Payne and Paul Sutton (London: Macmillan, 2001), 191.
7 Desmond Hoyte, cited in Kenneth O. Hall, ed., *Integrate or Perish! Perspectives of Leaders of the Integration Movement 1963–1999* (Kingston, Jamaica: UWI Mona, 2000), 330.
8 Andrew Cooper and Timothy Shaw, "The Summitry of Small States: Towards the Caribbean Summit," CIGI Policy Briefs no. 15, 2009, www.cigionline.org/publications.
9 Shridath Ramphal, cited in Terri-Ann Gilbert-Roberts, *The Politics of Integration: Caribbean Sovereignty Revisited* (Kingston, Jamaica: Ian Randle Publishers, 2013), 82.
10 Linden Forbes Burnham, cited in Hall, *Integrate or Perish!* 441.
11 Eugenia Charles, cited in Hall, *Integrate or Perish!* 431–433.
12 Observers suggest that the bureau has tended to concentrate more on agenda matters and liaising with the secretariat than on the politically sensitive task of following up on national implementation of CARICOM decisions.
13 Article 8, 1973; and Article 10, 2001.
14 Interview with retired senior CARICOM official, 26 March 2014. The regular meetings were expected to bring greater organization, discipline, and speed to the implementation of decisions and programs.
15 See www.caricom.org for details of quasi-Cabinet country portfolios. Information also gleaned from interview with CARICOM official, 27 March 2014.
16 Herbert Blaize, cited in Hall, *Integrate or Perish!* 238; and Jessica Byron, "The Caribbean Community's 'Fourth Pillar': The Evolution of Regional Security Governance," in *The Security Governance of Regional Organizations*, ed. Roberto Dominguez, Emil Kirchner (London: Routledge, 2011).
17 Grenada, July 1983; Barbados, September 1986.
18 Antigua, the Bahamas, Belize, Dominica, St Kitts, St Lucia, and St Vincent.
19 Payne, *The Political History of CARICOM*, 253–278; and Gilbert-Roberts, *The Politics of Integration*, 84–86.
20 Lloyd Erskine Sandiford, cited in Hall, *Integrate or Perish!* 273.
21 Michael Dash, "Paved with Good Intentions: Relations between Haiti and CARICOM 1986–96," in *Before and After 1865: Papers on Education, Politics and Regionalism in the Caribbean*, ed. Bryan Moore and Swithin Wilmot (Kingston, Jamaica: Ian Randle Publishers, 1998), 304–314; and interview with senior CARICOM official, 26 March 2014.
22 Hall, *Integrate or Perish!* 298–401.
23 Gilbert-Roberts, *The Politics of Integration*, 92–118.
24 CARICOM Grand Anse Declaration and Work Programme for the Advancement of the Integration Movement, Grenada, July 1989.

25 Holger Henke, "Drugs in the Caribbean: The Ship Rider Controversy and the Question of Sovereignty," *European Review of Latin American and Caribbean Studies* 64 (1998): 27–47.
26 CARICOM communiqué issued at Fifth Special Meeting of Heads of Government, Bridgetown Barbados, 16 December 1996.
27 CARICOM communiqué issued at 12th Meeting of Heads of Government St Kitts, 2–4 July 1991; and CARICOM communiqué issued at Summit of CARICOM Heads of Government, the G-3 and vice-president of Suriname, Trinidad, 13 October 1993.
28 CARICOM communiqué issued at Summit of CARICOM Heads of Government, the G-3 and vice-president of Suriname, Trinidad, 13 October 1993.
29 Gilbert-Roberts, *The Politics of Integration: Caribbean Sovereignty Revisited*, 94–95.
30 Gilbert-Roberts, *The Politics of Integration*, 92.
31 CARICOM Consensus of Chaguaramas, Trinidad, 27 October 1999.
32 Vere Cornwall Bird, cited in Hall, *Integrate or Perish!* 99–100.
33 Kenny Anthony, cited in Hall, *Integrate or Perish!* 74.
34 Byron, "The Caribbean Community's 'Fourth Pillar'."
35 CARICOM Nassau Declaration on Health, Bahamas, 6 July 2001.
36 CARICOM Liliendaal Statement of Principles on "Forward Together," Georgetown, Guyana, 5 July 2002.
37 The literature and interviews offer three reasons: summit agendas were overloaded, the encounters became confrontational, and some civil society groups were experiencing diminishing organizational capacity, as seen in Gilbert-Roberts, *The Politics of Integration*, 125.
38 Baldwin Spencer, CARICOM PR 108/2004, Address to 25th CARICOM Heads of Government Conference, St George's, Grenada, 4 July 2004.
39 Gilbert-Roberts, *The Politics of Integration*, 184–185.
40 CARICOM PR 23/2006 issued at conclusion of First Meeting of Committee of Heads of Government and Leaders of the Parliamentary Opposition, Kingston, Jamaica, 31 January 2006.
41 See CARICOM PR 47/2010, *Declaration of Paramaribo on the Future of Youth in the Caribbean Community*, 30 January 2010. The 2010 Paramaribo Youth Summit was overshadowed by the Haitian earthquake and poorly attended. Implementation of the report has been negatively affected by the economic recession.
42 Tyrone Ferguson, "The Guyana-Suriname Territorial Conflict: Is the Moment Opportune for Third Party Intervention?" in *Intervention, Border and Maritime Issues in CARICOM*, ed. Kenneth O. Hall and Myrtle Chuck-A-Sang (Kingston, Jamaica: Ian Randle Publishers, 2007), 111–126.
43 Colin Granderson, "The CARICOM Initiative towards Haiti: A Case of Small States Diplomacy," *Focal Point* 3, no. 6 (2004): 1–4.
44 Norman Girvan, "The Caribbean in a Turbulent World," in *Inter-American Cooperation at a Crossroads*, ed. Gordon Mace, Andrew Cooper, and Timothy Shaw (New York: Palgrave Macmillan, 2010), 60–80; and Dillon Alleyne, Michael Hendrickson, Willard Phillips, Kohei Yoshida, Macehl Pantin, and Nyasha Skerrette, "Preliminary Overview of the Economies of the Caribbean 2012–2013," *ECLAC Studies and Perspectives Series*, no. 24 (August 2013), LC/CAR/L.410.

Summitry in the Caribbean Community 105

45 CARICOM PR 192/2011, special summit in Guyana, 22 May 2011.
46 Shridath Ramphal, "The CARICOM Commission: Towards a Mature Regionalism," in *Caribbean Imperatives: Regional Governance and Integrated Development*, ed. Denis Benn and Kenneth O. Hall (Kingston, Jamaica: Ian Randle Publishers, 2005), 71–77.
47 CARICOM Rose Hall Declaration on Regional Governance and Integrated Development, Jamaica, 5 July 2003; and Havelock Brewster, "Mature Regionalism and the Rose Hall Declaration on Regional Governance," in *Caribbean Imperatives*, ed. Benn and Hall, 88–93.
48 Landell Mills Development Consultants, "Turning Around CARICOM: Proposals to Restructure the CARICOM Secretariat," Final Report, January 2012.
49 Interview with Jamaican foreign affairs official, 10 March 2014.
50 She complained about excessive, poorly organized meetings, ineffective management, and waste of regional resources. See in Eudine Barriteau and Alan Cobley, eds, *Enjoying Power: Eugenia Charles and Political Leadership in the Commonwealth Caribbean* (Kingston, Jamaica: UWI Press, 2006), 121.
51 John Compton, cited in Alicia Mondesire, "The Reluctant Feminist," *Enjoying Power*, ed. Barriteau and Cobley, 270–271.
52 Eugenia Charles, cited in Allan Cobley, "We are Kith and Kin," in *Enjoying Power*, ed. Barriteau and Cobley, 112.
53 Eugenia Charles, cited in Hall, *Integrate or Perish!*; Brewster, "Mature Regionalism and the Rose Hall Declaration on Regional Governance"; Landell Mills Development Consultants, "Turning Around CARICOM"; and interviews 2014.
54 George Michael Chambers, cited in Hall, *Integrate or Perish!*, 386–390; Freundel Stewart 2011 Address to 32nd CARICOM Heads of Government Conference, Basseterre, St Kitts, CARICOM PR 240/2011, 1 July 2011; and Bharrat Jagdeo, Address to 30th CARICOM Heads of Government Conference, CARICOM PR 264/2009, Georgetown, Guyana, 2 July 2009.
55 ACP-EU and FTAA negotiations, UN Climate Change negotiations, IFI consultations, and candidatures for international organizations.
56 Interview with Jamaican official, 10 March 2014.
57 Interview with CARICOM official, 26 March 2014.
58 Chrestia, "*Les Sommets Internationaux*"; and Berridge, *Diplomacy*.
59 Interviewees emphasized the regional public's unrealistic expectations for summit outcomes, pointed out shortcomings in CARICOM's communication strategies and in post-summit follow-up strategies.
60 Berridge, *Diplomacy*.
61 Payne, *The Political History of CARICOM*, 253.
62 Current associate applications are from the French and Dutch Caribbean territories. The president of Martinique's conseil régional attended the intersessional, March 2014 (CARICOM 2014). CARICOM PR 51/2014, issued at 25th Intersessional, Buccament Bay, St Vincent, 12 March 2014.

6 The impact of summitry on the governance of Mercosur

Marcelo de Almeida Medeiros, Rafael Mesquita de Souza Lima and Maria Eduarda Ferreira Cabral

- Mercosur: Institutional design and summitry in South America
- The functions of summitry in the Mercosur Council
- Conclusion

The Common Market of the South (Mercosur) provides a valuable example of summitry and presidential diplomacy in South America. With the increased interdependence caused by globalization, summits have become more and more frequent; as a result, they are today the main forums for direct interaction among heads of state around the world, including those of the Mercosur countries.

The institutional design of the Mercosur bloc follows a summitry framework: heads of state deal with matters of high politics in the top decision-making bodies, while technical matters are handled at lower levels of the organization. We argue that the dynamic of alliances and conflicts between member countries that characterizes Mercosur gives rise to an intergovernmental institutional structure which fosters the specialization of national bureaucracies over supranational ones. Consequently, the group's governance is effected primarily through presidential summitry. The decisions subsequently relayed to the rest of the bloc by its bureaucracies originate at such meetings.

In this chapter, we analyze Mercosur's structure, how it performs the main functions of summitry and how this performance affects its governance. It is worth underscoring that "summitry" within Mercosur refers exclusively to the meetings of its highest decision-making body, the Common Market Council (CMC). Although the various working groups that make up Mercosur hold periodic meetings of their own, it is the CMC summits that bring together the presidents of member countries; thus, the council is responsible for the political guidance of the bloc.

The chapter is divided as follows. First we describe Mercosur's origins, its institutional design, and the functioning of its council; then we indicate how the Mercosur Council carries out the four functions of summitry specified in the literature; and finally we offer concluding remarks on the importance of summitry for Mercosur's governance.

Mercosur: Institutional design and summitry in South America

Mercosur is a product of the rapprochement that took place between Brazil and Argentina when both countries overcame the mutual suspicion of their authoritarian years and sought to promote trade and democracy in the region. The road leading away from tense Cold War diplomacy and towards greater regional dialogue was constructed by means of bilateral meetings held throughout the 1980s. From its foundation in 1991 to the latter years of that decade, Mercosur was characterized by a convergence of "the domestic economic policies and the wider political objectives of its two biggest member states."[1] At the time, Brazil and Argentina underwent internal liberal reforms intended to attract foreign investment while favoring regional integration.[2] Furthermore, for its members Mercosur was also a pedagogical device on the subject of free trade. It became an antechamber of *hacia afuera* regionalism, where heads of states could put into practice the logic of liberal exchange and internalize the principles and norms of a new regional governance.

Because the economic and political aims of Brazil and Argentina were and remain decisive for the fate of the intergovernmental project, it is pertinent to underscore Brazil's persistent foreign policy concern with preserving its autonomy.[3] We argue that in the course of the regionalization process different alliances and conflicts are likely to arise, and the management of such relations will reflect national preferences, such as preserving autonomy. This process favors the formation of an intergovernmental institutional design that takes such preferences into account and also suits the summitry approach.

Although the founders of Mercosur arguably had the European model of integration in mind, they wanted to avoid the over-bureaucratization and exorbitant costs this might entail. Accordingly, they performed a counter-imitation of the European Union,[4] and, as a result, there was no supranational body responsible for coordinating or enforcing the integration project,[5] a task left to the domestic governments. Mercosur consequently has two enduring characteristics—a relatively weak institutional structure,[6] and dependence on presidential action—features that make it stand out once again as an institution working essentially through summitry.[7]

Mercosur's development, therefore, could be considered to some extent a case of "spill-around" integration, which Philippe Schmitter defines as "the proliferation of functionally specialized, independent, but strictly intergovernmental organizations."[8] This applies to Mercosur, but only in part, because its organs act less independently than Schmitter's definition implies and more in keeping with hierarchical subordination to the political decision-making bodies. As Malamud puts it, "Mercosur presents a process of non-conflictive complementarity between politicians and *técnicos*, albeit featuring a sharp supremacy of the former, without supplying a solid institutional framework."[9]

The Common Market Council summits

Mercosur's structure was outlined in the bloc's founding document, the 1991 Asunción Treaty (Art. 9),[10] and was further developed in the 1994 Ouro Preto Protocol.[11] The second article of the protocol instituted three decision-making bodies: the CMC, the Common Market Group (GMC) and the Mercosur Trade Commission (CCM). The Ouro Preto Protocol established the council—composed of heads of state—as the group's supreme organ; it embodies Mercosur's legal personhood (Art. 8), being responsible for the political guidance of the integration process and for fulfilling the bloc's integrationist purpose (Art. 3). The GMC and the CCM are subordinate to it, and the resultant pyramidal structure ensures that the orders coming down from superior hierarchical levels are followed.

As the main economic bloc in South America, Mercosur can be considered the greatest promoter of summits in the region. While there are other regional groups and myriad bilateral encounters that also take place in the Southern Cone, the council summits outweigh the other forums in terms both of the number of meetings and of their impact on regional governance.[12] For instance, Brazil and Argentina, the largest regional economies, have regular bilateral meetings, averaging 1.5 meetings annually over a period of 17 years. The Mercosur Council, meanwhile, had an average of 2.4 meetings per year over a 23-year period, as shown in Figure 6.1.

Based on these data, the council summits can be seen as the foremost example of summitry in South America. This is not a case of ad hoc diplomacy, but rather of an institutional body performing the essential functions of summitry. As underscored in the editors' introduction to this volume, such a degree of institutionalization helps the council to deliver tangible policy outcomes and have an impact on governance.

The functions of summitry in the Mercosur Council

The council plays a pivotal role in Mercosur's governance. Although the group has not made progress towards the achievement of some goals relating to deep integration mechanisms, it is thanks to the council's

The impact of summitry on the governance of Mercosur 109

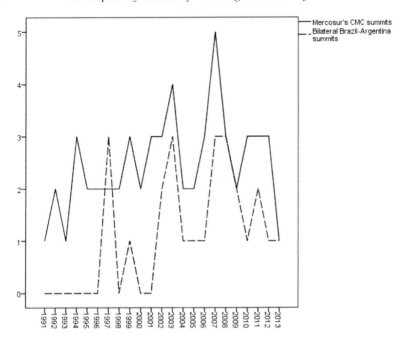

Figure 6.1 Frequency of bilateral Brazil–Argentina summits, 1997–2013, and Mercosur Council summits, 1991–2013
Note: No data were available for Brazil–Argentina bilateral summits between 1991 and 1997.
(Elaborated by the authors from data available at www.mercosur.int. *Listado de Reuniones Realizadas que generan documentación*, Mercosur, www.mercosur.int/innovaportal/v/5662/1/secretaria/registro_de_reuniones; press releases, Ministry of Foreign Affairs, Argentina, www.mrecic.gov.ar/es/comunicados-de-prensa; and press releases, Ministry of Foreign Affairs, Brazil, www.itamaraty.gov.br/index.php?b_start:int=9040&-C=&lang=pt-BR.)

summitry-oriented outlook that the bloc continues to be alive and active in regional and international arenas. As noted in the introduction to this volume, functions can be used to measure to what degree summitry and governance are linked. Among the many functions that could be attributed to the summits, the literature identifies four main ones. These four functions and how the Mercosur Council fulfills them are discussed below.

Dialogue and socialization

According to Peter Weilemann, one of the distinguishing features of summits is the face-to-face contact among high-level decision makers.[13]

These events help to introduce newcomers to the political neighborhood, while allowing them to get a personal impression of fellow leaders.[14] There is a widespread image of summits as opportunities for presidents to "get to know each other better," making it possible to reduce animosities. The literature warns, however, that deeply rooted differences will hardly be solved by brief encounters, which actually can worsen relations in some cases.[15] Divergences among participants, therefore, should be key variables in determining the outcome of a summit.

In Mercosur, the number of countries participating in the council and the asymmetries among them have significantly impacted on the bloc's governance. It is possible to expect that smaller states would act so as to constrain the action of larger states, more specifically, by proposing a design for the regional institution such that the decision-making powers of larger members would somehow be curtailed or, alternatively, by using their veto power strategically.

Regarding socialization, the council summits fulfill this function directly. The participation of the presidents of member states is stipulated in the Ouro Preto Protocol (Art. 6), which provides that they should meet at least once a semester. Concerning Mercosur's governance, while it is true that the council summits are the most frequent of all such meetings held in the region (as shown in Figure 6.1), one also needs to know who attends these summits, how representative they are, and what their impact is on the governance of Mercosur. If the adoption of a common set of practices by a number of states is an indicator of governance, then it is important to know how many countries participate in the institution where such practices are determined.

The representativeness of the council summits is illustrated in Table 6.1, showing how many meetings were held annually from 1991 to 2013, and which members sent delegations. The table also indicates each country's status in Mercosur over the years: white cells stand for non-member status, light gray for associate membership, and dark gray for full membership.

The four founding members have perfect attendance records, except for Paraguay, which was suspended from Mercosur in 2012. Venezuela, admitted as an associate member in 2004 and as a full member in 2012, also had a perfect score as of 2006—very different behavior from that of other associate countries.[16]

As the number of active countries in the council is small, we can hypothesize that its summits are relatively homogeneous and cohesive. The fact that all council "Decisions" must be made consensually (Art. 16 of the Asunción Treaty and Art. 37 of the Ouro Preto Protocol) adds a formal incentive for members to pursue unity. As will be shown

Table 6.1 Total Mercosur Council summits and number of participating states, 1991–2013

	1991	1992	1993	1994	1995	1996	1997	1998	1999	2000	2001	2002	2003	2004	2005	2006	2007	2008	2009	2010	2011	2012	2013	Total
Meetings in the year	1	2	1	3	2	2	2	2	3*	2	3	3	4**	2	2	3	5	3	2	3	3	3	1	57
Argentina	1	2	1	3	2	2	2	2	2	2	3	3	3	2	2	3	5	3	2	3	3	3	1	55
Brazil	1	2	1	3	2	2	2	2	2	2	3	3	3	2	2	3	5	3	2	3	3	3	1	55
Paraguay	1	2	1	3	2	2	2	2	2	2	3	3	3	2	2	3	5	3	2	3	3	–	–	51
Uruguay	1	2	1	3	2	2	2	2	2	2	3	3	3	2	2	3	5	3	2	3	3	3	1	55
Venezuela	–	–	–	–	–	–	–	–	–	–	–	–	–	–	–	3	5	3	2	3	3	3	1	23

(*Listado de Reuniones Realizadas que generan documentación*, Mercosur, www.mercosur.int/innovaportal/v/5662/1/secretaria/registro_de_reuniones. Compiled by the authors.)

Notes: * In 1999 there was one extraordinary summit but its communiqué did not indicate which members were present. ** In 2003 there were four meetings, one of which posted no communiqué on the Mercosur website.

below, the council has indeed enabled the development of a certain ideological solidarity among full members, but regional asymmetries have also revealed the summits' shortcomings when it comes to promoting actual convergence.

The ideological cohesion in Mercosur's summits is best reflected in the way that its agenda has been diversified over the years, a topic examined more fully in the next section. As for the group's asymmetries, they are most visible in the economic sphere. The smaller economies—Uruguay and especially Paraguay—have used the council summits as opportunities to demand their more prosperous counterparts to take action in order to reduce the inequality between them. At the twenty-fourth ordinary meeting of the council in 2003, Paraguay stressed the fact that although the disparities between members were mentioned in its founding documents, Mercosur remained "the only integration process of the hemisphere in which asymmetries are not recognized in practice," whereas other regionalist alternatives, such as the Free Trade Area of the Americas (FTAA) project, did acknowledge the disparities.[17] Some of the council's Decisions made in the mid-2000s sought to address this matter, most notably through the creation in 2004[18] of Mercosur's Structural Convergence Fund (FOCEM) and, in 2007, of a high-level group tasked with designing a strategic plan for overcoming asymmetries.

Nevertheless, the capacity of the less powerful members to voice their objections regarding certain subjects seems limited. For example, upon returning to Mercosur after its suspension, Paraguay softened its criticism of Venezuela's entry, claiming its disagreement was only juridical and not political.[19] This move can be seen as an indication that vulnerable members—in spite of their veto power, which in theory puts them on an equal footing with all other members—may back down so as not to jeopardize their position in the bloc, given their heavy dependence on their partners.

Lastly, it should be emphasized that the council summits and the plethora of parallel meetings that they trigger foster dialogue and socialization among heads of states and, by the same token, between actors of regional civil society. The Mercosur Social Forum and the Mercosur Entrepreneurial Forum, which also rely primarily on summits, are good examples of this process. The Social Forum has promoted, since 2006, meetings between representatives of governments and from different sectors of civil society and interest groups, while the Entrepreneurial Forum focuses on the region's industry and business leaders. Indeed, the council summits can be viewed as the epicenter of an archipelago of social relations brought about by Mercosur's institutional arrangement. On one level, there is socialization among heads of state; on another, there is a dialogue between governments and civil society that can only have a positive effect on regional governance.

Agenda-setting and orientation

Coordinating agendas and promoting unity are core functions of summits.[20] Mercosur has played a major role in harmonizing the foreign policies of its members and in identifying common issues to be addressed, inside and outside the trade sphere. Compared with the kind of diplomacy traditionally practiced by career diplomats in multilateral institutions, presidential diplomacy, as exercised in Mercosur, is more flexible. It allows changes to the agenda to be made faster, and those changes can be broader and arguably better adapted to the complex issues of globalization.[21] We can thus infer that council summits have enabled Mercosur to remain responsive to external and internal political changes.

An early and important example of Mercosur's capacity to coordinate regional preferences in the face of external political changes was its resistance to the FTAA, which was proposed at the 1994 Miami Summit of the Americas. Mercosur was in its first years and was yielding positive results; its member countries acted as bulwarks against the United States' project to create a continental free trade zone, which was brought to a standstill in 2004.[22]

Mercosur's opposition was a display of foreign policy coordination aimed at halting what was interpreted as yet another attempt by Washington to impose its own interests.[23] Additionally, the FTAA project was launched during a period marked by economic stagnation and skepticism regarding the potential of liberalism to promote development in the region. As well, in the large South American economies the FTAA was understood to be a menace to their ongoing industrialization processes.[24] In sum, Latin American opposition to the FTAA project was rooted in the seminal alliance first established by Mercosur and later followed by other countries.

Other alliances formed within the council tended to reflect members' concerns as to autonomy, regional stability and the maintenance of the democratic order. This was visible in their unanimous condemnation of the deposition of Honduran President Manuel Zelaya in 2009, and of the decision by the United Kingdom to carry out military exercises on the Falkland Islands in 2010.

As Mercosur involved a growing number of actors and issues, the council summits covered a widening range of regional concerns, including security, human rights, democracy, and others. Two-thirds of the 808 Decisions taken by the council from 1991 to 2013 dealt with issues related to "institutional, legal and technical standards" and "trade, customs and cooperation affairs," as shown in Figure 6.2.

It is telling that from Mercosur's foundation until now, these two topics have been the main concerns of the council; nonetheless, its agenda has been more diversified in recent years. For instance, during Mercosur's first decade (1991–2001), the topic of "security"[25] ranked third, accounting for 9 percent of all Decisions. During the second decade (2002–12), Decisions on this subject dropped to 1.7 percent of the total. Meanwhile, "labour issues, social security and development," which during the first decade represented only 3.9 percent of all Decisions, became the third top-ranking issue from 2002 onwards, representing 11.2 percent of the Decisions.

These agenda changes were responses to international pressures and to political shifts inside Mercosur countries. The high volume of Decisions dealing with "security" (most of which were reached toward the end of Mercosur's first decade) can be seen as part of the worldwide

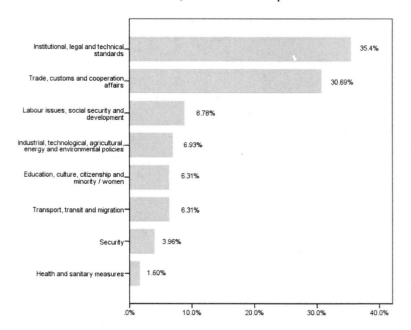

Figure 6.2 Decisions taken by the Mercosur Council, divided by topic, 1991–2013
(Mercosur Council, www.mercosur.int/innovaportal/v/383/1/secretaria/busqueda_avanzada. Compiled by the authors.)

trend triggered by the attacks against the United States on 11 September 2001. Furthermore, in the wake of those events, the United States expressed a growing apprehension about the Brazil–Argentina–Paraguay triple border, where it was believed that jihadist cells were operating. In this context, the council summits have fulfilled a coordinating function, identifying new and pressing issues and responding to them. Several of the council's Decisions of that period list specific actions and programs addressing international crime, terrorism, intelligence cooperation, and border surveillance.

During the second decade, the number of Decisions related to "labour issues, social security and development" rose considerably. In general, increased awareness of these topics in the 2000s can be attributed to the rise in member countries of left-wing governments attentive to such issues. The more numerous Decisions made in that decade concerning development coincide with the creation of FOCEM, which was emblematic of the shift in Mercosur's integration paradigm. More specifically, the bloc departed from its original liberal approach of promoting integration via free trade, supporting instead more actively state-led efforts to reduce inequalities among countries.

In short, the council summits have created a setting for ideological solidarity among South American presidents, who have then been able to identify and address regional problems in a coordinated fashion, based on their shared worldview. This can be seen in the reaction to external threats (e.g. the FTAA) and in the agenda shifts that took place over the years, which also reveal how responsive Mercosur summitry is to changing interests and to external factors.

Negotiation and coordination

The decisions taken at summits are more likely to be carried out if presidents have enough discretionary power to strike effective deals.[26] Powerful presidents are a constant in Latin America, and their role in Mercosur has been paramount from the bloc's inception to this day. Mercosur was the offspring more of political will than of a gradual regional enmeshment, and presidents have long been the primary agents of decisions, enforcement, and dispute resolution.[27] Moreover, the most practical way to incorporate Mercosur norms in the domestic legislation of member states has been to leave this unclear and painstaking process mainly in the hands of the executives of each state, thereby further favoring presidential diplomacy. At the same time, heads of state need a diplomatic corps to handle technical matters, and to ensure that promises are realized.[28] This explains why Mercosur has a system of organs that effectuate council Decisions, either by implementing them or by addressing technical issues in the council's place.

The division of labor between the council and its subsidiary organs can be clearly observed in the way that high politics is addressed in comparison with low politics. Here, we have identified as high politics matters relating to the central and strategic concerns for Mercosur member states, and which therefore cannot be settled by lower-level decision makers. These are issues pertaining to state interests and external relations, but also those that bear on the relationship between the state and civil society, and involve the mobilization of key resources.[29] Consequently, we have categorized (1) security; (2) trade, customs and cooperation affairs; and (3) industrial, technological, agricultural, energy and environmental policies, as "high politics," and all other questions as "low politics."

Over a period of 22 years, more than 41 percent of the council's Decisions have been in the field of high politics. Most technical issues have been left in the hands of lower-level groups, such as the CCM, the bloc's third-ranking decision-making body. Nearly 85 percent of the commission's Directives issued from 1994 to 2013 have dealt with institutional, legal and technical standards—a low politics subject. The findings of this section are summarized in Table 6.2, which compares the percentage of Decisions by the council with the "Directives" by the commission, thus indicating which topics are central to each hierarchical level.

Mercosur's intergovernmental design makes the process of implementing its legislation domestically very slow and cumbersome, thereby compounding the oft-mentioned weak point of summits: translating words into actions. Its norms must be evaluated and assimilated at the legislative or executive level of each state before they can become part of their national legislations; however, there are cases where this is not required—for instance, when a country already has an identical law.

By forcing regional legislation to pass through domestic bottlenecks, the bloc's institutional design favors presidential action, which is relatively quicker. A study carried out by Deisy Ventura, Janina Onuki, and Marcelo A. Medeiros found that in approximately 90 percent of cases the domestic processing of Mercosur norms has been carried out by the executives of the member states.[30] The same study also pointed out that the council has sought to minimize the participation of the legislatures in this procedure. Approximately half of the council's Decisions did not need to be integrated to the domestic legislation of member countries, and 27 percent of the Decisions that did were processed through executive decrees. In low politics issues, presidential action is much less prevalent: over 61 percent of Mercosur's Trade

Table 6.2 Comparison between Mercosur Council Decisions, 1991–2013, and Commission Directives, 1994–2013

	Mercosur Council Decisions 1991–2013 (%)	Mercosur Trade Commission Directives 1994–2013 (%)
Institutional, legal, and technical standards	35.40	84.36
Trade, customs, and cooperation affairs	30.69	11.54
Labor issues, social security, and development	8.79	–
Industrial, technological, agricultural, energy, and environmental policies	6.93	0.26
Transport, transit, and migration	6.31	2.82
Education, culture, citizenship, and minority/women	6.31	–
Security	3.96	0.51
Health and sanitary measures	1.61	0.51
Low politics	58.42	87.69
High politics	41.58	12.31

(Mercosur Council and Trade Commission, www.mercosur.int/innovaportal/v/383/1/secretaria/usqueda_avanzada. Compiled by the authors.)

Note: Numbers are the percentage of total decisions made, classified by topic and identified as high or low politics.

Commission Directives have been integrated into domestic legislation through ministerial or infra-ministerial action.

To sum up, it is important to visualize the council embedded in an institutional network, where it is connected to secondary intergovernmental bodies (e.g. the commission, but also the GMC and the secretariat) that relay high politics summit decisions to agencies in charge of technical matters and implementation. Because it is linked with regional and national bureaucracies, the council can better fulfill its function of negotiation and coordination, as it gives heads of state considerable autonomy and discretionary power to discuss the bloc's agenda, courses of action and mobilization of resources.

Legitimation

Summits have a legitimizing function due to their media exposure and symbolic nature.[31] They can improve a leader's image at home, but they can also emphasize appearances over substance and thus inflate society's expectations as to their outcome.[32] In the case of intergovernmental entities such as Mercosur, summitry gives legitimacy not only to individual heads of state, but also to the institution itself. Such events are opportunities to present the organization's position regarding current issues, display its capacity to provide solutions, and reinforce its norms and procedures.

Although council summits strive to fulfill such functions, Mercosur's concern with legitimacy goes beyond summitry and is manifested in particular in three areas: agenda, membership, and institutional design. The first two concern the council summitry directly, while the third regards Mercosur as a whole, since several of its organs and commitments are aimed at democratizing the bloc or involving more actors in its processes.

To begin with, the previously discussed shifts in the council's agenda can be seen as efforts by national governments to enhance presidential legitimacy in the eyes of domestic populations (e.g. devoting more attention to labor and development issues in accordance with the expectations of a growing left-wing electorate), or of the international community (e.g. showing readiness to improve security policies). Second, legitimacy is linked to representativeness,[33] and representativeness is the underlying reason for the recent rise in the number of member countries. Nonetheless, as we will show, membership criteria and norms have of late become rather controversial matters affecting the council's institutional legitimacy.

When considering the relationship between agenda, membership, and legitimacy, the role of national interests must be kept in mind. Originally conceived as a common market project, Mercosur went from a trade-dominated agenda to one with many subjects, notably in the area of high politics. This rise of political issues relative to commercial ones is in tune with the interests of the region's number-one player, Brazil, whose latest administrations have valued Mercosur more for the political clout it can provide than for the "commercialist character" that defined its early years.[34] Consequently, more countries have been invited to join the bloc so as to expand Brazil's influence and, hence, bolster its international legitimacy.

Yet, according to the literature, adding actors and topics to the agenda can compromise decisional capacity or even erode the group's original purpose if its membership becomes too heterogeneous.[35] Because legitimacy also depends on efficiency, the expansion of Mercosur may entail a trade-off between representativeness and efficiency.

Paraguay's suspension and Venezuela's entry as a full member constitute a good illustration of this tension. The procedure whereby Venezuela joined the council in 2012 was criticized by Paraguay on the grounds that such a decision had to be made unanimously, which for Paraguay meant "by all members," including itself. The fact that the vote had been held during Paraguay's suspension from the council was perceived by Paraguay as political opportunism. Although Venezuela's inclusion greatly increased Mercosur's representativeness in South America—while granting some international legitimacy to Chávez's regime—Frizzera argues that it ultimately weakened the bloc by exposing the lack of clarity in its rules and norms (i.e. the proper interpretation of admission criteria and voting procedures)[36] and, by the same token, diminished its institutional legitimacy.[37]

Finally, regarding its institutional features, Mercosur's concern with legitimacy was expressed when its member states signed the Ushuaia Protocol, committing themselves to democracy. Also, if democracy—described by Held as "the fundamental standard of political legitimacy in the current era"[38]—is taken to mean a greater openness to civil society participation, then several of the group's organs are also instruments of democracy, for example, the Economic-Social Consultative Forum (FCES), the Consultative Forum for Municipalities, Federated States, Provinces and Departments of Mercosur (FCCR), and the Mercosur Parliament (Parlasur). Though they all have serious operational shortcomings,[39] they help to enforce the council's Decisions and to project an image of regional commitment to democracy.

In short, considering the hierarchical primacy of the council summits, they are a source of legitimacy for regional practices and norms, as well as for leaders. Still, critical situations such as Venezuela's admission show how Mercosur's low institutionalization can give rise to ad hoc justifications for its practices and, hence, undermine its institutional legitimacy.

Conclusion

Mercosur can be viewed as a regional bloc whose architecture favors a logic of summitry. It is characterized by a division of jurisdictions and by intergovernmental structures that give the council the central political role in the bloc's governance. Our analysis of this body has shown that its summits perform the main functions identified in the literature.

By bringing together heads of state, ministers and technical staff more frequently than other regional groupings, Mercosur promotes dialogue and socialization among these decision makers. The council summits are responsive to both external and internal changes and enable coordination among member countries, as evidenced in the episodes concerning the FTAA, Honduras, and the Falkland Islands, and also in the diversification of the council's agenda over the years.

According to Fen Osler Hampson, there is a natural tendency of summits to diversify as they mature. In Mercosur's case, this tendency has been strengthened by the preferences of its members (e.g. Brazil's concern with political clout rather than regional trade).[40] The broadening of the agenda and of the membership can potentially dilute a summit's purpose and coherence.[41] However, council Decisions have steadily multiplied over the years (from 256 in 1991–2001 to 534 in 2002–12), a sign that the group is increasingly active and responsive, in spite of its diversification. This, as we have seen, may be because Mercosur's representativeness seems to be limited to the hard core of full members, which would facilitate greater cohesion on most (but certainly not all) topics. The economic asymmetries among member countries have proven to be a bone of contention (motivating some targeted responses by the council). Also, even though all members are formally equal, there are indications that the smaller economies' dependence on Mercosur may make them less willing to express disagreement.

Finally, several of the subjects addressed and organs created over the years reflect Mercosur's concern with increasing its domestic, regional, and international legitimacy. Yet, events like Venezuela's entry demonstrate that the low degree of institutionalization and definition of the council's procedures and norms have a negative impact on its legitimacy.

In conclusion, the council is Mercosur's institutional cornerstone. The interaction among heads of states and their decisions have been instrumental in framing the main issues of the bloc's governance. This indicates that the summitry system has clearly predominated over any supranational tendency in Mercosur. In the end, it is Mercosur's tendency toward cooperation—rather than integration[42]—that makes it, and especially the council, essential instruments of presidential diplomacy while serving, at the same time, as central means of regional governance.

Notes

1 Marc Schelhase, "The Successes, Failures and Future of Mercosur," in *Inter-American Cooperation at a Crossroads*, ed. Gordon Mace, Andrew F. Cooper, and Timothy M. Shaw (New York: Palgrave Macmillan, 2010), 172.
2 Andrew Hurrell, "Regionalism in Theoretical Perspective," in *Regionalism in World Politics*, ed. Louise Fawcett and Andrew Hurrell (Oxford: Oxford University Press, 1995), 70. According to Hurrell's typology: "Convergence

The impact of summitry on the governance of Mercosur 121

theories understand the dynamics of regional co-operation and especially regional economic integration in terms of converging domestic policy preferences among regional States."
3 See Gelson Fonseca Jr., *A legitimidade e outras questões internacionais* (São Paulo: Paz e Terra, Brazil, 1998); and Tullo Vigevani and Gabriel Cepaluni, "A Política Externa de Lula da Silva: a Estratégia da Autonomia pela Diversificação," *Contexto Internacional* 29, no. 2 (2007): 273–335.
4 Olivier Dabène, *The Politics of Regional Integration in Latin America* (New York: Palgrave Macmillan, 2009), 90.
5 Marcelo A. Medeiros, *La Genèse du Mercosud* (Paris/Montreal: L'Harmattan, 2000).
6 Schelhase, "The Successes, Failures and Future of Mercosur,"176.
7 Andrés Malamud, "Presidential Diplomacy and the Institutional Underpinnings of Mercosur: An Empirical Examination," *Latin American Research Review* 40, no. 1 (2005): 138–164.
8 Philippe C. Schmitter, "Neo-neo-functionalism," in *European Integration Theory*, 1st edn, ed. Antje Wiener and Thomas Diez (Oxford: Oxford University Press, 2003), 32, unila.edu.br/sites/default/files/files/05%20Neo-Neo7_final.pdf.
9 Andrés Malamud, "Spillover in European and South American Integration: A Comparative Evaluation," CIES e-Working Paper 1/2005, CIES-ISCTE, Lisbon, 2005, 13.
10 Asunción Treaty, Mercosur (1991), www.mercosul.gov.br/normativa/tratados-e-protocolos/tratado-de-assuncao-1.
11 Ouro Preto Protocol, Mercosur (1994), www.mercosul.gov.br/normativa/tratados-e-protocolos/protocolo-de-ouro-preto-1.
12 In comparison with other regional groups (CAN, UNASUR, CELAC, etc.), Mercosur summits are the most frequent. See Chapter 2 in this volume for a comparison.
13 Peter R. Weilemann, "The Summit Meeting: The Role and Agenda of Diplomacy at its Highest Level," *NIRA Review* 7, no. 2 (2000): 16–20.
14 Kenneth L. Adelman, "Summitry: The Historical Perspective," *Presidential Studies Quarterly* 16, no. 3 (1986): 437.
15 Richard Nixon, "Superpower Summitry," *Foreign Affairs* 64, no. 1 (1985): 1–11; and Weilemann, "The Summit Meeting."
16 Because we are interested in studying primarily the council summits, Table 6.1 does not include data on Mercosur's associate members (Chile, Bolivia, Peru, Colombia, and Ecuador), since they play no part in the council's Decisions. Still, it is noteworthy that the attendance rate of the associate members has been very low. Of a total of 57 summits, 49 took place in the absence of a delegation from those five countries. This indicates that the centripetal force of the council summits is much greater for the hard core of full member states than for the associate members.
17 Mercosur, *XXIV Reunión ordinaria del Consejo del Mercado Común Acta 1/03 Anexo V* (June 2003), 3, www.mercosur.int; and see also Sônia Unikowsky Teruchkin, "Ampliação do Mercosul: a adesão da Venezuela," *Indicadores Econômicos FEE* 34, no. 3 (2006): 45–50.
18 The FOCEM was created through a Brazilian initiative to finance structural projects that involve integrating and modernizing productive chains, improving social indicators and updating common norms and procedures.

It is structured so that larger economies contribute more and, inversely, smaller economies are entitled to greater benefits. Thus, of the current total of 41 projects, worth approximately US$1.5 billion in total, 29 projects (accounting for 90 percent of that sum) are set to benefit Uruguay and Paraguay directly.

19 Guilherme Frizzera, "A Suspensão do Paraguai no MERCOSUL: Problema Interno, Solução Externa," *Conjuntura Global* 2, no. 3 (2013): 160.
20 Robert D. Putnam, "Western Summitry in the 1990s: American Perspectives," *The International Spectator* 39, no. 2 (1994): 81–93; Adelman, "Summitry"; and Ulrich Schneckener, "The Opportunities and Limits of Global Governance by Clubs," *SWP Comments* 22 (September 2009): 1–8.
21 Francisco Rojas and Paz Milet, "Diplomacia de Cúpulas: o Multilateralismo Emergente do Século XXI," *Contexto internacional* 21, no. 2 (1999): 291–359; and Mercedes Botto and Diana Tussie, "Las Cumbres de las Américas: una Nueva Plataforma para la Sociedad Civil," *América Latina Hoy: Revista de Ciencias Sociales* 40 (August 2005): 73–91.
22 For more on Mercosur's objection to the FTAA, see Chapter 3 in this volume.
23 Cecilia Alemany, "Diplomacia de Cumbres y Diplomacia Ciudadana en la Asociación Birregional desde la Perspectiva del Mercosur: una Historia que Contar," *Nueva Sociedad* 190 (March–April 2004): 136–150.
24 José Briceño Ruiz, "Strategic Regionalism and Regional Social Policy in the FTAA Process," *Global Social Policy* 7, no. 3 (2007): 294–315; and Jean Grugel, "Regionalist Governance and Transnational Collective Action in Latin America," *Economy and Society* 35, no. 2 (2007): 209–231.
25 Barry Buzan and Lene Hansen, *A Evolução dos Estudos de Segurança Internacional* (São Paulo: Editora Unesp, 2012), 24. "Security" is understood here as also encompassing non-military matters that involve perceived threats and vulnerabilities.
26 Robert D. Putnam, "Diplomacy and Domestic Politics: the Logic of Two-level Games," *International Organization* 42, no. 3 (1988): 427–460; Karl Magnus Johansson and Jonas Tallberg, "Explaining Chief Executive Empowerment: EU Summitry and Domestic Institutional Change," *West European Politics* 33, no. 2 (2010): 208–236; and Laurence Whitehead and Alexandra B. de Brito, "Las Cumbres Mundiales y sus Versiones Latinoamericanas: ¿Haciendo una Montaña de un Grano de Arena?" *América Latina Hoy: Revista de Ciencias Sociales* 40 (August 2005): 15–27.
27 Malamud, "Presidential Diplomacy and the Institutional Underpinnings of Mercosur," 148.
28 Rojas and Milet, "Diplomacia de Cúpulas."
29 Michael Barnett, "High Politics is Low Politics: The Domestic and Systemic Sources of Israeli Security Policy, 1967–1977," *World Politics* 42, no. 4 (1990): 529–562.
30 Deisy Ventura, Janina Onuki, and Marcelo A. Medeiros, et al., "Internalização das Normas do MERCOSUL," *Série Pensando o Direito* 45 (2012): 52–54.
31 Jeffrey G. Giauque, "Bilateral Summit Diplomacy in Western European and Transatlantic Relations, 1956–63," *European History Quarterly* 31, no. 3 (2001): 427–445; and Weilemann, "The Summit Meeting."

32 Alemany, "Diplomacia de Cumbres y Diplomacia Ciudadana en la Asociación Birregional desde la Perspectiva del Mercosur: una Historia que Contar"; Nixon, "Superpower Summitry"; Whitehead and de Brito, "Las Cumbres Mundiales y sus Versiones Latinoamericanas"; Adelman, "Summitry: The Historical Perspective"; and Rojas and Milet, "Diplomacia de cúpulas."
33 Fonseca Jr., *A Legitimidade e outras Questões Internacionais*; and Andrew Hurrell, *On Global Order: Power, Values and the Constitution of International Society* (New York: Oxford University Press, 2007).
34 Miriam G. Saraiva, "A Diplomacia Brasileira e as Visões sobre a Inserção Externa do Brasil: Institucionalistas Pragmáticos x Autonomistas," *Mural Internacional* 1, no. 1 (2010): 50.
35 Fen Osler Hampson, "The Perils of Summitry," *Policy Options* (June 2010): 45–48; Putnam, "Diplomacy and Domestic Politics"; and Whitehead and de Brito, "Las Cumbres Mundiales y sus Versiones Latinoamericanas."
36 Most importantly, one of the reasons that Venezuela's entry faced opposition in the legislatures of Mercosur countries was because some parties saw Chávez's government as anti-democratic, hence not fit to join the bloc, in accordance with the Ushuaia Protocol. Ushuaia Protocol, Mercosur (1998), www.mercosur.int/innovaportal/file/2485/1/cmc_1998_protocolo_es_ushuaia.pdf.
37 Frizzera, "A Suspensão do Paraguai no MERCOSUL."
38 David Held, *Models of Democracy* (Stanford, Calif.: Stanford University Press, 1987), xi.
39 See Botto and Tussie, "Las Cumbres de las Américas: Una Nueva Plataforma para la Sociedad Civil" concerning the FCES; Marcelo A. Medeiros, Natália Leitão, Henrique Sérgio Cavalcanti, Maria Eduarda Paiva, and Rodrigo Santiago, "A Questão da Representação no Mercosul," *Revista de Sociologia e Política* 18, no. 37 (2010): 31–57, on the FCCR; and Marcelo A. Medeiros, Maria Eduarda Paiva, and Marion Lamenha, "Legitimidade, Representação e Tomada de Decisão: o Parlamento Europeu e o Parlasul em Perspectiva Comparada," *Revista Brasileira de Política Internacional* 55, no. 1 (2012): 154–173, about Parlasur.
40 Hampson, "The Perils of Summitry."
41 Whitehead and de Brito, "Las Cumbres Mundiales y sus Versiones Latinoamericanas."
42 In the sense pointed out by Jean-Louis Quermonne. Jean-Louis Quermonne, *Le Système Politique de l'Union Européenne* (Paris: Montchrestien, 1994).

7 Presidential summitry in Central America
A predictable failure?

Kevin Parthenay

- **The origins of Central American summits**
- **Central American summitry in crisis**
- **Conclusion**

To appreciate properly the under-studied subject of Central America's political integration, it is crucial to consider the evolution of the region's presidential summits. The establishment of the Central American Integration System (SICA), underpinned by the whole set of internal rules and actors' relationships delineated in the 1991 Tegucigalpa Protocol, was a major step toward that integration. The protocol assigns a central role to the presidential summits as the "supreme organ" of the system (Art. 13), and specifies that the summits' main objective is "to define and direct Central American policy by establishing guidelines for the integration of the region as well as the provisions necessary to ensure the coordination and harmonization of the activities of the bodies and institutions of the region, and the verification, monitoring and follow-up of its mandates and decisions" (Art. 15a).

In Central America, presidential summits hold a "power of chair,"[1] combining two formal authorities—access to privileged information and control of procedures with the fundamental power to decide who has access to SICA's institutional setting. This power of chair exceeds the mere ability to control, as it enables the presidents to determine and circumscribe the exercise of power[2] in Central America. Theoretically, presidential summits have the capacity to steer the dynamics of change in SICA and to control some of its basic functions, specifically the guidance and coordination of its policies and actions.[3]

Although Central American summits have received little scholarly attention, whether at the empirical or the theoretical level, a study of their history can shed light on all the major changes concerning regional integration on the isthmus. First, in the early 1990s the summits helped to make peace and to reactivate the notion of Central American integration. Second, presidential summits are the institutional reflection of the region's national regimes,[4] which are generally presidential; indeed, presidentialism pervades the whole culture of Central American politics.[5] Third, presidential diplomacy has often been regarded as the main driving force of regional integration.[6] Central American states, like many of their Latin American neighbors, consider foreign policy to be an area reserved for presidents. Thus, presidential summits are arenas where leaders can deliberate and arrive at decisions, but also where national interests may clash or converge. Studying them can help us understand the relationships among Central American states and among their political leaders.

Between 1986 and 1991, presidential summits were held on an ad hoc basis, but when regional integration was officially reactivated in 1991 with the establishment of SICA, they became "serial summits" (to be held biannually), with traditional negotiation and diplomacy[7] functions. Presidential summits were seen as crucial to solving Central American conflicts in the 1980s, but have they been similarly effective in promoting regional integration since then?

The legitimacy that helped reactivate Central American integration has gradually waned since the early 1990s. Presidential summits have been the target of much criticism and disaffection—even on the part of the presidents themselves—and the reform of regional integration has been a constant bone of contention. Therefore, after nearly 23 years, it is necessary to examine the state of presidential summitry in Central America.

This chapter argues that the summits are in crisis. They have not contributed to the development of regional governance because they have failed to become privileged spaces for socialization, agenda setting, and for the coordination and legitimation of regional norms and practices. My discussion is empirically grounded and focuses on a single case study. I begin by outlining an historical narrative of Central American presidential summitry. Following an in-depth look at their functioning over the period 1991–2012, I present the main factors behind the crisis of the regional summits. Finally, I offer some concluding thoughts on the current situation and the pace of Central American regional integration.

The origins of Central American summits

Central American presidential summits started with the creation of the Central American States Organization (ODECA). Established by the San Salvador Charter in 1951, this regional organization was composed of Costa Rica, Nicaragua, Honduras, El Salvador, Guatemala, and Panama.

However, ODECA's regional influence was soon overtaken by the relative success of economic integration,[8] particularly through the Central American Common Market (CACM). Presidential summits—ODECA's supreme organ (Art. 2)—never got off the ground; as a result, regional integration has developed in more sectoral ways.[9] The 1969 "Soccer War" between Honduras and El Salvador occasioned a serious setback for Central American integration, which finally came to a halt with ODECA's breakdown in 1972. Over the ensuing decade, civil conflicts and authoritarianism obstructed presidential dialogue and coordination on the isthmus. During that time, the costs of cooperation were too high, and domestic realities impeded the advancement of regional aspirations.

Despite the prevailing turbulence, presidential dialogue was reactivated in 1986 thanks to the leadership of Guatemalan President Vinicio Cerezo, who initiated a solution by gathering all the region's presidents around the negotiation table at Esquipulas (Guatemala). The dialogue between Costa Rica, Nicaragua, El Salvador, Honduras, and Guatemala facilitated the resolution of the Central American conflict.[10] The assembled presidents adopted an electoral mechanism to help overcome the democratic impasse in Nicaragua and thus foster peace and democracy in the region. This small club of presidents—José Napoléon Duarte (El Salvador), Oscar Arias (Costa Rica), Vinicio Cerezo (Guatemala), Daniel Ortega (Nicaragua), and José Azcona de Hoyo (Honduras)—succeeded in setting a common agenda. They represented a new generation of leaders who shared the ambition of reducing the isolation and underdevelopment engendered by a decade of regional conflict, and they promoted political innovation with the aim of developing a regional perspective in the face of globalization. On that basis, presidential summits in Central America became a new and important political reality; they produced an innovative political toolbox that countered the region's international isolation, and successfully promoted peace and fresh social and economic development perspectives.

Given the region's previous background of conflict, the weak institutionalization of the new democratic regimes and the context of crisis in which presidential summits were reactivated, progress towards political integration was predictably slow, as the region settled into a more stable and peaceful period. As Olivier Dabène explains,[11] Central American integration was more an unintended consequence than a desired outcome of the initial summits. The presidents were more concerned with reinforcing peace and consolidating their national democratic institutions through dialogue and interdependence than with engaging in an intentional process of regional integration. Nevertheless, the series of political summits from 1986 to 1991 gave rise to many regional projects in the economic, cultural, social, and environmental sectors. Consequently, the Central American foreign ministers meeting in San Salvador in 1991 suggested the creation of a regional structure to institutionalize their growing interdependence. The presidents subsequently ratified the Tegucigalpa Protocol establishing the Central American Integration System on 13 December 1991.

It is my contention, however, that the idea of SICA presidential summits was characterized from the start by a great deal of confusion, which would lead to general inefficiency with respect to their intended outcome—that is, the production of regional public goods—and to widespread mistrust on the part of Central American citizens. The next part of this chapter presents an empirical analysis of how and why the crisis in presidential summitry came about.

Central American summitry in crisis

The dynamic set in motion by the initial series of presidential summits has gradually vanished to the point that the summits' usefulness for the consolidation of SICA as an institution has also diminished. There are five factors that can explain this crisis in presidential summitry: alternative instruments of regional diplomacy, minimal effectiveness, variable geometry integration, pragmatic alienation, and suboptimal decision making.

Alternative regional diplomacy instruments

Central American presidents have lost institutional control of SICA. Their use of alternative diplomatic mechanisms has led to a series of negative externalities: a lack of trust in SICA and in its procedural stability; misunderstanding of the rationale of regional integration; a disjointed and asymmetric institutional design; reduced implementation of the organization's agenda; the ineffectiveness of regular summits in promoting the integration agenda; and the divergence of member states' diplomatic positions, especially with regard to the pace of regional integration.

Although summit diplomacy developed in the context of regional peace, there has been a significant reduction in the number of presidential summits in the post-conflict period. The region's presidents met 11 times in ordinary summits between 1986 and February 1991 (when the new institutional integration system was formally created), but only another 11 times in the following 11 years (1992 to 2003), even though such meetings were meant to be biannual.

The initial achievements of summitry—presidential diplomacy brought peace to the region—and the multiplication of presidential summits generated a spillover effect[12] such that the Central American integration agenda expanded into the sectors of social development, the environment, and security. However, this trend gradually declined, as ordinary presidential summits became no more than annual events, with the concomitant lessening of the states' political interdependence. Given this dynamic, regional institutions were soon at risk of becoming empty shells; states would consequently grow less able to face regional challenges, such as environmental vulnerability or economic and social development.

In 1992, in response to the decreasing number of ordinary summits, a new multilateral diplomacy instrument appeared, the Extraordinary Summit of Central American Presidents and Heads of State, which has intended to compensate for the lack of ordinary summits. "Partial summits"—alternative summits with parallel and/or emergency agendas displaying varying levels of commitment among the different states—have also been held, further reducing the political interdependence and global coherence of the regional integration initiative.

In contrast, the ordinary summits organized between 1986 and 1990 expressed real and collective dynamics of cooperation, thanks to the states' common diagnosis of the Central American conflict and their determination to build a "community of destiny." However, the summits that followed were much less ideologically homogeneous, and the presidents were far from sharing a common vision of regional integration. The organization of extraordinary summits was an institutional reflection of this decreasing coherence.

For a better understanding of the particular effects of agenda prioritization and differentiated integration, a typology of Central American presidential summits, followed by a statistical overview of their distribution, are presented below. The typology identifies four types of high-level summit: ordinary summits, extraordinary summits, summits with third parties, and differentiated (or partial) summits. Each type has a particular logic, distinct from the dynamics of collective presidentialism that characterized the initial ad hoc summits:

- Ordinary summits (22 percent). These assemble the presidents of all member states and are organized each year on 1 January and 1 July, according to the official schedule, by the member state holding the SICA Pro Tempore Presidency (PTP). Each summit ensures the transfer of the PTP.

- Extraordinary summits (26.8 percent). These occur when unanimously called for and assemble the presidents of all Central American member states. They are convened mostly in response to specific political, economic, social, environmental, or defense situations. Despite the extraordinary nature of these meetings, the protocol remains that they are organized by the state holding the SICA PTP or, subject to that state's formal authorization, by another host.
- Summits with third parties (35.4 percent). These are high-level summits of the Central American states' presidents, non-member states (the United States, Mexico, Chile, Taiwan, Japan, Argentina, and Brazil), and international donors or international organizations (the European Union, the Organization of American States, Summits of the Americas, Ibero-American Summits). They are instruments for developing regional foreign policy but are not governed by the Tegucigalpa Protocol.
- Differentiated summits (15.9 percent). These events bring together a limited number of presidents to deal with bilateral or trilateral issues, such as the bilateral summit between Honduras and El Salvador, held on 10 September 1994 in San Salvador, concerning the Fonseca Gulf territorial dispute. Such summits tend to promote variable geometry dynamics, as evidenced by the Ostua Summit (Jutiapa, Guatemala on 24 August 1999), held between El Salvador and Guatemala with the aim of furthering the progressive materialization of the Central American Customs Union.

The emergence of alternative regional diplomacy instruments, and of extraordinary and differentiated summits in particular, signals the weakening of regional interdependence. Although such summits promote political exchanges, they are based on particular and differentiated logics. This is especially true of extraordinary summits, which tend to be fragmentary and selective.

A review of the official statements and resolutions of the extraordinary summits between 19 September 2001 and 25 October 2011 shows that they were all organized in response to particular events (for example: ES-19/09/2001,[13] following the attacks on the World Trade Center; ES-05/09/2005, following Hurricane Katrina), or highly significant political issues (for example, ES-26/09/2002 and ES-16/10/2004, in support of democracy and the fight against corruption in Nicaragua), or very technical and institutional matters (for example, ES-26/09/2002, on reform of the Central American Bank for Economic Integration (CABEI); ES-25/03/2009, on the SICA PTP).

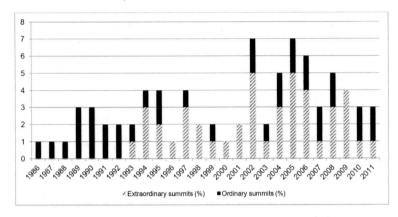

Figure 7.1 Evolution of Central American summits, 1986–2011
(Elaborated from data in Francisco Santos Carrillo, "El proceso de cumbres de presidentes centroamericanos como artífice del nuevo modelo de integración regional," in *El SICA y la UE: la integración regional en una perspectiva comparada*, ed. Pedro Caldentey del Pozo and Juan José Romero (El Salvador: Colección de Estudios Centroamericanos n°1, 2010), 263.)

The handling of such issues outside the regular agenda of the ordinary summits not only marks a lessening of the political interdependence and cohesion among states, but also illustrates the weakness of SICA's planning capacity. Addressing strategic and political issues outside the regular agenda subjects the summits (and SICA as a whole) to geopolitical and economic vagaries, and thereby makes the integration dynamic fragmentary and uncertain because the monitoring of commitments made at the extraordinary summits is lacking.

As a consequence, the ordinary summits no longer fulfill their priority mission of *defining and directing Central American policy* (Tegucigalpa Protocol Art. 15). Indeed, the large number of extraordinary summits suggests that the governing functions of the presidential summits are no longer being addressed; it also points to a major institutional weakness in the area of planning.

Minimal effectiveness

The presidential summit may be SICA's main regulator, but is it still a politically legitimate organ? The system's political legitimacy lies in its ability to foster change in societies and economies throughout the region. Currently, one of the major criticisms of SICA concerns the ineffectiveness of the presidential summits, particularly of their outputs—the presidential mandates—which are the organization's proper tools for promoting change in the region and for investing regional organizations with institutional authority and the legal obligation to implement regional public policies or institutional reforms.

As noted earlier, presidents set the agenda and control the execution of their mandates in order to guide regional integration. With the overall picture in mind, it should be noted that the Central American presidents have adopted 577 mandates since 1986. Yet this level of activism is only apparent. Despite the high figure, the proportion of unexecuted mandates has grown since 2006, while that of executed mandates decreased from 89 percent in 2002 to 40 percent in 2009 and to just 7 percent in 2011. At the same time, the list of ongoing mandates has substantially increased from 9 percent in 2002 to 70 percent in 2010, and many of them are "reiterated" year after year.

I have reviewed all the presidential mandates since 1993 and studied their main characteristics to understand whether or not they have been successful in promoting changes. My methodology involved comparing two sequences—the first covering the years 1993–2006 (n=247) and the second, the years 2006–12 (n=298)—in order to observe their evolution. The mandates were distributed, first, under two main categories of impact: integration agenda (IA) and institutional system (IS). Then, to understand to what levels the impacts apply, I classed the mandates according to their different political, operational, and consultative dimensions.[14] Finally, to assess the mandates' effectiveness, I isolated

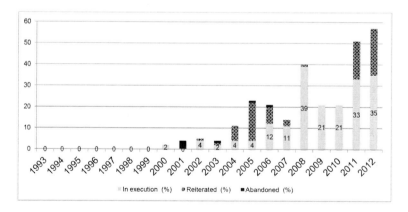

Figure 7.2 Evolution of unexecuted presidential mandates, 1993–2012
(Elaborated from data in Secretary-General, Central American Integration System (SG SICA), *Informe del Estado de Ejecución de los Mandatos Presidenciales*, Unidad de Planificación y Análisis, unpublished report (San Salvador, 2013).)

the status of their execution. In sum, for each mandate, I observed its type (IA or IS), its level (political, operational, or consultative), and its effectiveness (level of execution).

Regarding the first sequence (1993–2006), the majority of mandates (57.2 percent) are associated with operational considerations. In addition to defining and directing regional plans or public policies, the presidents regularly intervened in technical matters, despite the institutional logic defined in the Tegucigalpa Protocol. In doing so, they departed from their primary function and so tended to destabilize SICA's institutional structure. Regarding the levels of change and effectiveness in the first period, the presidents most often intervened at an operational level (53.7 percent), and their mandates can be seen as relatively effective, with an execution rate of 54.7 percent.

By contrast, during the second sequence (2006–12) the vast majority of presidential mandates (80.4 percent) addressed regional issues and only 17.6 percent the institutional system. Again, they deal mainly with operational issues (77.8 percent) and very few (16.7 percent) dealt with political matters; significant concentration on political matters would obviously have indicated greater interest in the integration agenda. Of the few mandates that deal with political considerations, most are quite discursive, being general statements about the necessity of reform. With reference to effectiveness, very little progress appears to have been made during this second period. The ratio of executed to unexecuted mandates is 3.24 between 1993 and 2006 (227 executed and 70 unexecuted), but only 0.47 for the 2007 to 2012 period (94 executed and 204 not executed).

The major findings of this comparison between periods are as follows. First, changes in the predominant type of the proposed mandates provide evidence of the lack of presidential activism. Second, by bending their political tools toward technical and operational questions, the presidents increasingly avoided dealing with regional politics and focused much more on instrumental and technical adjustments, thereby jeopardizing SICA's integration agenda. Finally, regarding effectiveness, the general decrease in the number of executed mandates and the concomitant increase of those categorized as "in execution" or "reiterated" accurately reflect SICA's inertia. These factors have progressively undermined SICA's legitimacy, consequently exposing the whole system to fierce criticism.

Variable geometry

The levels of presidential activism depend on regional institutional contexts that are both uncertain and differentiated. Institutional context has been conceptualized as "variable geometry" or "differentiated integration."[15] The uncertainty is due to the highly variable ratification by states of SICA instruments, especially its fundamental legal instruments. Of the seven fundamental pillars of SICA, only four have been fully ratified by all member states.[16] Some (such as the social treaty proposed in 1995) have only recently been fully ratified (Honduras' ratification came in 2010). Other instruments remain only partially ratified, for example, the Tegucigalpa Protocol (not ratified by the Dominican Republic) and the Guatemala Protocol (still to be ratified by Belize and the Dominican Republic). Both the security and democratic treaties and the court of justice convention await ratification, by Costa Rica, Panama and the Dominican Republic in the first case and by the same three states plus Belize in the second. As a consequence, instead of a single level of Central American integration there are differentiated integration levels across the region. Environmental integration is the pillar that has been ratified by the greatest number of member states, to a large extent, probably, because of the attractive effect of international aid flowing into that sector.

Another factor explaining this variable geometry is the fact that, in practice, endorsements and ratifications are not simultaneous. Delayed ratifications are commonplace among Central American states because some of their legal systems are weak, so that organizational commitments vary. For instance, the Honduran Congress endorsed the Social Treaty of Central American Integration in 1995 but did not ratify it until 2010, so the treaty was not binding there for 16 years after its ratification by the other member states. Similarly, only in September 2008—15 years after first endorsing it—did Guatemala ratify the relevant legal instrument and join the Central American Court of Justice. Still today, despite being a member state, Guatemala has still not yet appointed a representative to this regional institution. The endorsement or ratification of 52 (86 percent) of the 60 legal instruments that I reviewed for this study has been delayed in various Central American states; it takes four years on average for a treaty to be ratified.

Costa Rica and Panama can be singled out as the worst offenders, because of their pragmatic attitude and minimal commitment towards regional integration. Indeed, Luis Guillermo Solís, the ex-academic who is currently the president of Costa Rica, coined the expression "intervention without integration," which characterizes Costa Rican foreign policy;[17] the same could be said of Panamanian foreign policy.[18] Meanwhile, Honduras and Nicaragua are also responsible for major delays, a counter-intuitive situation inasmuch as the delays generally have been caused by their congresses, despite their political cultures' very strong inclination towards presidentialism.

Fundamentally, the variable geometry is an effect of the states' variable political and diplomatic interests. This explains why presidential summits cannot fulfill one of their basic functions, agenda setting, because dialogue between presidents is unlikely to lead to an agreement on political decisions. With each president promoting his state's specific vision of regional integration, summits have failed to become arenas where ideas could eventually converge.

It is true that parallel forums dealing with narrower intergovernmental matters have been developed. However, the setting of agendas and priorities continues to be complicated and obstructed by variable regional geometry,[19] with the effect of further undermining the central position and the legitimacy of Central American presidents' ordinary summits within the SICA system.

Pragmatic alienation

In response to SICA's decreasing effectiveness and the more radical positions taken by some states, some presidents have pragmatically distanced themselves from presidential summits, thus creating a vicious circle detrimental to regional integration. Major disparities exist between countries as regards their presidents' attendance at summits. Such disparities, I contend, are evidence of their varying expectations and commitments towards the overall regional integration initiative.

To verify my contention, I have examined the attendance records of presidents at all 19 ordinary summits held between 1999 and 2011.[20] The Salvadorian president has the best score, with a personal attendance rate of 94.7 percent (18 summits), which is consistent with the strategic interest (in both political and economic terms) that regional integration represents for this geographically small country. A similar observation can be made about Guatemala, whose president personally attended 16 summits or 84.2 percent of the total number. Guatemala and El Salvador benefit the most from the regional market (the CACM). The two states have become a driving force for integration (like the Franco–German duo in the European Union) and explicitly promote a supranational regional integration framework. Historically, they have assumed regional leadership: San Salvador (El Salvador) is an "institutional regional hub" (Central America's Brussels), and Guatemala is the original founder of the Central American Parliament.[21] The president of Honduras, which also has a strategic interest in regional integration, attended 15 ordinary summits (78.9 percent). Significantly, Honduras' influence was crucial for the establishment of SICA; between 1991 and 1993 it led the Preparatory Commission that laid down the basis of the current integration system. The so-called "Northern Triangle" (El Salvador, Guatemala and Honduras) exemplifies a supranational posture towards Central American integration.[22]

This supranational vision stands in radical opposition to the intergovernmental vision, which tends to encourage state-to-state relations based strictly on mutual interests. This stance—also called regional pragmatism—has been adopted by both Costa Rica and Panama, and it explains why their presidential attendance levels are only 63.2 percent and 42.1 percent, respectively, figures that underline their limited commitment towards regional integration.[23]

The symbolic and political dimensions of presidential summits are very important, and an empty chair or repeated absences are seen as highly significant, politically speaking. The rank of the representative that a state chooses to send also epitomizes the importance it attributes to the summit itself, and to the whole system. Diplomatic protocol differentiates the attendance of a vice-president, a minister, an ambassador, and a presidential special representative. Therefore, the fact that 58 percent of Panamanian summit attendances have been vice-presidential illustrates the country's relative lack of interest—until recently—in regional integration.[24]

Furthermore, comparing summit attendances adds to our understanding of the decreasing political interdependence between Central American states. Attendance is high in the Northern Triangle countries, and so is political interdependence, as suggested by the fact that a quarter of SICA's currently operative legal instruments are those ratified by El Salvador, Guatemala, and Honduras. However, political interdependence is much less pronounced throughout the system as a whole; empty presidential chairs add to the delegitimization of summits and reduce the intervention capacity of presidential mandates. The opting-out strategies applied by Costa Rica in 2001 vis-à-vis the security system, and by Honduras in 2004 vis-à-vis the regional Parliament and the Court of Justice, have contributed to discredit the system further.

Suboptimal decision making

The SICA intergovernmental decision-making process is based on consensus: each state is fully sovereign and so can veto the establishment of norms and institutions. Moreover, the need to reduce costs and to optimize the use of time often leads to contentious resolutions or declarations being pushed aside from the bargaining table. From a technical perspective, every possible effort is made beforehand to avoid discrepancies and conflicts between delegations at the summits, and agreements tend toward the lowest common denominator—that is, general and abstract principles—with the result that the system produces ineffective decisions.

What follows substantiates the point just made by showing how negotiations have led SICA to an institutional and normative imbalance. The case for reform is then presented. A presidential statement of 1997 proposed that all the regional secretariats for social and environmental issues and for tourism be moved to San Salvador (location of the SICA General Secretariat) so as to unify them and to prepare the ground for the creation of a Central American "Brussels."[25] At the same time, the presidents also decided to consolidate and rationalize regional institutions, a reform in line with the recommendations of an international report by the Inter-American Development Bank (IDB) and the Economic Commission for Latin America and the Caribbean (ECLAC),[26] which proposed two main changes to "adjust" or "reshape" the system. In this case, the inefficacy of the regional decision-making process led to two major paradoxes.

The first is that the unification process was decided and implemented without any reflection or declaration about the restructuring of the legal relations between actors within the system. This gave rise to a great deal of institutional confusion, which still persists.

The IDB-ECLAC report proposed two radical but opposing visions of regional integration: maximalism (Morazanism) and minimalism (intergovernmentalism). In the end, the presidents chose not to follow either route completely, taking instead a consensual approach that led to the adoption of an intermediate solution. Here is how José Sanahuja and José Sotillo describe the spirit of the negotiation that led to the reform: "The Presidents discussed the possibility of founding a 'Federation'—an entity that would take historical precedence over states' independence, but the unionist idea was chosen as they considered it would enable states to mix communitarian competences and intergovernmental cooperation and preserve national sovereignty."[27] Thus, the presidents opted in 1997 for a mixed reform calling for the creation of a regional financial mechanism and a Central American civil service (not yet created), while reducing the financial resources of the Central American Parliament (Parlacen) and the Central American Court of Justice, and eliminating some of their areas of jurisdiction. In sum, although the presidents' decision had binding effects, it was based on a loose and incoherent consensus.

The second paradox lies in the 1997 reform itself and stems from the presidents' desire to achieve a compromise that would gain Costa

Rica's political support for the promotion of political integration in Central America, a stance (as noted earlier) traditionally opposed by Costa Rican diplomacy. In 1997, however, El Salvador, Honduras, Guatemala, and Nicaragua (called the C4 Group) lobbied for political integration through the strengthening of SICA. Costa Rica was fiercely opposed to strengthening Parlacen and the Central American Court of Justice. To gain its support for greater political integration, the C4 Group yielded with respect to the two supranational institutions but went ahead with the reinforcement of SICA. However, this compromise produced unbalanced and incoherent reform. Hence, the summit failed to produce agreement among the presidents and generated a confused institutional structure; the institutional ambiguity explains why most of the 1997 reforms have not been implemented. It is, therefore, my contention that Central American presidential summits produce incoherent governance[28] at the regional level.

Lastly, Central American presidential summits have failed in their aim to legitimize regional norms.[29] Many regional organizations and integrationists have attacked the presidents fiercely for their decision to downsize the supranational elements of Central American integration.[30] Subsequent summits have also failed to realize the implementation of the 1997 reforms, and the small number of measures that have been implemented have been undone little by little. Central American presidents have not fulfilled their coordination function, and they have failed to mobilize either regional or national bureaucracies to implement their decisions, thereby contributing to delegitimizing further both their own position and that of their regional system.

Conclusion

Ultimately, what has been the impact of Central American summitry on regional governance? The 1986 Esquipulas Summit undoubtedly reactivated a mechanism that provided occasions for leaders to get to know each other and to exchange views directly. As a consequence, presidential summits fully realized their socialization function, even if such aspects of interdependence are less conditional on the existence of formal arenas in such a small region.

However, the summits have displayed many weaknesses and have proven unable to direct Central American policies towards regional integration. In fact, they have failed to create a space where political dialogue, multi-actor coordination and agenda-setting capacities can emerge. As a consequence, they have gradually lost the legitimacy that underpinned their initial actions, so that public opinion and even the presidents themselves have constantly questioned their effectiveness in fostering regional governance and producing regional public benefits.

Nor have the summits maintained stability and peace in the region, having proven unable to prevent either political crises (such as the 2009 Honduran *coup d'état*) or bilateral quarrels (such as the Rio San Juan conflict between Costa Rica and Nicaragua, which has persisted since 2010). Despite an accumulation of international strategies and plans, Central American summitry has still not found a way to erase violence or to prevent environmental vulnerability in the region.

Yet notwithstanding the ineffectiveness of presidential summits, some regional organizations have found ways to develop SICA's institutional structure and to consolidate its contribution to regional public policies. In fact, concerning institutionalization, SICA has made progress outside the structure of presidential summits and without the intervention of member states or assistance from national bureaucracies.[31] In this respect, Central American integration appears to be an atypical case of regional integration, inasmuch as a surprising level of success has been achieved without substantial presidential input. For many aspects of political life in Central America, change is often driven by external factors, and this is also true of regional integration, given that the mechanism of presidential summits is in crisis.

Notes

1 Jonas Tallberg, "The Power of the Presidency," *Journal of Common Market Studies* 42, no. 5 (2004): 999–1022.
2 Kevin Parthenay, "L'Intégration Régionale en Amérique Centrale. Une Sociologie Politique du Changement," doctoral dissertation in political science, Institut d'Etudes Politiques de Paris, Paris, 2013.
3 Geoff Berridge, *Diplomacy: Theory and Practice* (Basingstoke: Palgrave Macmillan, 2005); and Francisco Rojas and Paz Milet, *Diplomacia de Cumbres: El Multilateralismo Emergente del Siglo XXI* (Santiago de Chile: FLACSO-Chile, 1998).
4 Olivier Dabène, *The Politics of Regional Integration in Latin America: Theoretical and Comparative Exploration* (New York: Palgrave MacMillan, 2009).
5 Fabrice Lehoucq, *The Politics of Modern Central America: Civil War, Democratization, and Underdevelopment* (New York: Cambridge University Press, 2012); Jean Paul Vargas, "El Ocaso de los Presidencialismos Centroamericanos," *Anuario de Estudios Centroamericanos* 32 (2006): 37–79; and John Booth, Christine Wade, and Thomas Walker, *Understanding Central America: Global Forces, Rebellion, and Change* (Boulder, Colo.: Westview Press, 2009).
6 Andrés Malamud, "Presidentialism and Mercosur: A Hidden Cause for a Successful Experience," in *Comparative Regional Integration: Theoretical*

Perspectives, ed. Finn Laursen (London: Ashgate, 2003), 53–73; Andrés Malamud, "La Diplomacia Presidencial y los Pilares Institucionales del MERCOSUR: Un Examen Empírico," *Relaciones Internacionales*, no. 15 (2010): 113–138.
7   Berridge, *Diplomacy*.
8   James Cochrane, *Regional Integration in Central America* (Lanham, Md.: Rowman & Littlefield Publishing, 1972).
9   Philippe Schmitter, "Central American Integration: Spill-over, Spill-around or Encapsulation?" *Journal of Common Market Studies* 9, no. 1 (1970): 1–48.
10 Olivier Dabène, *La Région Amérique Latine. Interdépendance et Changement Politique* (Paris: Presses de Sciences Po, 1997).
11 Dabène, *La Région Amérique Latine*.
12 Schmitter, "Central American Integration."
13 "ES" for extraordinary summits.
14 Consultative mandates are marginal and so not taken into consideration in these statistics.
15 Katharina Holzinger and Frank Schimmelfennig, "Differentiated Integration in the European Union: Many Concepts, Sparse Theory, Few Data," *Journal of European Public Policy* 19, no. 2 (2012): 292–305.
16 The seven fundamental pillars of Central American integration are: the Tegucigalpa Protocol (1991, general political and institutional issues), the Guatemala Protocol (1993, economic issues), the social treaty (1995, social issues), the democratic security treaty (1995, security issues), the Alliance for Sustainable Development (1994, environmental and development issues), the Central American Parliament Convention (1987, political issues), and the Central American justice convention (1992, judicial issues).
17 Luis Guillermo Solís, "Historia e Integración Centroamericana: Las Visiones desde Costa Rica," Working Paper de la Escuela de Historia, Universidad de Costa Rica, San José, Costa Rica, 2009.
18 Kevin Parthenay, "The Unstable Panamanian Foreign Policy: So Far, So Close from Central America," Symposium, "'For the World's Benefit': Transnational Perspectives on the First Century of the Panama Canal," Paris, 28 November 2014.
19 ECLAC, *Regionalismo Abierto en América Latina y el Caribe. La Integración Económica al Servicio de la Transformación Productiva con Equidad* (Santiago, Chile: ECLAC, 1994).
20 Data available on SICA's website.
21 The General Captaincy of Guatemala, which ended with the independence wave of 1821, is a historical reference at a national level, and a cultural one at the regional level. The episode is often mentioned as an explanation for the necessity for Guatemala to exert regional leadership.
22 This strategic position is also described as "Morazanista" (or maximalist). Francisco Morazán was the Central American Simón Bolívar who helped to free and unify the region: the term refers to the old regional federal ideology that was formalized in the Central American Federal Republic (1821–38).
23 Nicaragua is an intermediate case, with 68.4 percent of presidential attendance at ordinary summits.

24 Panama's recent membership of the economic integration treaty is mainly the result of the free trade agreement signed with the European Union (Acuerdo de Asociación, May 2010).
25 Rafael Sánchez, *The Politics of Central American Integration* (New York: Routledge, 2009).
26 IDB-ECLAC, *La Integración Centroamericana y la Institucionalidad Regional* (Santiago, Chile: ECLAC, 1997).
27 José Antonio Sanahuja and José Angel Sotillo, *Integración y Desarrollo en Centroamérica. Más Allá del Libre Comercio* (Madrid: Los libros de la Catarata, Instituto Universitario de Desarrollo y Cooperación, 1998), 54. Author's translation.
28 Olivier Dabène, "Explaining Latin America's Fourth Wave of Regionalism: Regional Integration of the Third Kind," XXX International Congress of the Latin American Studies Association, San Francisco, 25 May 2012.
29 Peter Weilemann, "The Summit Meeting: The Role and Agenda of Diplomacy at the Highest Level," *Nira Review* 7, no. 2 (2000): 16–20.
30 Adolfo León Gomez, *El Anti-integracionismo en Centroamérica: Corte Centroamericana de Justicia* (Managua, Nicaragua: Corte Centroamericana de Justicia, 2003).
31 Parthenay, "L'Intégration Régionale en Amérique Centrale."

8 The anti-summitry of North American governance

Greg Anderson

- **Asymmetry**
- **Agenda buried, asymmetry intensified?**
- **Asymmetry, sovereignty, and an awkward marriage of security and economics**
- **Conclusion: Gulliver and the neoclassical state**

One of the most striking things about this contribution to a volume on summitry is the relative absence of summits as a mode of North American governance. Indeed, while the major organizing touchstones of this volume entail discussions of origins, expectations, goals, evolution, function, and governance structures created by summitry in different parts of the world, formal regularized summitry in North America was unheard of until 2005. Yet, its rarity in the context of a highly integrated region is especially meritorious of examination.

This chapter was drafted in the weeks immediately following the 2014 North American Leaders' Summit (NALS) in Toluca, Mexico. In most respects, it was like other summits: separate bilaterals, trilateral statements, photo-ops, and an official communiqué hammered out by staffers weeks prior. Yet, the NALS is not a well-entrenched institution, one indicator of which is the fact that US President Barack Obama was on the ground for less than seven hours, did not overnight in Mexico, and spent nearly all of his time in pursuit of his domestic agenda as he was followed by the American press corps.

More importantly, when the NALS was launched at Waco, Texas, in March 2005, it was alongside the summit's principal work program, the Security and Prosperity Partnership (SPP). On the surface, the SPP was an ambitious undertaking comprising leftovers from the economic integration of the 1990s and the new imperatives of post-9/11 security. An axiom of North American relations has long held that the sustained engagement of the leaders was critical to progress on any agenda, in part due to the stark asymmetries between the three countries.[1] Hence, the NALS was conceived in part as a means of animating progress on the SPP. Yet, after withering criticism on many fronts, the SPP was seldom mentioned at NALS meetings after 2007, and all references to the SPP were removed from government websites in August 2009. In 2010, the leaders decided not to hold a NALS, renewing doubts about the trilateral commitment to the idea of North America.

Neither the NALS, nor the evolving agendas that supposedly give the NALS purpose, have created institutional mechanisms that will ensure the summit's longevity. In fact, much like the evolution of North American integration, from which the NALS was largely derived, post-9/11 summitry has steadfastly avoided the pooling of sovereignty that would inherently extend the "shadow of the future" for the summit process.

The aim of this chapter is to examine the stark asymmetries of power as a major explanatory variable in the relative absence of summitry in North American governance. The region is certainly not without its governance mechanisms at virtually every conceivable level, but the regional governance architecture as driven by summitry has been uneven, and frequently in search of an agenda. The structure, function, and future of the NALS hinge on the dynamics of what has increasingly become a tale of two highly asymmetrical bilateral relationships, with the United States as the dominant player in both. The NALS, in fact, presents a test case for simple international relations theory positing the tensions between realism and liberal theory: the United States as the dominant, sovereign power, preserving its sovereign policy latitude and resistant to initiatives from its smaller, dependent neighbors for binding, high-level governance coordination.

America's dominance of the regional economic and security space has meant that most of the North American agenda is anchored in US domestic political and regulatory institutions. In the language of economists, Canada and Mexico have increasingly become reactive "price takers" where governance coordination is concerned. Moreover, Canada and Mexico have in recent years sought separately to strengthen bilateral ties with the United States, undermining the rationale for trilateral summitry. The NALS faces two major questions, both flowing from asymmetry, that this chapter seeks to explore. Has trilateralism effectively run its course? And is so much of the agenda setting now taking place in the United States itself that the idea of regional summitry has become moot?

Asymmetry

Cross-border economic, social, and political relationships, in part driven by proximity and simple necessity, have always transcended the arbitrary divisions of political borders, in a sense constantly reallocating power and sovereignty. However, the 1994 North American Free Trade Agreement (NAFTA) provided a significant boost to all of these impulses through shallow institutionalization that reallocated power and shifted the continent toward a more hierarchical form of sovereignty; a kind of "big bang" of institutionalization that had many wondering whether North America was lurching toward European Union (EU)-style governance.[2] Yet, rather than mitigating the effects of asymmetry as liberal institutionalism would suggest, NAFTA preserved and exacerbated North America as a tale of two highly asymmetric relationships for which high-level summitry has, especially for the United States, seemed unnecessary.[3]

Tables 8.1 and 8.2 present standard measures of economic openness and vulnerability to shifts in the global economy for all three NAFTA countries, but also depict a major source of asymmetry. Where the United States is less "open" in terms of dependence on international trade—exports + imports/gross domestic product (GDP)—and has a more diversified set of trading partners, Canada and Mexico are both open and dependent on a single market.

Table 8.1 NAFTA asymmetries, by GDP, 1975–2012

	1975	1987	1994	2000	2012
Canada GDP (US$ billion)	170	420	560	770	1,780
% of North American GDP	9.0	7.9	7.0	6.5	9.3
Exports + imports as % GDP	47	53	67	85	63
Mexico GDP (US$ billion)	88	140	420	581	1,178
% of North American GDP	4.7	2.6	5.9	5.2	6.1
Exports + imports as % GDP	17	33	38	64	66
United States GDP (US$ billion)	1,600	4,700	7,017	9,764	16,240
% of North American GDP	86.0	89.3	87.7	88.2	84.5
Exports + imports as % GDP	16	19	22	26	29

(World Bank, Data Bank (data.worldbank.org), and author's calculations.)

Table 8.2 NAFTA export partners, 2012

	Canada (%)	Mexico (%)	United States (%)
Exports to	United States (74.5) China (4.3) UK (4.1)	United States (80.5) Canada (3.6) Germany (1.4)	Canada (18.9) Mexico (14) China (7.2) Japan (4.5)
Imports from	United States (50.6) China (11) Mexico (5.5)	United States (49.9) China (15.4) Japan (4.8)	China (19) Canada (14.1) Mexico (12) Japan (6.4) Germany (4.7)

(Elaborated by the author from data available at CIA World Factbook, "Country Profiles," www.cia.gov/library/publications/the-world-factbook/.)

Moreover, patterns of integration in North America have also been unequal. Since NAFTA began its implementation phase in 1994, north-south commercial linkages between Canada and the United States have grown at a much faster pace than those flowing from south to north.[4] In other words, Canada has become far more integrated into the US economy than the United States has become integrated into the Canadian.

Another way to think about how the stark asymmetries of power affect the incentives for summitry and the pooled sovereignty that might flow from it comes from the theory of the firm in economics, and specifically literatures on mergers and acquisitions. Summitry has a number of qualities in common with the merger of two firms. For businesses, the incursion of either spot-market or investment-specific transactions costs in exchange suggests the rationale for the rise of the firm itself or the merger of any two firms engaged in exchange. The greater the investment-specific nature of an exchange relationship (e.g. few other exchange partners), the stronger are the incentives for both integration and robust institutional design to govern the relationship.[5] Yet, who bares the burden of those investment-specific transactions costs may depend on which party's asset specificity is greater. In other words, if one party has fewer options for exchange than another, the asset-specificity of the relationship is higher for one party relative to the other. In short, one party needs the other more.

Examples of this kind of asymmetry are everywhere in mergers and acquisitions in which a weak firm may have few options other than to be sold to a specific, healthier firm, or risk going out of business.[6] In short, the asset-specific transactions costs of exchange will be more heavily borne by the weaker party.

The relative dependence of Canada and Mexico on US market access entails a form of investment specificity in their relations full of transactions costs. For the United States, the investment specificity of relations with Canada and Mexico is relatively low; in other words, there are many potential partners to which assets could be deployed and few incentives to invest in the construction of institutions with Canada and Mexico. International relations scholars, and realists in particular, would argue that the unwillingness of the United States to engage in institutions or formal summitry is mainly about hegemony, power, and preservation of sovereignty. Yet, looked at through principles of the theory of the firm, the dynamics of asymmetrical power can also be seen in terms of investment-specificity driving the relative institutionalization of bi- and trilateral relations.[7]

Embedded within these asymmetrical relations is a near-bottomless pit of lower-level forms of governance, many of which are driven by much less investment specificity than we see in more high-profile governance such as summitry. Such forms of governance in North America are everywhere, expanding, and include the growing activism of sub-federal governments, a range of cross-border business-to-business relationships, and network-like activity in domains such as the environment or regulatory harmonization.[8]

Getting there requires a significant investment of resources in a single exchange relationship and is fraught with a high-risk burden for the smaller/weaker party. By contrast, the larger, more powerful party to a negotiation has a lower risk burden, but may be unwilling to commit the asset-specific resources necessary.[9]

NAFTA contributed significantly to making North American sovereignty more hierarchical, by instilling new rules of economic governance in trade and investment relations that have drawn Canada and Mexico deeper into the American economic orbit. Politically, the symbolism of both Canada and Mexico each abandoning decades of nationalist economic policies and integrating themselves into the US sphere was considerable, and not without controversy. NAFTA softened some effects of asymmetrical power by entrenching much of the trade and investment relationship in a set of rules that have governed the evolution of economic exchange relations since. Establishing formal summitry such as the NALS "extends the shadow of the future" of the relationship, effectively guaranteeing that it will continue.[10]

Yet because NAFTA was limited to just trade and investment, and never contemplated supranational institutions, and, with the exception of regular meetings among trade ministers, did not institutionalize summitry between each nation's leaders, NAFTA deepened integration without the pooling of sovereignty that would have mitigated asymmetry's other effects.

Put differently, the trade liberalization of the late 1980s and early 1990s mitigated the need for high-level summitry by taking some of the most important irritants—summit agenda items—in trilateral relations off the table. America had arguably obtained most of what it wanted from high-level contact upon completion of NAFTA: shallow institutionalization, economic irritants managed, and few issues of significance to merit the sustained attention of the US president.[11]

For Canada and Mexico, the rationale for the NALS was obvious: keep the United States engaged and cooperative. Canadian economic history, in particular, is partly a tale of alternately trying to ensnare its southern neighbor in formal arrangements or walling itself off through protectionism.[12]

Mexico has confronted a similar set of tensions with the United States, albeit framed by the additional legacy of invasion, warfare, and the loss of territory. Such is the potency of nationalism vis-à-vis the United States in both countries, that it has frequently altered electoral outcomes and generated a paradigm of dependency and dominance through which relations with the United States are viewed.[13]

International relations theorists have for years been making the case that one way to reduce the effects of asymmetry is by fostering increased interdependence and institutionalization among states.[14] It is through this basic liberal institutional framework that we can view the postwar integration of Europe, as well as understand elements of the interdependence fostered by the rapid expansion of the global economy.[15]

Similarly, as Canada contemplated free trade with the United States, and the likely consequence of deepening dependence on the US market through trade liberalization with a single country, restraining the arbitrary use of trade remedy law against Canadian exports was a matter of economic necessity.[16] When Mexican president Carlos Salinas subsequently proposed free trade with the United States in 1990, immunity from US trade remedy laws was also high on the list of Mexican priorities, and for many of the same reasons.[17]

Canadian governments routinely devote significantly more resources (investment-specific assets) to interactions with the United States, in the case of the Canada–United States free trade negotiations of the 1980s actually reorganizing part of the federal bureaucracy to focus on the talks.[18] The dynamics across the negotiating table represented a near-total contrast of styles and strategies: hardened, experienced, high-profile, and determined Canadian negotiators with direct access to the prime minister versus a relatively inexperienced and under-resourced

American team with little access to decision-making authority.[19] The Canada–United States free trade negotiations barely registered in Washington, DC, much less the rest of the country. In Canada, the agreement was of monumental importance, virtually transforming the 1988 federal election into a single-issue referendum on Canada's relationship with the United States.[20]

One of the great challenges for Canada and Mexico in North America is actually getting issues of importance to them the high-level attention in Washington needed to effect change. The large trade liberalization exercises of the late 1980s and early 1990s were significant enough to attract the attention of high-level US officials, albeit only at the eleventh hour.[21] Likewise, the post-9/11 security agenda in North America was similarly significant enough that the United States was willing to create the NALS to move that part of the SPP forward.[22] However, combining the security agenda with a mature trade agenda may undermine the NALS as security also matures.

As Geoffrey Hale has pointed out, economic integration with the United States has meant that most issues of importance to Canada are dealt with in the US domestic regulatory system.[23] Canada is left in the awkward position of needing the same status as US domestic stakeholders, but hampered in doing so by its status as "foreign." This in turn is compounded by America's vast foreign policy agenda that inherently preoccupies the highest levels of government, and the many domestic institutional foundations of hegemony that make US policy-making slow and laborious, one consequence of which has been the management of important issues to Canada and Mexico by lesser officials in the US bureaucracy.[24]

While trade liberalization projects like NAFTA went some distance toward regularizing the flow of goods, services, and capital across North America's borders, both were shallow forms of integration that did not create the kind of binding institutional arrangements Canada and Mexico sought.[25] Hence, NAFTA routinized economic relations in a set of rules, but did so by avoiding the kind of Europe-like, supra-national institutions where pooled sovereignty is thought to be effective in rebalancing power asymmetries.[26]

Nevertheless, NAFTA did provide a set of rules by which trade and investment relations have become more predictable. Indeed, even the dispute settlement mechanisms designed to deal with trade remedy laws, imperfect as they are, have been broadly successful in smoothing the incidence of trade disputes among the three countries.[27] All of this has been in line with both liberal institutionalist scholarship and real-world experience (Europe) in terms of the salutary effects of integration and institutionalization on the arbitrary exercise of power. However, NAFTA also left much unfinished business. In January 2008, the final phase-ins of NAFTA were completed, but little had been done to advance NAFTA beyond its limited ambition as a free trade agreement, one of the shallowest stages of integration.

Agenda buried, asymmetry intensified?

NAFTA created the shallowest forms of institutionalization, which largely preserved many traditional patterns of Westphalian sovereignty while simultaneously dismantling others. It established regular ministerial-level meetings, but entrenched management of the agreement in the respective national bureaucracies, making elements of the relationship not covered by the agreement (the built-in agenda) difficult to elevate onto the political agenda. Bunched together, these outstanding agenda items created a "tyranny of small differences" that were a serious drain on North America's competitiveness, but were not politically significant enough in the United States to address.[28] Moreover, NAFTA reallocated decision-making power by creating a series of ad hoc dispute settlement mechanisms with limited scope to arbitrate disputes.[29]

Hence, NAFTA went some distance toward mitigating the effects of asymmetry by restricting policy latitude (negative integration) in a limited number of areas. However, with no real institutional teeth to forcibly govern economic conflict in North America, the weaker partners to NAFTA effectively deepened their economic dependence on the United States without winning the kind of institutional depth (positive integration) that would have augmented their decision-making power, thereby moving the continent toward a more hierarchical form of sovereignty, arguably exacerbating the asymmetrical distribution of decision-making power in the process.

The immediate aftermath of the 11 September terrorist attacks on the United States reinvigorated discussions of how to institutionalize North American governance. The North American Leaders' Summit, for now, remains a byproduct of that period.

Asymmetry, sovereignty, and an awkward marriage of security and economics

North America's citizenry would be right to assume that the leaders of the three countries see each other regularly. The presidents, prime ministers, foreign ministers, secretaries of state, and economic ministers of all three countries meet regularly, over 100 times since 2001, on the margins of meetings held under the auspices of a variety of international organizations of which they are members.[30] Much of the public also assumes trilateral "Leaders' Summits" have long been institutionalized under the auspices of NAFTA. While NAFTA negotiations typified the high-level attention to trilateral issues sought by Canada and Mexico, the post-NAFTA agenda has instead been dominated by a kind of ad hoc governance that privileges traditional lines of communication and jurisdictions of control within and between governments.[31]

The closure of US airspace and border access in the days after 11 September 2001 laid bare Canadian and Mexican dependence on US market access. The closure of several auto assembly plants in the United States in the days following the attacks revealed the extent of cross-border integration among the three countries as just-in-time assembly broke down amidst parts shortages in all three countries.[32] However, the dependence of Canada and Mexico on the US market for their economic survival put the political and economic stakes in sharp relief for policymakers.[33]

At Canada's suggestion, a number of ideas from the failed or incomplete "next steps" processes from the 1990s were pulled off the shelf and presented to the George W. Bush Administration as a means of handling the new imperatives of security in an integrated North American marketplace.[34] The Bush Administration agreed and the result was the December 2001 US–Canada Smart Border Declaration and the 30 point Action Plan.[35] In early 2002, the United States and Mexico agreed to a similar list of 22 proposals known as the US–Mexico Border Partnership Action Plan. Between 2001 and 2005, the blending of security and economics re-stimulated significant thinking and debate about what North America could be.[36] For some, the insertion of security made it logical that the next steps in North American integration would entail the initiation of a common security perimeter, perhaps including a customs union and the attendant supranational, pooled sovereignty that went along with it.[37] Yet, the securitization of the stagnant post-NAFTA economic agenda failed to pool sovereign decision making.

In March 2005, at Waco, Texas, a mature, but shallow economic agenda rooted in NAFTA was formally linked to an evolving security agenda with the launch of the SPP, and seemed to herald a new era of high-level attention to regional governance. The SPP's 300+ agenda items, divided into distinct agendas (security and prosperity), looked like an ambitious, pragmatic program to deal at once with NAFTA's left-overs and emerging security imperatives. Yet the SPP itself generated no new institutional mechanisms, involved no legislative oversight of activities, and did not formally incorporate private sector or civil society input.[38] As importantly, responsibility for management of the SPP was left, as under NAFTA, in the hands of the respective national bureaucracies: in the United States this meant security would be handled by the Department of Homeland Security and prosperity by the Department of Commerce. As a process, the SPP suffered from numerous faults that effectively doomed it after just a few years.[39]

Formal summitry seemed to be a natural complement to a lengthy and ambitious agenda.[40] In reality, the entire process was hardly a process at all. A major reason for the NALS was to animate the SPP agenda, in part by signaling its importance; principals' devotion of scarce time to an issue inherently signals its importance to their respective bureaucracies. However, the SPP agenda circumvented national legislatures, sidelined civil society, and only ventured progress in areas with residual or latent administrative authority.[41] By 2008, all references to the SPP in NALS declarations had disappeared, and the SPP itself was purged from government websites the following year. In each of the succeeding years after 2005, the NALS declined in importance and was actually skipped in 2010 in favor of bilateral meetings on the margins of the G20 summit in Toronto. The lack of enthusiasm for the NALS is, in part, also linked to the demise of the SPP in 2009, and the fact that none of the current leaders had a hand in establishing it. Without the SPP, the NALS has no formal agenda and risks becoming even more ad hoc and irregular.

Since 2009, the NALS has been further undermined by the so-called "rebilateralization" of North American relations in which Ottawa and Mexico City have pursued issues with Washington on their own rather than in a trilateral setting. The result has been the de facto end of trilateralism and the return of North American governance patterns via two separate, asymmetrical relationships.[42] These developments have led a number of scholars to lament the demise of a trilateralized North America, arguably calling into question the longevity of summitry as well.[43] Early 2011 saw the establishment of two separate high-level contact processes, two separate regulatory harmonization processes, and two separate clean energy and climate change dialogues.[44]

Tellingly, both the NALS Joint Statement and the Fact Sheets of "deliverables" from the 2014 Toluca meeting acknowledge all of this activity, but gloss over the fact that many are distinct bilateral processes separate from the NALS itself.[45] For advocates of trilateralism, Toluca repeated a familiar and:

> ... unproductive pattern whereby bureaucrats negotiate the fine points of a "Declaration" in which the details camouflage its

vacuousness. Then, bureaucrats justify the Summits as necessary to keep the heads of state engaged and pushing the bureaucracies ... Summits have been more photo-opportunities than substantive discussions.[46]

Indeed, a comparison of the SPP Signature Initiatives and the "Deliverables" from the Toluca meeting reveals a kind of shared DNA in the broad themes being discussed, but it is increasingly difficult to ascertain whether the NALS process is behind the "progress" being made since none of it requires the launch of a political project needing the imprimatur of the leaders. Much like the SPP agenda itself, which sidestepped the national legislatures, sidelined private sector and civil society groups, and contemplated no new tri-national governance institutions, all that the NALS considers "deliverables" is taking place within existing legislative and administrative authorization. Almost by definition, the stark asymmetries of power operational in North America mean those "deliverables" will be set mostly in the United States.

Conclusion: Gulliver and the neoclassical state

Wherever we look in the global political economy, we see significant variance in degrees of integration and pooled sovereignty aimed at managing the transactions costs incurred between states. For example, no two free trade areas are exactly alike in terms of the depth of tariff liberalization or the shallowness of institutionalization. However, with each stage of integration, the institutional constraints on policy for the state multiply.

Therein resides a kind of "Gulliver" effect for states of varying size and power in the international trading system. For small states, engaging larger trading powers in ever-deeper forms of integration can restrict the arbitrary application of policy by larger powers. Increasing levels of institutionalization of economic relations breeds interdependence between states, but also facilitates a more predictable application of domestic law within the confines of the agreement. Large states, by contrast, are less dependent on small states for their economic prosperity and tend to resist encumbering institutionalization both in form and practice.

Stephen Krasner argues that there are very different incentives for states of varying size within the international trade regime and that large, powerful states have a significant advantage in both setting the structure of the regime and reaping the benefits from it. However, the creation and maintenance of an open trading regime does not entail the accumulation of most benefits by large states. In fact, it is small open economies that reap the largest gains from an open regime, while larger states benefit from additional openness on the margins. Specifically, Krasner argues:

> ... the utility costs [of openness] will be less for large states because they generally have a smaller proportion of their economy engaged in the international economic system ... a state that is relatively large ... will find its political power enhanced by an open system because its opportunity costs of closure are less.[47]

Small states, Krasner argues, are likely to opt for an open regime, even one undergirded by hegemonic power, because the benefits of openness for small economies are so large and the opportunity costs of closure significant.[48] The result is the marginal accumulation of power by the hegemonic state while small states weigh the significant costs of remaining outside the trade regime's structure. Contrary to depictions of the international trade regime suggesting that interdependence was softening the use of power, Krasner persuasively argues that it is in the design and operation of the system itself that we see hegemonic power being wielded. In other words, small states might look at the rules-based regime as a means of bringing additional predictability to their economic relations with larger states, but the reality is that the many Lilliputians engaged with Gulliver are having little impact on the underlying utility of power within the regime.

We see this set of dynamics within the anti-summitry of North American integration. The stark asymmetries between the United States and its North American neighbors have generated very different incentives in terms of any rationale for further institutionalization of trilateral relations, and for further summitry that might promote it.

This chapter has argued that North American governance has been, and largely remains, characterized by the absence of formal summitry. The region's major bout of institutionalization in the early 1990s, NAFTA, was not the byproduct of a summit process, nor did it create one in its wake. Instead, and much to the disappointment of advocates of deeper levels of institutionalization in North America, governance has remained the byproduct of an uneven, sporadic set of initiatives that few would identify as formal, high-level summitry. There is no shortage of interaction among the NAFTA partners on a range of issues, but genuine trilateral governance remains the exception rather than the rule, in part because of the stark asymmetries among the three countries that drive divergent interests and outlooks, even in the presence of robust cross-border interaction.

Cast in realist terms, the United States largely has what it wants from its relationship with Canada and Mexico; economic benefits from the addition of members to a system America underwrites, shallow institutionalization that eschews pooled sovereignty, and the technocratic management of "foreign relations" with its closest neighbors. The NALS has emerged only recently and has neither the institutional foundation nor the big-ticket agenda to justify the contribution of future US presidents. While the region's Gulliver may be getting what it wants out of existing levels of interaction and institutionalization, the region's frustrated Lilliputians have gone their separate ways, undermining the limited trilateralism that exists, and casting doubt on the utility of the NALS as a trilateral summit.

Notes

1 Allan Gotlieb, *I'll be With You in a Minute, Mr. Ambassador: The Education of a Canadian Diplomat in Washington* (Toronto: University of Toronto Press, 1991); and Derek Burney, *Getting it Done* (Montreal: McGill-Queen's University Press, 2005), 177–191.
2 Greg Anderson, "Securitization and Sovereignty in Post-9/11 North America," *Review of International Political Economy* 19, no. 5 (2012): 711–741.
3 Greg Anderson, "NAFTA on the Brain: Why Creeping Integration Has Always Worked Better," *American Review of Canadian Studies* 42, no. 4 (2012): 450–459.
4 Aaron Sydor, "An Index of Canada–U.S. Economic Integration," Analytical Paper Series, Foreign Affairs and International Trade Canada, Office of the Chief Economist, Foreign Affairs and International Trade Canada, Ottawa, 2008, 10.
5 Oliver Williamson, "Transaction-Cost Economics: The Governance of Contractual Relations," *Journal of Law and Economics* 22 (1979): 239.
6 Shameen Prashantham and Julian Birkinshaw, "Dancing with Gorillas: How Small Companies Can Partner Effectively with MNCs," *California Management Review* 51, no. 1 (2008): 6–23; Tyrone Callahan and Thomas Moeller, "Who's Cheating Whom in Mergers and Acquisitions?" unpublished working paper, University of Texas at Austin (July 2009); and Melissa Graebner, "Caveat Venditor: Trust Asymmetries in Acquisitions of Entrepreneurial Firms," *Academy of Management Journal* 52, no. 3 (2009): 435–472.
7 Anderson, "Securitization and Sovereignty in Post-9/11 North America," 711–741.
8 Chris Kukucha, *The Provinces and Canadian Foreign Trade Policy* (Vancouver: UBC Press, 2008); Neil Craik, Isabel Studer, and Debora Van Nijnatten, *Climate Change Policy in North America* (Toronto: University of Toronto Press, 2013); and Greg Anderson, "Expanding the Partnership?: State and Provinces in U.S.–Canada Relations," *Canadian American Public Policy* 80 (2014): 1–44.

9 Kenneth Oye, "Explaining Cooperation under Anarchy: Hypotheses and Strategies," *World Politics* 38, no. 1 (1985): 1–24; and Robert Axelrod and Robert Keohane, "Achieving Cooperation under Anarchy: Strategies and Institutions," *World Politics* 38, no. 1 (1985): 226–254.
10 Pedro Dal Bo, "Cooperation under the Shadow of the Future: Experimental Evidence from Infinitely Repeated Games," *American Economic Review* 95, no. 5 (2005): 1591–1604.
11 Michael Hart, Bill Dymond, and Colin Robertson, *Decision at Midnight: Inside the Canada-U.S. Free Trade Negotiations* (Vancouver: UBC Press, 1994), 36–53.
12 Kenneth Norrie and Douglas Owram, *A History of the Canadian Economy*, 2nd edn (Toronto: Harcourt Brace & Company, Canada, 1996); and D.F. Barnett, "The Galt Tariff: Incidental or Effective Protection," *Canadian Journal of Economics* 9, no. 3 (1976): 389–407.
13 Jack Lawrence Granatstein, *Yankee Go Home? Canadians and Anti-Americanism* (Toronto: Harper Collins, 1996); Sidney Weintraub, *Un-Equal Partners: The United States and Mexico* (Pittsburgh, Penn.: University of Pittsburgh Press, 2010); Stephen D. Morris and John Passe-Smith, "What a Difference a Crisis Makes: NAFTA, Mexico, and the United States," *Latin American Perspectives* 28, no. 3 (2001): 124–149; and Roger Bartra and Susan Casal-Sanchez, "Culture and Political Power in Mexico," *Latin American Perspectives* 16, no. 2 (1989): 61–69.
14 Ernst Haas, *The Uniting of Europe: Political, Social, and Economic Forces, 1950–1957* (Stanford, Calif.: University of California Press, 1968); and Wayne Sandholtz and Alec Stone Sweet, "Neo-functionalism and Supranational Governance," working paper, April 2010, ssrn.com/abstract=1585123.
15 Frederic Fransen, *The Supranational Politics of Jean Monnet: Ideas and Origins of the European Community* (Freeport, NY: Greenwood Press, 2001); Richard Cooper, *The Economics of Interdependence: Economic Policy in the Atlantic Community* (New York: Council on Foreign Relations, 1968); Barry Eichengreen, "Toward a More Perfect Union: The Logic of Economic Integration," *Essays in International Finance* 198 (June 1996); and Thomas Zeiler, *Free Trade Free World: The Advent of the GATT* (Chapel Hill, N.C.: University of North Carolina Press, 1999).
16 Hart et al., *Decision at Midnight*, 318–342.
17 Maxwell Cameron and Brian Tomlin,*The Making of the NAFTA: How the Deal Was Done* (Ithaca, NY: Cornell University Press, 2000), 88–89, 117; and Carlos Salinas de Gortari, *Mexico: The Policy and Politics of Modernization* (Barcelona: Plaza & Janes Editores, 2000), 99–103.
18 Hart et al., *Decision at Midnight*, 133–151; and Gordon Ritchie, *Wrestling with the Elephant* (Toronto: Macfarlane, Walter & Ross, 1997), 55–59, 70–71.
19 Hart et al., *Decision at Midnight*, 36–53, 154–157, 190, 193, 204, 239, 270–271, 314; and Steve Dryden, *Trade Warriors* (Oxford: Oxford University Press, 1995), 340–343.
20 Brian Mulroney, *Memoirs, 1939–1993* (Toronto: McLelland & Stewart, 2007), 622–644; and Hart et al., *Decision at Midnight*, 389.
21 See Hart et al., *Decision at Midnight*, 36–53, 328–340.
22 Paul Martin, *Hell or High Water: My Life in and Out of Politics* (Toronto: McLelland & Stewart, 2008), 93–100.

The anti-summitry of North American governance 155

23 Geoffrey Hale, *So Near and Yet So Far* (Vancouver: UBC Press, 2012).
24 Stephen Haggard, "The Institutional Foundations of Hegemony: Explaining the Reciprocal Trade Agreements Act of 1934," *International Organization* 42, no. 1 (1988): 91–119; and Greg Anderson, "Did Canada Kill Fast Track?" *Diplomatic History* 36, no. 3 (2012): 583–610.
25 Greg Anderson, "Can Someone Please Settle this Dispute: Canadian Softwood Lumber and the Dispute Settlement Mechanisms of the NAFTA and the WTO," *The World Economy* 29, no. 5 (2006): 585–610; and Greg Anderson, "The Reluctance of Hegemons: Comparing the Regionalization Strategies of a Crouching Cowboy and a Hidden Dragon," in *China and the Politics of Regionalization*, ed. Emilian Kavalski (Farnham, Surrey: Ashgate Publishing Ltd, 2009): 91–107.
26 Isabel Studer and Carol Wise, *Requiem or Revival: The Promise of North American Integration* (Washington, DC: Brookings Institution Press, 2007), 64–65; and Robert Pastor, *Toward A North American Community* (Washington, DC: Institute for International Economics, 2001).
27 Anderson, "Can Someone Please Settle this Dispute," 585–610; and Patrick Macrory, "NAFTA Chapter 19: A Successful Experiment in International Dispute Resolution," *The Border Papers C.D. Howe Institute Commentary*, no. 168 (2003).
28 Michael Hart, "A New Accommodation with the United States: The Trade and Economic Dimension," in *Art of the State II: Thinking North America: Prospects and Pathways*, ed. Thomas J. Courchene, Donald J. Savoie, and Daniel Schwanen (Montreal: Institute for Research on Public Policy, 2004), 1–70; and Michael Hart, "Steer or Drift? Taking Charge of Canada–US Regulatory Convergence," *The Border Papers C.D. Howe Institute Commentary*, no. 229 (2006): 1–36. See also Robert Pastor, "The Future of North America: Replacing a Bad Neighbor Policy," *Foreign Affairs* 87, no. 4 (2008): 84–98.
29 Martin, *Hell or High Water*, 376–379; Weintraub, *Un-equal Partners*, 121–126; Barbara Kotschwar, "Trade Rift Deepens With Mexico," Peterson Perspectives: Interviews on Current Topics, 19 March 2009, www.iie.com/publications/papers/pp20090319kotschwar.pdf; and Anderson, "Can Someone Please Settle this Dispute," 585–610.
30 Author's calculations.
31 See Robert Pastor, *The North American Idea* (Oxford: Oxford University Press, 2011); and Robert Pastor, *Toward A North American Community*.
32 "11 Lives, Manning the Bridge," *Time*, 1 September 2002; and Robert Bonner, "Testimony before the Seventh Public Hearing," National Commission on Terrorist Attacks on the United States, 26 January 2004.
33 See Maureen Molot "The Trade-Security Nexus: The New Reality in Canada-U.S. Economic Integration," *American Review of Canadian Studies* 33, no. 1 (2003): 27–62.
34 Martin, *Hell or High Water*, 93–100.
35 Martin, *Hell or High Water*, 12–14.
36 John Manley, Pedro Aspe, William Weld, and Chairs, *Building a North American Community* (New York: Council on Foreign Relations, 2005); Wendy Dobson, "Shaping the Future of the North American Economic Space," *C.D. Howe Institute Commentary*, no. 162 (2002); and Jeff Heynen and John Higginbotham, "Advancing Canadian Interests in the United

States: A Practical Guide for Canadian Public Officials," Action-Research Roundtable, Canadian School of Public Service, Ottawa, 2004.
37 Pastor, "The Future of North America," 84–98; Thomas J. Courchene, Donald J. Savoie, and Daniel Schwanen, "Thinking North America," *The Art of the State*, Vol. II (Montreal: Institute for Research in Public Policy, 2005); and Dobson, "Shaping the Future of the North American Economic Space."
38 Greg Anderson and Christopher Sands, "Negotiating North America: The Security and Prosperity Partnership," Hudson Institute White Paper, Washington, DC, 2007; Jason Ackelson and Justin Kastner, "The Security and Prosperity Partnership of North America," *American Review of Canadian Studies* 36, no. 2 (2006): 207–232.
39 Anderson and Sands, "Negotiating North America."
40 Anderson and Sands, "Negotiating North America."
41 Anderson and Sands, "Negotiating North America."
42 Pastor, "The Future of North America"; and Pastor, *The North American Idea*.
43 Pastor, *The North American Idea*, 156; Stephen Clarkson, *Does North America Exist: Governing the Continent After NAFTA and 9/11* (Toronto: University of Toronto Press and Woodrow Wilson Center Press, 2008); Studer and Wise, *Requiem or Revival*; and Jeffrey Ayres and Laura Macdonald, *North America in Question: Regional Integration in an Era of Economic Turbulence* (Toronto: University of Toronto Press, 2012).
44 See Pastor, *The North American Idea*, 162–166; and "Canada–US: Beyond the Border: A Shared Vision for Perimeter Security and Economic Competitiveness," the Regulatory Cooperation Council, and the Clean Energy Dialogue; US–Mexico: High Level Regulatory Cooperation Council, Bilateral Framework on Clean Energy and Climate Change (formalized March 2011).
45 See Joint Statement by North American Leaders—21st Century North America: Building the Most Competitive and Dynamic Region in the World, www.whitehouse.gov.
46 Pastor, *The North American Idea*, 193.
47 Stephen Krasner, "State Power and the Structure of International Trade," *World Politics* 28 (April 1976): 322.
48 Krasner, "State Power and the Structure of International Trade," 317–347.

Part III
Case studies—World

9 ASEAN summits and regional governance in comparative perspective[1]

Richard Stubbs

- ASEAN summits, consultation, and negotiations
- ASEAN's agenda and summits
- Successful ASEAN summits, socialization, and legitimacy
- Conclusion

The Association of Southeast Asian Nations (ASEAN) has been one of the most successful regional organizations of the global South.[2] While it has had its problems, ASEAN has, on the whole, been a positive element in the regional relations of Southeast Asia and more recently East Asia. It has also provided specific benefits for its members. This analysis explores the role that ASEAN summits as "institutionalized multilateral leaders' meetings"[3] have played in the development of the regional organization. More specifically, it reviews how ASEAN summits have established the way in which relations among members should be conducted and set the overall goals of the organization. Finally, the analysis assesses why ASEAN summits have been relatively successful in promoting ASEAN's development and what other regions, including Latin America, can learn from ASEAN's experience with summits.

ASEAN was established at a meeting of the foreign ministers of the five original members—Indonesia, Malaysia, the Philippines, Singapore, and Thailand—at Bangkok in August 1967, but the First ASEAN Summit was not held until 1976. The Second Summit was held in 1977, but the Third Summit did not take place until ten years after that, in 1987. However, as the workload of summits increased and as the summit process gained momentum and legitimacy, more meetings of leaders became necessary. Moreover, as the Introduction to this volume indicates, the increased frequency of ASEAN summits was also prompted by greater regional interdependence brought on by the end of the Cold War and the advent of globalization. At the Fourth

Summit in 1992 it was agreed that summits should, henceforth, be held every three years, and indeed the Fifth, Sixth, and Seventh Summits took place in 1995, 1998, and 2001. At the same time, in the "off" years of 1996, 1997, 1999, and 2000 leaders' meetings did take place, although they were designated as "informal summits." After the Seventh Summit in 2001 the association's leaders' meetings officially became annual affairs, and with the advent of the ASEAN Charter in December 2008 it was decided to hold ASEAN summits twice every year in one of the member states on a rotating basis. For example, in 2014 the two summits were held in Myanmar.

Since its inception ASEAN has expanded its membership, with Brunei joining in 1984, Vietnam in 1995, Laos and Myanmar in 1997, and Cambodia in 1999. ASEAN summits have also been augmented by meetings with leaders of major powers—in what are often referred to as ASEAN + One leaders' meetings—and by the ASEAN Plus Three (APT) process, which brings together ASEAN leaders with those of China, Japan, and South Korea. In addition, the formation of the East Asian Summit (EAS) in 2005 brought together the leaders of the APT grouping and Australia, New Zealand, and India. At the Sixth EAS in 2011 membership of the summit meetings was expanded to include the United States and Russia. ASEAN summits, then, have not only increased in frequency over the years but have also taken on the crucial role of integrating ASEAN into the wider East Asian region and providing a link to ASEAN's neighbors and to the world's major powers. In some ways, then, ASEAN exemplifies Jan Melissen's observation that "summitry breeds summitry"; but although ASEAN has not been short of critics, in the case of ASEAN and East Asia the increased use of summits may not be such a bad turn of events.[4]

ASEAN summits, consultation, and negotiations

The First ASEAN Summit held in Bali in 1976 was crucial for a number of reasons but most notably because it set out a code of conduct for members in their relations with each other. The First Summit also set the tone of informality, consensus building, and friendly discussions that characterized the early summits. This so called "ASEAN Way" set the trajectory for the manner in which ASEAN leaders and their ministers and officials should interact.[5]

The Bali Summit took place in a region that was in some turmoil. Indeed, the summit was prompted by the US withdrawal from Vietnam, communist forces moving into South Vietnam as well as into Cambodia and Laos, and the continuing uncertainty across Southeast Asia. There was clearly a sense among the ASEAN members that if they were to be taken seriously by their neighbors and the international community, they needed to demonstrate at the highest possible level their unity and solidarity.[6] In the face of communist expansion in the region, the five ASEAN leaders decided against a military pact but sought to underscore ASEAN's original aim of cooperating to promote peace, stability, and neutrality. It was agreed to set out a code of conduct for regional relations. This was done in the Treaty of Amity and Cooperation (TAC).

The TAC expressed "the need for cooperation with all peace-loving nations, both within and outside Southeast Asia." It specifically called for: (1) "mutual respect for the independence, sovereignty, equality, territorial integrity and national identity of all nations"; (2) the right to be "free from external interference, subversion or coercion"; (3) "non-interference in the internal affairs of one another"; (4) the "settlement of differences and disputes by peaceful means"; (5) the "renunciation of the threat or use of force"; and (6) "effective cooperation among members."[7] Just as importantly, the leaders acknowledged in the treaty's preamble that the principles laid out in the TAC had their roots in the Charter of the United Nations, the Ten Principles adopted by Asian and African leaders at the 1955 Bandung Conference, the original Bangkok Declaration that established ASEAN, and the 1971 Kuala Lumpur Declaration that set out Southeast Asia as a Zone of Peace, Freedom and Neutrality (ZOPFAN). The aim was to keep the region "free from any form or manner of interference by outside powers."[8] In other words, then, the leaders at their First Summit saw the TAC as the culmination of a movement toward a set of principles for conducting regional relations that had been discussed and debated for some time.[9]

The TAC quickly became a touchstone agreement for ASEAN members. As the Introduction to this volume indicates, the consensus of values and worldviews was crucial to ASEAN's development. The TAC has been amended three times: in 1987 to allow countries outside Southeast Asia to accede, in 1998 to ensure that all members gave their consent, and in 2010 to allow regional organizations—specifically the European Union (EU)—to join. Each new member of ASEAN automatically signed on to the TAC. Papua New Guinea signed on to the TAC in 1989 but the big breakthrough came in 2003 when both China and India acceded to the treaty. Since then nearly 20 other countries have signed on, including Russia, Japan, South Korea, Pakistan, Australia, New Zealand, Canada, the United States, and the EU. The ASEAN leaders have, therefore, underscored their collective influence over regional affairs and, indeed, to some extent international relations more generally.[10]

The First and Second Summits also reinforced the way in which business was to be conducted in ASEAN from the leaders on down. Ironically, the TAC was unusual in that it was one of the few treaties signed among ASEAN members. Its relatively legalistic wording ran counter to the prevailing norms that emphasized unstructured, non-confrontational discussions and relatively loose arrangements that all could live with.[11] At early summit meetings, as with many ASEAN meetings at all levels, apart from the opening and closing ceremonies, relatively little time was given over to formal presentations and debate. Discrete discussions in informal settings around meals or while golfing were much preferred as the best way to do business at the early summits. The preference was for "sports shirt diplomacy" over "Western business shirt diplomacy."[12]

This predilection for informality at ASEAN summits has only gradually been transformed. As the membership of ASEAN has increased and as the frequency of ASEAN summits has risen, inevitably greater formality has been introduced. Just as importantly, the agendas of summits have become more crowded with formal meetings taking place not just of the ASEAN leaders themselves but also with other leaders in various formats—e.g. ASEAN + One, APT, and various ad hoc summits. In addition, the EAS is held in conjunction with the second of the twice-yearly ASEAN summits. Formal meetings are certainly an important part of each summit schedule, but the tradition of informality is still important.

One of the key features of ASEAN summits is that it is usual for exhaustive consultations to have taken place before decisions are taken. These consultations take place through a number of mechanisms. The ASEAN Secretariat, which was established at the First ASEAN Summit in 1976 and which might have been thought of as the obvious vehicle for promoting consultation, was at first relatively small and incapable of coordinating region-wide discussions. Indeed, many of the initial consultations within ASEAN were undertaken by officials charged with dealing with ASEAN in each of the member states.

Over the last ten years or so, as a consequence of the leaders promoting the development of the ASEAN Community and the ASEAN Charter, the secretariat has grown. This expansion was most evident under the direction of Dr. Surin Pitsuwan, who was ASEAN secretary-general for five years from 1 January 2008. Yet by international standards the secretariat is still relatively small and its responsibilities are limited, with leaders reluctant to hand too much power to a central agency. Consultations continue to take place at all levels, however, from the summit on down, with ASEAN sponsoring an ever-increasing number of committee meetings, panels, workshops, and so forth, at which issues are discussed at length. Indeed, summits are in essence the tip of the consultation iceberg, with each ASEAN initiative, from its founding to the most recent, accompanied by extensive discussions and debates.[13] The culmination of the consultation process is a decision made at a summit. Increasingly, the leaders have to make a commitment to a policy before it can be formally adopted and fully implemented.

Decision making at ASEAN summits is by consensus. One commentator notes that "an ASEAN policy is actually a synthesis or amalgam of the policies of the different members so that a common stand is projected."[14] National positions are first developed and then "feelers" are sent out to see where other members stand. Through discussion and adjustments to national positions a consensus is sought. If no consensus emerges then the issue is shelved until common ground can be found. Summits generally confirm the policy that has been developed but on occasion may be the forum for arriving at the final position. However, summits can be crucial if an issue is seen as driven by rapidly changing external circumstances. For example, the agreement to adopt the ASEAN Free Trade Agreement (AFTA) at the 1992 summit was pushed by the Thai prime minister, Anand Panyarachun, out of concern that much of the foreign direct investment (FDI) flowing into ASEAN would be redirected to China if the ASEAN members did not make the movement of goods across regional boundaries much easier and less costly.[15]

The consensus imperative has been criticized as too rigid and limiting. However, a former ASEAN secretary-general, Rodolfo Severino, has argued that in practice consensus does not always mean total unanimity. Rather, he points out that consensus can mean that "enough members support [a decision] even when one or more members have misgivings about it, but do not feel strongly enough about an issue to block action on it."[16] This approach has been made more formal in terms of economic issues and is labeled the "ASEAN minus X" principle. It means that any member or group of members may not join an initiative but allow it to go ahead nonetheless. The ASEAN minus X principle was enshrined in the ASEAN Charter signed by leaders at the Thirteenth Summit in Singapore in November 2007. It should be noted, however, that there has to be a consensus that the ASEAN minus X principle is applicable.

The one caveat that needs to be entered in terms of the importance of consensus as a principle guiding decision making is the importance of the role of the chair at each summit.[17] The member, and therefore the leader, charged with hosting ASEAN summits rotates on an annual basis. The chairs can be quite influential in promoting particular issues which often derive from their own specific interests. The chair is also in charge of assessing whether a consensus on a particular topic has emerged or not, and this can give a leader some leverage, although it has to be underscored that chairs generally take the task of mobilizing a consensus very seriously indeed.

Overall, then, the early summits, most notably the First Summit of 1976, set the tone for both the conduct of relations among Southeast Asian states and the way in which negotiations were conducted at ASEAN-sponsored meetings. This "ASEAN Way" approach to regional governance has been distinctive and, by the standards of the global South, reasonably effective. Certainly, the ASEAN Way and the TAC gave the association a set of norms and practices that brought a level of coherence to the organization that other regional groupings such as the Organization of American States (OAS), the Caribbean Community (CARICOM), and the Southern Common Market (Mercosur) have been unable to generate.[18]

ASEAN's agenda and summits

A number of themes stand out in terms of the issues discussed by the leaders at ASEAN summits. First, from the outset ASEAN leaders have been preoccupied with managing their relations with the major powers and more generally limiting their own and the region's vulnerability to external pressures. The ASEAN members are relatively small states on the international stage and have a history of being the object of great power intrigue, whether during colonial times or during the Cold War. ASEAN's first 20 years were taken up with dealing with the consequences of the Cold War in Asia through the signing of the TAC. It was a clear indication of how ASEAN leaders wanted their relations with the major powers to proceed. Intriguingly, at the Second and Third Summits in 1977 and 1987 a key feature of the agenda was a meeting with the prime minister of Japan at the time. Japan's cooperation in aiding the economic development of ASEAN was seen as crucial.

After the end of the Cold War in Asia ASEAN leaders became concerned with the newly emerging powers in international affairs. The emphasis within ASEAN was increasingly placed on the development of "competence power" or the ability not so much to exercise dominance over others but to shape ASEAN members' political, security, and economic environment in ways that were beneficial to them.[19] The

Asia-Pacific Economic Cooperation (APEC) forum, which was initiated in 1989 and which moved to regular annual summits in 1993, had an ASEAN leader as host every second or third year until very recently.[20] Starting in 1996, and in conjunction with China, Japan, and South Korea, ASEAN established regular summit meetings every other year with the leaders of the EU at the Asia-Europe Meetings (ASEM). In 1997, leaders of each of the individual "Plus Three Members"—China, Japan, and South Korea—met with ASEAN leaders annually at the ASEAN summit. Building on what were termed dialogue partnerships, which had been held at the level of foreign ministers since the 1970s, ASEAN heads of state and government met with a number of other leaders including those from India, Australia, New Zealand, the United States, and Russia. Many of these meetings became more formalized when the annual EAS was established in 2005. In addition, there have also been some ad hoc summits, such as the one that brought ASEAN leaders together with the Chinese leadership over SARS in April 2003, and various commemorative summits marking an anniversary of ASEAN's relations with a particular country.

In other words, then, starting in the mid-1990s, ASEAN heads of state and government have very successfully used summits to maintain strong relations with key players in the region and on the international stage. Most of the summits were held in ASEAN with the ASEAN host setting the agenda, being responsible for probing for a consensus on particular issues prior to the meetings, ensuring that the "ASEAN Way" approach infused negotiations, and issuing the all-important final communiqué. Significantly, in terms of ASEAN's role in determining the pace and direction of East Asian regionalism, the general refrain has been that ASEAN has been in the "driver's seat."[21] While it has by no means been foolproof or worked to the benefit of ASEAN all the time, the constellation of summits generated by the ASEAN leaders has on the whole allowed the organization's members to gain a level of autonomy as well as a certain amount of leverage in regional and international affairs that they would otherwise not have been able to achieve.

A second theme that has consistently been on the agenda of ASEAN summits is the need to promote regional harmony and cooperation. Given the region's history of regional conflicts, especially over border issues, there has always been the possibility of the region devouring itself. The TAC was obviously an initial attempt to set out the ground rules for trying to ensure that harmony within the region was maintained. The vision of an inclusive and cooperative region also drove the leaders to expand the membership of ASEAN to include all Southeast

Asian countries. Hence, despite considerable external criticism, ASEAN leaders chose to admit Vietnam, Laos, Myanmar, and Cambodia to ASEAN in the 1990s as a way of ensuring "one Southeast Asia."[22] The only conditions that the new members had to fulfill in joining ASEAN was that they accede to the TAC and sign the AFTA, although they were allowed additional time to bring their tariff rates down to the 0–5 percent levels.

With the advent of the new millennium, external and internal forces have continued to threaten to undermine ASEAN's solidarity. The forces of globalization, the fallout from the 9/11 attacks in the United States, and the rise of China have all produced tensions in the association. As a consequence, at the Ninth ASEAN Summit in 2003, in an attempt to keep at bay the centrifugal forces that were at work in the region, the leaders intensified their commitment to regional cooperation by agreeing to establish a formal "ASEAN Community." It was proposed that the community would have three pillars: one centered on political and security cooperation, one on economic cooperation, and one on socio-cultural cooperation. The aim was that the community would be in place by 2015 and so ensure a "durable peace, stability and shared prosperity in the region."[23]

In 2007, spurred on by the commitment to develop the ASEAN Community, as well as by the need to reinforce the idea of regional unity, ASEAN leaders also agreed to the creation of the ASEAN Charter. The charter makes ASEAN a legal entity and acts as a constitution for the association. The charter came into force in December 2008. Moreover, as Alice Ba perceptively notes, around this time the leaders felt compelled to underscore their unity by producing mottos for their summits.[24] The motto for the Eleventh Summit in December 2005 was "One Vision, One Identity, One Community"; that for the Twelfth Summit in January 2007 was "One Caring and Sharing Community"; and that for the Thirteenth Summit in November 2007 was "One ASEAN at the Heart of Dynamic Asia." In other words, ASEAN leaders were determined to overcome the perceived fragility of their regional enterprise and preserve their "oneness." This concern to repel any possibility of regional fragmentation has continued with the motto for the Twenty-second and Twenty-third Summits in Brunei in 2013 being "Our People and Our Future Together"; with the 2005 motto of "One Vision, One Identity, One Community" becoming the official ASEAN motto; and with the leaders continuing to work, even if a little too slowly for some, towards the 2015 deadline for the ASEAN Community.

A third theme that has been on the agenda of the ASEAN leaders has been the need for economic cooperation and even an increasing measure of integration. This need for cooperation is widely seen as a way of managing the forces of globalization and links into a key point made in the Introduction to this volume that globalization is a major factor in promoting the holding of regional summits. In the first few summits, economic cooperation was only paid lip service, with relatively little actually being accomplished. It was not until the Fourth Summit in Singapore in 1992 that the leaders showed a commitment to regional economic integration. At Singapore they signed the AFTA, which was essentially a framework document outlining the key elements of a regional trade agreement. Negotiations over AFTA were accelerated at the Fifth Summit in 1995, with a number of political compromises being worked out to make AFTA more acceptable to individual countries.[25] A free trade agreement among ASEAN members was viewed as necessary to compete with the signing of the North American Free Trade Agreement, the move to a Single European Market, and the rise of China. The aim of ASEAN's leaders was to attract FDI by creating the possibility for regional production networks to flourish in a globalizing world. Further calls for even greater economic integration led to the announcement at the Ninth ASEAN Summit in 2003 of an ASEAN Economic Community (AEC) to be established by 2020. At the Thirteenth ASEAN Summit in Singapore in 2007, new agencies to help implement the AEC and a new goal of implementation by 2015 for the more advanced members of ASEAN were revealed.

As Helen Nesadurai argues, ASEAN leaders and their "governments have always tried to balance their liberalisation initiatives with policies that served domestic purposes."[26] The goal was to manage the forces of globalization without exacerbating domestic tensions and having them spiral out of hand. The AFTA/AEC negotiating and implementing processes demonstrated that the need to balance various interests required a specific approach. The preference was for general "framework" agreements that set out basic principles to be followed and a target date for the full realization of the commitments. The parties to the agreement would then work their way toward full implementation, taking all the domestic and international factors into account, as pragmatically and expeditiously as possible. This is what ASEAN leaders refer to as negotiating in a "sequential manner."[27] This is a very different approach to the North American/European legalistic perspective, which sees free trade negotiations leading to a final document—referred to as a "single undertaking"—which is enforceable by law.[28]

There are numerous instances of a sequential negotiating process at work as ASEAN leaders have sought to promote regional economic prosperity and greater regional economic integration. For example, based on the mandate of the Fifth ASEAN Summit a framework agreement on the ASEAN Investment Area Scheme was signed in 1998. Similarly, a framework agreement was signed between China and ASEAN in 2002 with the goal of establishing free trade among the ten ASEAN members and China by 2010, and a framework agreement for a comprehensive economic partnership was signed between Japan and ASEAN in 2003 with the objective of implementing an agreement covering trade in goods and services as well as investment and economic cooperation by 2008.[29] At the Bali Summit of November 2011, the leaders set in motion the negotiations for the EAS-based Regional Comprehensive Economic Partnership.[30]

Finally, ASEAN leaders had to deal with an array of specific problems that came up at each of the summits. These issues ranged from the need for cooperation in the face of terrorism, to concerns about climate change, to problems that might be associated with over-fishing or food security. Generally, the leaders would agree on a suitable declaration or agreement that gave ministers, senior officials, or the secretary-general guidance on how to proceed with dealing with each issue. Summits were seen, therefore, as a key part of the process of moving an issue along to some resolution or as contributing in some way to resolving a problem. Indeed, ASEAN leaders have been busy promoting policies to address various concerns.

Certainly, over the last few years, driven in good part by the imperatives of overseeing the implementation of the ASEAN Charter and the move toward an ASEAN Community, summit agendas have become increasingly crowded. While summits have always been a key component of the development of ASEAN, they are now an integral part of the association's development in ways that were not envisaged when the leaders first started meeting on an irregular basis. The summits now play a pivotal role not just in the regional governance of Southeast Asia but of East Asia and beyond. The regional architecture of East Asia, and indeed the wider Asia-Pacific, still puts ASEAN near or at the center of unfolding events, with the ASEAN summits instrumental in these developments.

Successful ASEAN summits, socialization, and legitimacy

Why have ASEAN summits been relatively successful? There are obviously "skeptics," who point to ASEAN as being simply a "talk shop" which is weighed down by its norms of non-interference and the requirement of unanimous decision making. They also argue that its glacial pace of development and apparent need to overcome regional distrust mean that the association is in constant need of rejuvenation.[31] In a sense they question not only the effectiveness of ASEAN but also its legitimacy, and by extension the effectiveness and legitimacy of the ASEAN summits. It is perhaps possible to detect a certain amount of Eurocentrism in aspects of these criticisms which needs to be resisted.[32] In its own relatively modest way, ASEAN, by most measures and certainly by the standards set by regional organizations in the global South, has produced a number of notable achievements. What is it that has allowed ASEAN summits to play an increasingly significant role in the development of ASEAN, the APT grouping, and the EAS?

First, David Reynolds's injunction to think of summitry as intercultural communication puts considerable emphasis on the backgrounds of the leaders involved in summits.[33] In the case of ASEAN summits there is one remarkable factor that helps to explain their relative success. Many of the early ASEAN leaders held their positions for many years and came to know each other relatively well. Lee Kuan Yew was the prime minister of Singapore from 1965 to 1990 and his successor, Goh Chok Tong, was in power from 1990 to 2004. Ferdinand Marcos was president of the Philippines from 1965 to 1986. Suharto was president of Indonesia from 1967 to 1998. Mahathir Mohamad was prime minister of Malaysia from 1981 to 2003. The Sultan of Brunei, Hassanal Bolkiah, has been in power from the time Brunei joined ASEAN in 1984 to the present. Similarly, Hun Sen has been Cambodia's prime minister and representative to ASEAN summits since his country joined the organization in 1999. In commenting on this phenomenon, Alice Ba has noted that "longevity has helped insulate ASEAN processes, which in turn have helped incubate and grow ideas, relationships, and core consensuses that were key to ASEAN's survival during its formative years."[34]

However, there is another important element of continuity that also helps to perpetuate the key features of ASEAN summits to which Ba alludes. This can perhaps best be identified as the significance in ASEAN of dynastic political families. The current prime minister of Singapore, Lee Hsien Loong, who has been in office since 2004, is the son of the influential former prime minister, Lee Kuan Yew. The current prime minister of Malaysia, Najib Razak, is the son of Abdul Razak, who is a former prime minister, but also, as deputy prime minister, the person who signed the original Bangkok Declaration for Malaysia that established ASEAN in 1967. The current president of the Philippines is Benigno Aquino, the son of a former president of the Philippines, Corazon Aquino, who hosted the Third ASEAN Summit in 1987. Hence, in recent years, while the ASEAN leaders come from diverse cultures and backgrounds, there are important commonalties and a familiarity with each other and ASEAN's traditions that have encouraged norms of consultation, consensus, informality, and respect for sovereignty and territorial integrity to be adhered to and nurtured. And, as Amitav Acharya has also noted, the role of summits in ASEAN reflects "the highly elitist nature of Southeast Asian decision making."[35]

Some analysts see a crucial socialization process at work that has been a critical factor in educating new participants in the summit process.[36] The extensive discussions that take place at all levels in ASEAN, not least at ASEAN summits, have the impact of educating members to the overall consensus about how to conduct themselves both regionally and domestically. Indeed, bringing China into the APT and ensuring that it acts as a responsible power, and helping Myanmar move down the road to greater democratization can be seen as indicative of this process at work.

A second factor enabling summits to play a crucial role in regional developments was the economic prosperity that has permeated the region from the late 1960s onwards. This is in contrast to the economic fortunes of many other regions of the global South, including Latin America and the Caribbean.[37] More specifically, the first two summits in 1976 and 1977 took place against the backdrop of rising oil prices and commodity prices more generally. This development was particularly important for Indonesia, a major oil producer; Malaysia, an emerging oil producer; and Singapore, whose shipyards serviced the regional off-shore oil fields. The next few summits, in 1987, 1992, 1995, and 1996, all took place as massive waves of FDI poured into the ASEAN economies, first from Japan, then from the United States, Hong Kong, South Korea, and Taiwan, and then from Europe. While the Asian Financial Crisis of 1997–98 took its toll, ASEAN economies were revived by the strong demand from the United States at the turn of the century and then from the very positive impact the expansion of the Chinese economy had on Southeast Asia. Hence, as the frequency and work load of summits increased from the turn of the century onwards, ASEAN economies were buoyed up by a continued influx of growing regional production networks and expanding trade with China.

There were a number of specific consequences of this regional prosperity. Significantly, there was a virtuous circle created with prosperity promoting regional stability, which in turn encouraged further investment in the region. The growing regional economic pie and the general sense of well-being it created made it easier for ASEAN leaders to reach compromises over what in earlier days could have been seen as zero-sum conflicts. There was also a virtuous circle which helped ASEAN leaders more directly. The longevity in power of various ASEAN leaders can be attributed to what has been termed "performance legitimacy."[38] In other words, after the chaos and lean years of the first three decades following World War II, people in the region valued the prosperity and stability that came to the region from the Vietnam War onwards. The performance of a number of ASEAN leaders was rewarded with continued public support, which in turn gave ASEAN stability and helped it develop as a regional organization.

Regional prosperity also attracted the attention of other leaders. ASEAN's participation was perceived as crucial to the development of APEC. European leaders were more than happy to take part in the ASEM summits, the Plus Three leaders have been regular attendees at the APT and ASEAN + One summits, and Australia, New Zealand, India, Russia and the United States have valued their participation in the EAS. ASEAN leaders have gained leverage in the international community from ASEAN's increasing centrality in regional affairs. With all the resulting summits, the fact that the region was relatively prosperous gave leaders and their governments the resources to put on a seemingly endless round of regional summits. Talk is not cheap in the sense that arranging summits, and the many ministerial and bureaucratic meetings that buttress them, can be an expensive undertaking; ASEAN has been fortunate in generally having the funds to put them on.[39]

Finally, and a point that is intimately connected to the previous point, it needs to be underscored that a crucial reason for the success of ASEAN's summits is that being a member of the association has conferred benefits on the region's leaders, their governments, and their societies. The positive feedback from the work of the summits, not just in terms of economic outcomes but also in terms of regional stability and enhanced international status for themselves and their countries has given the leaders the incentive to continue and even accelerate their use of ASEAN as part of the regional governance structure. In addition to some of the points already noted, among other achievements summits have enabled leaders to promote the development of the Mekong Basin sub-region; initiate infrastructure projects designed to integrate ASEAN economies physically and tie them into the Chinese economy; and to begin to bridge the development gap between the original, more developed ASEAN members and the newer members—Cambodia, Laos, Myanmar, and Vietnam. Moreover, while ASEAN by itself may not have been a factor in promoting the long period of regional stability and prosperity, it is widely understood to be a contributory factor.[40] Prior to the emergence of ASEAN as an important regional institution, Southeast Asia was generally thought of as a backwater in world affairs, only notable as an arena for proxy battles in the Cold War. Now ASEAN has acquired a reputation as an influential player in the global economy and ASEAN summit meetings, to which many world leaders would like to be invited, as key venues for managing regional and international affairs.

These benefits, then, have given ASEAN summits a good deal of legitimacy.[41] Summit decisions do not necessarily have the force of law as it is understood in the West. However, given the importance of social trust to relations within Southeast Asia, it can be said that decisions taken at summits have considerable influence on the way member states conduct themselves. Members generally do their best to follow ASEAN declarations, resolutions, and other commitments made at ASEAN summits not only because they are made by heads of state and government who themselves are seen as legitimate, but also because ASEAN summits have shown that they can steer the membership in the direction of greater regional stability and prosperity.

Overall, then, the reason for the success of ASEAN summits, in contrast perhaps to those in other parts of the world, including Latin America, comes down to the fact that the leaders themselves feel comfortable with their fellow participants, the general economic environment has been positive, and the work done by the summits has benefited the leaders and their governments.

Conclusion

Like all regional projects ASEAN has had its ups and downs, with its membership, goals, norms, and future direction all being contested at one time or another. Certainly, as the Introduction to this volume notes has happened to all regions, ASEAN has been buffeted by external influences and internal debates about its future. Of course, there has been ample room for those in John Ravenhill's skeptical camp to dismiss ASEAN as underachieving at best and impotent at worst—a minor regional organization that is of little consequence in world affairs.[42]

Yet ASEAN has gained a profile and legitimacy in Southeast Asia and the international community that warrants attention. It has helped to promote regional stability and prosperity, as well as the stability and prosperity of its members. It has established a code of conduct for the region that has allowed regional leaders to come to appreciate the values they share and their common worldview. ASEAN has also been at the hub of many of the key developments in East Asia and the Asia-Pacific region more generally.[43] In particular, ASEAN can be said to have been central to developing East Asia's regional institutions.[44]

Leading ASEAN from the front—especially since the mid-1990s—has been the function of ASEAN summits. The summits have been the main vehicle by which ASEAN has set its goals and maintained its forward momentum as a regional project. Increasingly, ASEAN summits have staked out the association's place on the international stage. ASEAN summits have also led the way in terms of helping members to manage the forces of globalization and encourage a level of stability within Southeast Asia.

What are the lessons for other regions, including Latin America? Although it might be said that ASEAN has been fortunate in developing in the context of regional prosperity, it has taken advantage of this good fortune to use the summits to provide a regional focus for a relatively disparate, heterogeneous group of member states to find solutions to common problems. However, ASEAN's ability to perform the key functions normally associated with summits—dialogue and socialization, agenda setting and orientation, negotiation and coordination, and legitimation[45]—developed only very slowly.

The crucial point that needs to be taken from the ASEAN experience is that generating a reasonably successful summit process for any regional body takes time. It took ten years for ASEAN to be able to craft a consensus around a set of values and a common worldview which was expressed in the TAC and the "ASEAN Way." These have mutated over the years but crucially remain important benchmarks. Significantly, they have guided regional negotiations and formed the basis of the summits' role as a socializing agent for the region's political elite. Again, though, this process has been by no means instantaneous. It has taken time for relationships to develop. Similarly, it is only through developing practices over many years that ASEAN summits have proven successful in exchanging information, setting the regional agenda, and coordinating policies, especially economic policies. Finally, the extent to which the ASEAN summits have become, over an extended period, associated with regional stability and prosperity has allowed them to build up considerable legitimacy. In other words, then, after nearly 50 years in existence and nearly 40 years of holding summits, ASEAN is able to claim a number of significant accomplishments for its summit process.

Notes

1. I am grateful to Amitav Acharya, Alice Ba, and Helen Nesaduari for discussing some of the ideas developed in this chapter, to the participants at the summits workshop in Quebec City, and particularly the editors, for their comments; and to the Social Sciences and Humanities Research Council (SSHRC) for research funds. However, I alone am responsible for any errors in fact or interpretation.
2. Helen E.S. Nesadurai, "The Association of Southeast Asian Nations," *New Political Economy* 13, no. 2 (2008): 225–239.
3. Richard Feinberg, "Institutionalized Summitry: When Leaders Matter," in *The Oxford Handbook of Modern Diplomacy*, ed. Andrew F. Cooper, Jorge Heine, and Ramesh Thakur (Oxford: Oxford University Press, 2013), 303–318. See also the discussion of the definition of "summits" in the Introduction to this volume.
4. Jan Melissen, *Summit Diplomacy Coming of Age* (The Hague: Netherlands Institute of International Relations Clingendael, 2003).
5. Amitav Acharya, "Ideas, Identity, and Institution-Building: From the 'ASEAN Way' to the 'Asia-Pacific Way'," *The Pacific Review* 10, no. 3 (1997): 319–346; David Capie and Paul Evans, "The 'ASEAN Way'," in *The 2nd ASEAN Reader*, ed. Sharon Siddique and Sree Kumar (Singapore: Institute of Southeast Asian Studies, 2003), 45–51; Nesadurai, "The Association of Southeast Asian Nations," 225–239; and Richard Stubbs, "The ASEAN Alternative? Ideas, Institutions and the Challenge to 'Global' Governance," *The Pacific Review* 21, no. 4 (2008): 451–467.
6. Khaw Guat Hoon, "The Evolution of ASEAN 1967–75," in *The ASEAN Reader*, ed. K.S. Sandhu, Sharon Siddique, Chandran Jeshurun, Ananda Rajah, Joseph L.H. Tan, and Pushpa Thambipillai (Singapore: Institute of Southeast Asian Studies, 1992), 38–42.
7. ASEAN "Treaty of Amity and Cooperation," Jakarta, 24 February 1967, www.aseansec.org/news/item/treaty-of-amity-and-cooperation-in-southeast-asia-indonesia-24-february-1976-3.
8. M.C. Abad Jr., "The Role of ASEAN in Security Multilateralism: ZOPFAN, TAC and SEANWFZ," paper presented at the ASEAN Regional Forum, Professional Development Programme for Foreign Affairs and Defence Officials, Bandar Seri Begawan, 23–28 April 2000, www.asean.org/archive/arf/7ARF/Frof-Dment-Programme/Doc-10.pdf.
9. Stubbs, "The ASEAN Alternative?" 451–467.
10. Stubbs, "The ASEAN Alternative."
11. Rudolfo C. Severino, *Southeast Asia in Search of an ASEAN Community* (Singapore: Institute of Southeast Asian Studies, 2006), 13.
12. Capie and Evans, "The 'ASEAN Way'," 46.
13. Alice D. Ba, *(Re)Negotiating East and Southeast Asia: Region, Regionalism, and the Association of Southeast Asian Nations* (Stanford: Stanford University Press, 2009), 224; and Melissen, *Summit Diplomacy Coming of Age*, 7.
14. Pushpa Thambipillai, "Negotiating Styles," in *The ASEAN Reader*, ed. Sandhu, Siddique, Jeshurun, Rajah, Tan, and Thambipillai, 73.
15. Richard Stubbs, "Signing on to Liberalization: AFTA and the Politics of Regional Economic Cooperation," *The Pacific Review* 13, no. 2 (2000): 297–318.

16 Severino, *Southeast Asia in Search of an ASEAN Community*, 34.
17 Sanae Suzuki, "Chairmanship in ASEAN+3: A Shared Rule of Behaviour," Discussion Paper No. 9, Institute of Development Economics-JETRO, Chiba, Japan, October 2004.
18 See Chapters 3, 5, and 6 in this volume.
19 Sarah Eaton and Richard Stubbs, "Is ASEAN Powerful? Neo-Realist Versus Constructivist Approaches to Power in Southeast Asia," *The Pacific Review* 19, no. 2 (2006): 135–155.
20 All ASEAN members are members of APEC except Cambodia, Laos, and Myanmar.
21 Barry Wain, "Wen Drives his Way into ASEAN Hearts," *Straits Times*, 7 May 2011, web1.iseas.edu.sg/?p=3525; and Richard Stubbs, "ASEAN Leadership in East Asian Region-Building: Strength in Weakness," *The Pacific Review* 27, no. 4 (2014): 523–541.
22 Amitav Acharya, *The Making of Southeast Asia: International Relations of a Region*, 2nd ed. (Singapore: Institute of Southeast Asian Studies, 2012): 214–224; and Ba, *(Re)Negotiating East and Southeast Asia*, 103–131.
23 ASEAN, "Treaty of Amity and Cooperation."
24 Ba, *(Re)Negotiating East and Southeast Asia*, 246.
25 Helen E.S. Nesadurai, *Globalization, Domestic Politics and Regionalism: The ASEAN Free Trade Area* (London: Routledge, 2003); and Stubbs, "Signing on to Liberalization."
26 Nesadurai, "The Association of Southeast Asian Nations," 232.
27 ASEAN, "ASEAN Framework for Regional Comprehensive Economic Partnership," ASEAN Secretariat, Jakarta, November 2011, www.asean.org/news/asean-framework-for-regional-comprehensive-economic-partnership.
28 ASEAN, "ASEAN Framework for Regional Comprehensive Economic Partnership." See also the discussion of the contrast in Judith Cherry, "Upgrading the 'Software': The EU–Korea Free Trade Agreement and Sociocultural Barriers to Trade and Investment," *The Pacific Affairs* 25, no. 2 (2012): 258.
29 Greg T. Chin and Richard Stubbs, "China, Regional Institution-Building and the China–ASEAN Free Trade Area," *Review of International Political Economy* 18, no. 3 (2011): 227–298; Paige McClanahan, Alexander Chandra, Ruben Hattari, and Damon Vis-Dunbar, *Taking Advantage of ASEAN's Free Trade Agreements* (Winnipeg: International Institute for Sustainable Development, 2014); and Nesaduari, "The Association of Southeast Asian Nations."
30 ASEAN, "ASEAN Framework for Regional Comprehensive Economic Partnership"; and ASEAN Secretariat, "Regional Comprehensive Economic Partnership (RCEP) Joint Statement The First Meeting of Trade Negotiating Committee", 10 May 2013, www.asean.org/news/asean-statement-communiques/item/regional-comprehensive-economic-partnership-rcep-joint-statement-the-first-meeting-of-trade-negotiating-committee.
31 See, for example, Mark Beeson, "ASEAN's Ways: Still Fit for Purpose," *Cambridge Review of International Affairs* 22, no. 3 (2009): 333–343; David Martin Jones and Michael L.R. Smith, "Making Process not Progress: ASEAN and the Evolving East Asian Regional Order," *International Security* 32, no. 1 (2007): 148–184; Shaun Narine, "ASEAN in the Twenty-First Century: A Sceptical Review," *Cambridge Review of International*

Affairs 22, no. 3 (2009): 360–386; and John Ravenhill, "East Asian Regionalism: Much Ado About Nothing?" *Review of International Studies* 35, Supplement S1 (2009): 215–235.

32 John M. Hobson, "Part 1—Revealing the Eurocentric Foundation of IPE: A Critical Historiography of the Discipline from the Classical to the Modern Era," *Review of International Political Economy* 20, no. 5 (2013): 1024–1054; and John M. Hobson, "Part 2—Reconstructing the non-Eurocentric Foundations of IPE: From Eurocentric 'Open Economy Politics' to Intercivilizational Political Economy," *Review of International Political Economy* 20, no. 5 (2013): 1055–1081.

33 David Reynolds, "Summitry as Intercultural Communication," *International Affairs* 85, no. 1 (2009): 115–127.

34 Ba, *(Re)Negotiating East and Southeast Asia*, 246.

35 Amitav Acharya, *Constructing a Security Community in Southeast Asia: ASEAN and the Problem of Regional Order* (London: Routledge, 2001), 64.

36 Amitav Acharya, "Arguing About ASEAN: What Do We Disagree About?" *Cambridge Review of International Affairs* 22, no. 3 (2009): 493–499; and Alice D. Ba, "Who's Socializing Whom? Complex Engagement in Sino–ASEAN Relations," *The Pacific Review* 19, no. 2 (2006): 157–179.

37 The recent economic success is the one notable exception to this generalization. See Chapter 11 in this volume.

38 Helen E.S. Nesadurai, "The Global Politics of Regionalism: Asia and the Asia Pacific," in *Global Politics of Regionalism: Theory and Practice*, ed. Mary Farrel, Björn Hettne, and Luk Langenhove (London: Pluto, 2005), 155–170; and Richard Stubbs, "Performance Legitimacy and 'Soft Authoritarianism'," in *Democracy, Human Rights, and Civil Society in South East Asia*, ed. Amitav Acharya, B. Michael Frolic, and Richard Stubbs (Toronto: Joint Centre for Asia Pacific Studies, 2001), 37–54.

39 Melissen, *Summit Diplomacy Coming of Age*, 17.

40 Timo Kivimäki, "The Long Peace of ASEAN," *Journal of Peace Research* 38, no. 1 (2001): 5–25; and Timo Kivimäki, "East Asian Relative Peace and the ASEAN Way," *International Relations of the Asia-Pacific* 11, no. 1 (2011): 57–85.

41 Stubbs, "Performance Legitimacy and 'Soft Authoritarianism'."

42 Ravenhill, "East Asian Regionalism: Much Ado About Nothing?" 220.

43 Acharya, "Arguing About ASEAN."

44 Stubbs, "ASEAN Leadership in East Asian Region-Building."

45 See the Introduction to this volume.

10 Assessing the role of G7/8/20 meetings in global governance

Processes, outcomes, and counterfactuals

Emmanuel Mourlon-Druol

- Processes: The G7/8/20 as a diplomatic instrument
- Outcomes: What were the results of the G7 summits?
- Untying the "process vs. outcome" knot: Blurred boundaries in the G7/8/20 functions
- Counterfactuals: What if the G7/8/20 did not exist?
- Conclusion

"Previous summits have been useless," wrote Jacques Attali, advisor to French President François Mitterrand, in preparing the 1981 Ottawa summit, the first to be held since Mitterrand's election.[1] Summits of the G7 had not just been useless in the relations between the seven powers, Attali argued, but also in the relations between developed countries and in the North–South dialogue. Interestingly, Attali went on to say that problems—rather than the G7 itself—should be tackled differently: by adopting a more political approach and focusing on unemployment, among other issues. In spite of a provocative start, Mitterrand's adviser therefore did not condemn the institution of the G7 as such.

Attali's stocktaking of G7 summitry when Mitterrand took power highlights the central issue that lies in any assessment of multilateral summitry: distinguishing the outcome and the process. That a G7 was unable to reach an agreement is not automatically the responsibility of the G7 as an institution, although most of the time one will read, as Attali indeed himself wrote, that a G7 has been "useless." This statement should not, however, be interpreted as an assessment against multilateral summitry per se—Attali did not suggest putting an end to G7 summitry—but rather to the frustrating result that a specific summit had come to.

Assessing multilateral summitry therefore depends on a prior detailed examination of what functions the G7/8/20 was and is meant to fulfill.[2] The literature on summitry, both in political science and history, has outlined a range of functions already, as the editors of this volume mentioned in the Introduction, but most of these functions were self-assigned from the start: the actors themselves wanted to achieve a number of goals through routine heads of government meetings when the G7 emerged in the mid-1970s. The rise of regular summitry, understood as the frequent and regular meeting of heads of government at the international level, was an entirely new practice that emerged in the peculiar context of the mid-1970s.[3] The leaders of the time did not have a clear template on which they could model the new sort of gathering they had in mind; their frames of reference were the so-called Library Group meetings—the unofficial meetings of the finance ministers of Britain, France, Germany, Japan, and the United States in the White House library—and the "fire-side chat." However, they did have specific goals in mind as to what the G7 meetings would be used for. From 1975 onwards, Rambouillet became the main frame of reference, and from one year to the next, each new host tried to make some improvement to the summit's organization. Together with this improvement emerged a clearer sense of what the G7 could actually achieve: specific agreements, greater socialization of leaders, improved cooperation—to name but a few.

This sense of novelty, and the piecemeal definition of the functions that such summits would fulfill, lay at the heart of the beginnings of the G7, and had important consequences as to its later evolution. Helmut Sonnenfeldt, advisor in the US State Department, very aptly summarized both the dilemma and the objective of a summit shortly before the Rambouillet meeting. His analysis largely applies to later G8/20 meetings, and deserves to be quoted in full:

> The essential *dilemma of the summit* is that it will try to project publicly that Western leaders are able to manage current problems at a time when they do not fully understand the nature of the new types of problems they confront. The trick will be for the leaders to avoid both deluding themselves by boldly confident statements (which could tend to divert them from serious inquiry into their common problems) and lapsing into a categorization of their frustrations (which if made public would further erode confidence in democratic leadership).
>
> *The summit's objective* should be a serious inquiry into common problems to achieve better understanding of them and how to resolve them. The *result* can be an improvement in public confidence, a realization by public opinion that all nations face similar

difficulties which cannot be overcome by painless panaceas, and a recognition by the assembled leaders that if they act together they can strengthen their hands internally, take stronger action than they might otherwise be able to do, and buy time and domestic support to work their way through their difficulties.[4]

Following on Sonnenfeldt's perceptive remarks, which largely coincide with many other reports from actors of the time and the literature on the topic, a range of functions that were and are assigned to the G7/8/20 clearly emerge: socialization (of the leaders and of their diplomatic personnel), agenda setting, reaching agreements, coordination/cooperation, and psychology/trust.[5] In order to reach a qualified assessment as to whether G7/8/20 meetings fulfilled these functions, this chapter tries to distinguish between those functions that belong to the G7 as a process (that is, the G7 as a diplomatic instrument, which chiefly concerns socialization and agenda setting), and those that belong to the G7 as an outcome (namely, what the G7 contributed to global governance, which chiefly concerns the results). Inevitably, some of the functions do not fit neatly into one of these two categories only, which largely explains why the G7 is often considered to be inefficient—the process is confused with the outcome, one being successful and the other not. Such blurred functions concern cooperation/coordination and psychology/trust. This chapter finally explores the issue of counterfactuals in the assessment of multilateral summitry—what would have happened had the G7/8/20 not been created?—which lies at the heart of the most common frame of reference used for highlighting the need for multilateral summitry, namely the crises of the 1930s.

Processes: The G7/8/20 as a diplomatic instrument

Socialization and agenda setting are among the main functions assigned to G7 summits, but before turning to those functions, it is necessary to tackle the primary task that summitry had to fulfill: that of actually creating a forum where heads of government could routinely meet. With the benefit of hindsight, this may seem nothing but a platitude. Yet as French President Valéry Giscard d'Estaing put it retrospectively in 2007 in a *New York Times* article, "the original idea was for them [G7 heads of government] to actually talk."[6] In the mid-1970s, there existed no international forum of the type that the leaders of the most industrialized countries were looking for: informal, relatively small, exclusively at heads of government level, and dealing with economic matters. In addition, international travel became easier and easier from the 1970s, and contributed to making such regular meetings the rule rather than the exception. During the Rambouillet conference itself, Giscard thus stated that "the most important [thing] is that this meeting took place."[7] It should therefore not be overlooked that the very fact of actually meeting on a routine basis at heads of government level was an entirely new phenomenon half a century ago, and represents the first function successfully fulfilled by the G7.

Such a success should not be taken for granted. The repetition of G7 meetings, in the early years, was not automatic. The first Rambouillet meeting, held on 15–17 November 1975, was mostly considered a one-off. Confronted with intertwined economic crises—the breakdown of the Bretton Woods system, the 1973 oil shock, and the 1975 recession—Western leaders tried to coordinate their response in calling for a summit meeting at heads of government level. The French government chiefly wanted to try to find a solution to the debates about the reform of the international monetary system, while the German government, supported by the British and the United States, managed to enlarge the goals of the conference to wider economic issues.[8] The holding of another G7 meeting in Puerto Rico the following year was largely due to US President Gerald Ford's personal electoral considerations and was not considered a success. It was only from 1977 that it became clear that the G7 would become an annual gathering. As a consequence, the very regularity and frequency of the G7 as an instrument in the diplomatic "toolbox" took a few years to happen. In spite of all the criticisms that may have been voiced against the G7/8/20 as such, these meetings still exist, showing that their regularity is something that is valued.

The logical corollary to the emergence of such regular and frequent meetings was the socialization of heads of government and their staff ("sherpas" and diplomatic personnel).[9] This was again a key function, in that these persons, prior to the 1970s, did not meet very often. Ministers, by contrast, did: foreign ministers repeatedly gathered in Brussels for meetings of the Council of Ministers of the European Economic Community (EEC); and finance ministers met in the framework of the International Monetary Fund (IMF) or the Organisation for Economic Co-operation and Development (OECD). However, heads of government did not have a forum where they could, on a regular basis, freely exchange their views.

This personal dimension of G7/8/20 summitry contributes to creating good working relationships, even among leaders from opposite political cultures, as most famously between Mitterrand and US President Ronald Reagan, or Mitterrand and German Chancellor Helmut

Kohl. It even tended to "educate leaders," as Robert Putnam and Nicholas Bayne put it.[10] At the sherpas' level—the sherpas are the personal representatives to the G7/8/20 leaders in charge of the summit's preparation—this socialization created a "sense of camaraderie" that went again beyond political lines, and perhaps most importantly highlighted the profound embeddedness of the G7 in the international system.[11] Indeed, many sherpas continued their careers in international institutions (European Commission sherpa (1985–1994) Pascal Lamy at the World Trade Organization or German sherpa (1990–93) Horst Köhler at the IMF, to name two) and thereby further underscored that the G7 had become yet another instrument in the international system. The summit's socialization function bears even more importance with the creation of the G20, since it enables the personal acquaintance of the diplomatic personnel of developed and developing countries. The G7/8/20 therefore successfully fulfilled its socialization function, in that it allowed for the meeting, on a regular basis, of policymakers who had previously been little acquainted with each other. It should be noted, however, that this was not the most difficult issue to assess, as the summits merely needed to offer an opportunity for these leaders and diplomats to meet; the extent to which this socialization contributed to a harmonization of their views is another matter, particularly difficult to gauge.

A final function of the G7/8/20, and one that relates more to the process than its outcome, is agenda setting. Looking at the various items on the G7's agenda since 1975 (and also more recently that of the G20), it is quite striking to see the variation. This ever-widening agenda constituted a classic criticism against the G7 itself in its early years, especially when it progressively moved away from an economic-centered agenda to one including all sorts of issues that were of interest to its members. The presence of some items is particularly striking, with the benefit of hindsight, such as the emergence of environmental issues as early as 1979 in Tokyo, mostly because of the second oil shock.

The widening of the G7's agenda should not, again, be taken for granted. It may seem quite logical that a meeting of heads of government, who by nature can deal with all sorts of issues, ended up tackling such a diverse agenda. It is, however, important to note that ever since the emergence of the G7, the French government, in a bipartisan fashion—both Giscard d'Estaing and Mitterrand sustained the same position—had maintained that G7 summits should remain *economic*, and as a consequence exclude any subject that was political in character from the agenda.[12] For a few years, the French government reluctantly accepted the inclusion of political issues on the agenda, claiming that these were one-off exceptions due to international circumstances: the situation in Afghanistan (discussed in Venice in 1980, and then again in Ottawa in 1981), and international terrorism (tackled in London in 1984, and then again in Tokyo in 1986), for instance. As a consequence, the agenda-setting function of the G7 can be considered a success for all G7 members but France, for which it remains a conspicuous failure. The agenda-setting capacity of the G7 quite obviously did not foretell the actual agreements that a meeting could reach, as the next section will show.

Outcomes: What were the results of the G7 summits?

G7 summits are probably most frequently judged by the actual results and agreements they have achieved. G7 leaders themselves, from the start, called for concrete results. "What we want is results, not public acclaim," explained US President Gerald Ford in 1975 to his Japanese counterpart, Takeo Miki, a few months before the Rambouillet summit.[13] This partly explains why G7 summits are not always well regarded: the discrepancy is too wide between their final communiqués and the concrete results. G7 summits have produced countless calls to fight against unemployment, while unemployment rates in G7 members have not consequently fallen. True, this may not be the exclusive responsibility of the G7, but media coverage magnifies the centrality of the meeting of the world's so-called most powerful leaders as well as their inability concretely to change the course of events—a situation that Sonnenfeldt had presciently exposed.

Putnam and Bayne have already assessed the G7 summits by their outcome, and there is no need to question their ranking here.[14] They assigned grades, from A+ to E, to the different G7 summits. In terms of "outcomes," the most highly regarded are indeed the most famous, although only two received an A grade: Rambouillet in 1975 (where an agreement was found on the international monetary system), and Bonn in 1978 (for the coordinated economic re-launch, although it has not really been put into practice). The G20 meeting in London in 2009 could well feature in that list, as it reached an important agreement on international finance and economic stability.[15]

Looking into the detail of the grading over the period 1975–2002, Bayne's ranking highlights just how difficult it is to provide a clear-cut assessment of the G7's performance.[16] Looking at the overall marks over that period, one finds only three grades at both extremes: the two As mentioned above and one E (Bonn summit in 1985). Bs constitute the largest bulk of summits (13 meetings receive that grade, that is 46.4

percent), then come the Cs (eight meetings, 28.6 percent) and Ds (four meetings, 14.3 percent). If looking at the G7 cycles, that is the seven-year period during which each G7 member will host one summit, the average grade is not very high: B- (1975–81), C- (1982–88), C+ (1989–95) and B (1996–2002). In terms of concrete results, therefore, the track record of the G7 until 2002 looks "average"—neither particularly good nor particularly bad—and reflects the basic difficulty for the G7 to reach a consensus among all its members on a very wide agenda.

Untying the "process vs. outcome" knot: Blurred boundaries in the G7/8/20 functions

The distinction made above between the process and the outcome allows seeing rather clear patterns of success and failure: G7/8/20 meetings did contribute to a better socialization of their leaders and their diplomatic personnel; the G7/8/20's agenda-setting capacity is clear; and the G7's track record is uneven, to say the least. However, for two other functions (cooperation/coordination and psychology/trust), this distinction between process and outcome does not work as neatly. This section tries to untie the knot between process and outcome for these two functions, so as to reach a qualified assessment as to whether or not G7 meetings fulfilled their functions.

G7 summitry emerged as an attempt to avoid uncoordinated reactions among the leaders of the most industrialized countries. Giscard mentioned this aspect to Ford about a year prior to the Rambouillet meeting: "We could mention closer cooperation to reestablish control of the general economic development. If the situation developed in dangerous ways, we would meet ... at Presidential level, if necessary, to deal with it ... We need to have some new approach. The Group of 20 [on international monetary reform] failed."[17] Whether or not the G7 achieved this function of "close cooperation" is difficult to assess. This difficulty—and its solution—stems from the definition of what "cooperation"—that is, in broad terms, the process of working together—exactly entails. The sharing of information? Commonly agreed actions? Their implementation? Or simply the fact that leaders meet on a regular basis?

Richard Cooper has identified six types of cooperation in central banking, but some of these apply to multilateral summitry as well.[18] Cooperation can be more or less intense, ranging from a simple exchange of information to something more forward looking, such as an exchange of views on how the world works, the economic outlook, or the process of standardizing concepts. Finally, the most advanced form of cooperation concerns commonly agreed actions.

Bearing these distinctions in mind, it is clear that the broad function of "closer cooperation" assigned to the G7 may concern in fact very different tasks. The socialization function mentioned above can thus be associated with the "exchange of information" dimension of cooperation, while the "commonly agreed actions" by and large fit with the concrete results mentioned in the last section. This distinction helps qualify the degree to which G7 meetings have successfully fulfilled, or not, their functions: the low-intensity part of cooperation, which is mostly about information sharing and exchange of views, has been rather successfully achieved, while the track record of the high-intensity part of cooperation is much more uneven.

"Coordination," the other word often put forward as a function of the G7, has a slightly different meaning from "cooperation." In broad terms, it means the attempt to organize the work of different bodies or activities more effectively; it thus relates more to the institutional dimension rather than the personal. In that sense, it applies best to transatlantic and North-South relations, as well as relations between the G7 and other institutions and groupings in the international system (such as the IMF) and regional summits.[19] The latter involves, for instance, European summitry, namely the rise of the European Council. As Giscard explained to Ford before the Rambouillet meeting, but shortly after the creation of the European Council: "The diplomatic problem remains for you to establish relations with a single Europe. We engaged in an objectively frustrating enterprise. Previously the will to establish a strong, unified Europe wasn't very strong. We are planning EC summit meetings three times a year for consultation."[20] Coordination pertains to a diplomatic-institutional game, in which the G7/8/20 has to find its place in an already complex international framework, but here again it is useful to distinguish between the process and the outcome. The longevity of the G7/8 meetings indicates that, in practice, they have found their place and filled an institutional gap in the diplomatic process. The emergence of the G20 shows that further gaps existed and its continued relevance tends to show that it fulfills its functions. However, this does not prejudge as to whether this new tool available to improve international coordination can always be effectively used.[21]

The psychological dimension of multilateral summitry has been a central function of G7 meetings ever since 1975, as well as G20 meetings since their creation. Fostering confidence and trust in the international system and in the participating governments' policies, is an essential feature of G7/8/20 summits.[22] During the first G7 meeting in France, Ford explained thus: "Rambouillet can send a message of interdependence and cooperation which would contribute to a feeling of international confidence."[23] He came back later on to this idea, as if it were a leitmotiv of the meeting: "There are also steps that we can take at this meeting to aid in rebuilding confidence."[24] West German Chancellor Helmut Schmidt also declared that "the psychology is as important as mechanical moves."[25] This theme has remained central to G7/8/20 meetings to the present day. "The G20 ... helped to preserve confidence," declared French President Nicolas Sarkozy in 2011.[26] Even more recently, on the occasion of the G20 summit of Saint Petersburg on 5–6 September 2013, the president of the European Council, Herman Van Rompuy, and the president of the European Commission, José Manuel Barroso, wrote a joint letter in which they called on "G20 leaders to unite around a common purpose to improve global confidence."[27]

The psychological/trust function of summitry is Janus-faced: it is aimed at restoring confidence in the international system, the stability of which may be put at risk by multifaceted crises, as the Van Rompuy/Barroso letter highlights; and it is aimed at fostering trust among the G7 participants themselves. As in the previous cases of cooperation and coordination, it could be argued that part of the trust function falls under the "process," while another part falls under the "outcome": trust between the G7 members is part of an ongoing process, while trust vis-à-vis the Western liberal capitalist system should be able to bring tangible results more swiftly. On this occasion, however, the distinction between process and outcome does not seem to be fruitful, as contradictory examples can be found in each case: G7 summits may have nurtured mistrust between some leaders as well as fostering unexpected trust between others; while some meetings may have reinforced disillusionment in the Western liberal capitalist economy, others have produced just the opposite. This uneasy assessment arguably comes from the concept of trust itself, which is transient by nature. It is therefore difficult to draw any clear-cut conclusion as to whether G7/8/20 meetings fulfilled this function: multilateral summitry cannot quite institutionalize trust.[28] However, as a key result, G7/8/20 meetings did allow cooperation even without trust, a point that is further developed in the next section.

Counterfactuals: What if the G7/8/20 did not exist?

A final way of trying to assess whether G7 meetings have fulfilled their aims is very open to debate, but surely deserves to be mentioned: what would have happened had the G7/8/20 not existed? This counterfactual could lead to endless debates and options; it is not the goal of this section to enter into this creative thinking. However, what this section can do is reflect on one of the implicit counterfactuals that European, Japanese, and North American policymakers most frequently raised when preparing G7/8/20 summits: that is, the crises of the 1930s. This parallel is not so much about the policy substance of the two periods: the economic and political issues dealt with in the 1930s were very different from those tackled in the 1970s and 1980s. Rather, it relates to the overall interpretation of the dynamics of that decade. The crux of the interwar period had been the "dual crisis": the simultaneous collapse of the international economic system *and* the international political system.[29] The breakdown of international cooperation and the inability of policymakers to address these issues has remained a central reference ever since the end of World War II.

It is indeed striking to see that the parallel with the 1930s has survived multiple decades. Not only did the "founders" of the G7 make repeated references to it in the mid-1970s, but also their successors in the 1980s, and finally contemporary leaders after the 2008 financial crisis. In virtually all instances policymakers referred to the crux of the 1930s, namely the simultaneous collapse of the international economic and political systems. True, the references post-2008 have also been geared towards concrete economic and financial policy measures, reminiscent of the need for coordinated international action that was lacking in the 1930s, but that was not so much on the agenda of the 1970s and 1980s. Heads of government in the 1970s did not want to revert back to the vicious circle that occurred in the 1930s, characterized by a lack of cooperation and coordination in both the political and economic realms. Schmidt was the most vocal in this, and reported to Ford before the Rambouillet meeting that he was "deeply worried": "this is the greatest depression since 1932. And in some countries we can expect social unrest. I am deeply worried. 1975 is very different from 1932, but the behavior of governments—trying to ride it out—could be similar. We can't use the methods of recent years for a situation that none of us have lived through."[30] Japanese Prime Minister Takeo Miki also said during the Rambouillet meeting itself: "But now we should make a clear stand not to resort to protectionist measures. We must avoid the mistakes of the 1930s."[31]

The parallel with the 1930s continued to haunt the generations that replaced the "founders" of G7 summitry. Robert Hormats, US sherpa at the G7 meeting in Versailles in 1982, talking to the US Congress, thus declared:

> There are those in this country, as in others, who counsel disengagement from the institutions and rules which make up the world

economy. They tend to forget the tragic lessons of the inter-war period, but there are still others who, I believe, remain in the majority in most countries, who recognize that while we have high unemployment and inflation today, a breakdown in the international economic system, and a move to protectionism, would seriously worsen both of those problems. I profoundly share that point of view.[32]

Closer to us, the frame of reference of the 1930s has remained ever since the outbreak of the 2008 financial crisis—which has been described on countless occasions as "the worst since the Great Depression." Policymakers this time admittedly referred to the 1930s with reference to the economic policy options available, but in order to examine these options, international cooperation and coordination were needed.[33]

Thinking about the G7/8/20 in terms of counterfactuals brings us back to the notion of "trust": if such multilateral meetings do not always contribute to fostering trust among their participants, they importantly allow cooperation *without* trust. This was an institutional option that did not really exist before. The list of difficult interpersonal relationships among G7 leaders is long: one may think, with varying degrees of mistrust in each case, of Giscard and Canadian Prime Minister Pierre Trudeau, Schmidt and US President Jimmy Carter, British Prime Minister Margaret Thatcher and Mitterrand, and French President François Hollande and German Chancellor Angela Merkel. However, in spite of their difficult relationships, these leaders did carry on meeting on a routine basis in a multilateral framework. This crucially allowed for the G7 *process*—regardless of potential deceiving *outcomes*—to carry on too. Such continuity was key, in particular since it is unlikely that the entire administration of the respective heads of governments shared their leaders' personal predisposition against (or indeed in favor of) his or her counterparts, and as a consequence permitted the continued fulfillment of some other key functions of the G7, such as the sharing of information and socialization.

One way to counter the risk of another "dual crisis" was hence to facilitate the meetings of heads of government of the most developed countries, able to deal simultaneously with the international economic *and* political system. The same reasoning can be applied to the emergence of the G20. Ford had declared at the beginning of the Rambouillet summit that "it was necessary to work together in the economic field in order to stabilize the political background."[34] Takeo Fukuda, the Japanese prime minister, said during the London G7 summit of 1977 that he recalled his time in London between 1930 and

1933, and "thought that there was now [in 1977] a better chance of international economic cooperation."[35] Of course, it did not go far sometimes, and it just appeared as nonsense, but at least there was some attempt at cooperating in an international forum on a regular basis to discuss political economy—which was not really the case in the 1930s.

In spite of all its weaknesses and imperfections, the G7/8/20, as an instrument of global governance, importantly avoided any debacle in international cooperation/coordination comparable with that which happened in the 1930s. The G7/8/20 process has managed to maintain a minimum level of cooperative behavior throughout the crises of the 1970s, 1980s, and since 2008, in spite of disappointing and limited concrete results at times. This may certainly not definitively predict what would have happened without multilateral summitry over these timeframes, but it does provide a useful *longue durée* comparison against which the G7/8/20 can be assessed.

Conclusion

This chapter tried to provide a qualified reading grid to help assess whether the G7/8/20 have fulfilled their functions, both self-assigned by the participants, and later on in the literature. This chapter argued that distinguishing between the G7/8/20 processes and outcomes helps better evaluate whether these summit meetings have achieved their functions. In general terms, they have best fulfilled their functions in relation to processes rather than results. The existence and persistence of routine summitry, socialization, and agenda setting have all been fulfilled, while the evaluation of the concrete results achieved by G7 summits can only be done on a case-by-case basis. When "cooperation" is understood as a process (e.g. exchanging information) it has been rather successful, while when it is considered as an outcome (e.g. commonly agreed action) the track record is uneven. The function of trust is the most difficult to gauge, as it is by nature transient, but the G7/8/20 framework crucially allows for the continuing of cooperation even without trust—a feature that was not really present before the mid-1970s.

Does that uneven track record, in terms of concrete results, really matter—or, put differently, have G7 participants ever claimed that they would solve many international issues thanks to the establishment of the G7? The fact that the G7 should be able to bring effective solutions is an expectation that largely goes beyond what G7 meetings can realistically give. Patrick Nairne, a British official in the Cabinet Office, put it nicely, with reference to the European framework: "we should not look to the European Council for more than it can give."[36] The same could be argued for the G7: the expectation that its meetings can provide adequate responses on every occasion, instead of giving birth to frustrations as they most often do, is excessively ambitious. Ford quite lucidly explained this during the very first G7 meeting in Rambouillet in 1975: "This summit is designed to deal with economic questions but in a more fundamental sense it springs from the enormous interdependence of our societies and the common values which we share ... We cannot resolve all our problems, but we can achieve a better understanding of them."[37] In short, what matters most in the G7/8/20 meetings is the process rather than the result, and in that sense, summit meetings have fulfilled their functions.

This analysis of the structural forces at play in G7/8/20 summitry helps finally sketch some reflections as to the future of such multilateral meetings. It is unlikely that the evolution of multilateral summitry will fundamentally alter the situation analyzed above. The very nature of G7/8/20 meetings—intergovernmental gatherings (possibly) reaching non-binding agreements—implies perforce a very uneven track record. G7/8/20 meetings cannot provide magical solutions to longstanding problems; their outcomes will likely remain dependent upon the goodwill of their participants. As far as the G7/8/20 process is concerned, the situation is again likely to remain similar. There is little reason—apart from a member permanently leaving the structure—for the socialization, exchange of information and tentative building of interpersonal trust suddenly to stop. The G7/8/20 will continue to offer a useful, albeit often frustrating, additional instrument in the global governance toolbox—an instrument that provided the highest level of international cooperation ever witnessed in world politics when it emerged in the mid-1970s.

Notes

1 Archives nationales, site de Pierrefitte (thereafter AN), 5AG4/CD61, "Attali to Morel, Esquisse du discours du Président à Ottawa," 4 June 1981. My translation.
2 The G6, G7, G8, and G20 are often compared in this chapter, but their respective backgrounds and timeframes deserve to be briefly explained here: the G6 emerged after the mid-1970s economic crises and consisted of Britain, France, Italy, Japan, the United States, and West Germany at its first meeting in 1975 (Rambouillet); it became the G7 with the inclusion of Canada in 1976 (Puerto Rico); the G7 became the G8 between 1998 and 2014 as it included Russia; and the G20 referred to in this chapter is the meeting at heads of government level of the G8 members plus Argentina, Australia, Brazil, China, the European Union, India, Indonesia, Mexico, Saudi Arabia, South Africa, South Korea, and Turkey, and started in 2008.

3 Emmanuel Mourlon-Druol, "'Managing from the Top': Globalisation and the Rise of Regular Summitry, Mid-1970s–early 1980s," *Diplomacy & Statecraft* 23, no. 4 (2012): 679–703.
4 National Archives and Records Administration (thereafter NARA), Department of State, Office of the Counsellor, Helmut Sonnenfeldt, Entry 3, Memorandum from Robert Hormats to Henry Kissinger, 24 October 1975. Original emphasis.
5 Admittedly most of these functions could well apply to other types of summits. The literature on the topic is large: among the sources that mention these functions, one can refer to David Reynolds, "Summitry as Intercultural Communication," *International Affairs* 85, no. 1 (2009): 115–127; David Reynolds, *Summits: Six Meetings that Shaped the Twentieth Century* (New York: Basic Books, 2007); Robert D. Putnam and Nicholas Bayne, *Hanging Together: Cooperation and Conflict in the Seven-Power Summits*, 2nd edn (London: Sage, 1987); Emmanuel Mourlon-Druol and Federico Romero, *International Summitry and Global Governance: The Rise of the G7 and the European Council, 1974–1991* (London: Routledge, 2014); Noël Bonhomme and Emmanuel Mourlon-Druol, "Institutionalising Trust? The G7 Summits and the European Council Meetings, 1975–1990," in *"Trust but Verify": The Politics of Uncertainty and the Transformation of the Cold War Order, 1969–1991*, ed. Christian Ostermann, Reinhild Kreis, and Martin Klimke (forthcoming); Enrico Böhm, *Die Sicherheit des Westens: Entstehung und Funktion der G7-Gipfel (1975–1981)* (München: Oldenbourg Wissenschaftsverlag, 2013); Johannes von Karczewski, *"Weltwirtschaft ist unser Schicksal": Helmut Schmidt und die Schaffung der Weltwirtschaftsgipfel* (Bonn: Dietz, 2008); Peter I. Hajnal, *The G7/G8 System: Evolution, Role, and Documentation* (Aldershot: Ashgate, 1999); and Nicholas Bayne, *Staying Together: The G8 Summit Confronts the 21st Century*, G8 and Global Governance Series (Aldershot: Ashgate, 2005).
6 Valéry Giscard d'Estaing, "The Original Idea was for them to Actually Talk," *The New York Times*, 4 June 2007.
7 AN, 5AG3 886, Handwritten notes of Giscard, Rambouillet summit (1975).
8 Elizabeth Benning, "The Road to Rambouillet and the Creation of the Group of Five," in *International Summitry and Global Governance*, ed. Mourlon-Druol and Romero, 39–63; and Putnam and Bayne, *Hanging Together*, 11–43.
9 On international socialization, see for instance Jan Beyers, "Problèmes Conceptuels et Méthodologiques dans la Recherche sur la Socialisation Internationale," in *La Fabrique des "Européens". Processus de Socialisation et Construction Européenne*, ed. Hélène Michel and Cécile Robert (Strasbourg: Presses Universitaires de Strasbourg, 2010), 29–64.
10 Putnam and Bayne, *Hanging Together*, 257.
11 For more details, see Emmanuel Mourlon-Druol, "Less than a Permanent Secretariat, More than an Ad-Hoc Preparatory Group: A Prosopography of the G7's Personal Representatives, 1975–1991," in *International Summitry and Global Governance*, 64–91.
12 Emmanuel Mourlon-Druol, "La Normalisation des Sommets: Rôle, Atouts et Limites des Sommets Institutionnalisés (G7 et Conseil

Européen), 1974–1986," in *La France Entre Guerre Froide et Construction Européenne, 1974–1986*, ed. Christian Wenkel (forthcoming).
13 Gerald Ford Digital Library (thereafter FDL), National Security Advisor (NSA), Memoranda of Conversations, Box 14, Miki-Ford, 5 August 1975, www.fordlibrarymuseum.gov/library/guides/findingaid/Memoranda_of_Conversations.asp.
14 Summits were graded according to agreement on policy issues and on "durable institutional innovations" in Bayne, *Hanging in There*, 195, the table that is referred to is in this chapter. For the different rankings, see Putnam and Bayne, *Hanging Together*; Bayne, *Hanging in There*, 195; Hajnal, *The G7/G8 System*, 68; Nicholas Bayne, "The G7 Summit's Contribution: Past, Present and Prospective," in *Shaping a New International Financial System: Challenges of Governance in a Globalizing World*, ed. John J. Kirton, Karl Kaiser, and Joseph Daniels (Aldershot: Ashgate, 2000), 19–36; and Nicholas Bayne, "The G7 and Multilateral Trade Liberalisation: Past Performance, Future Challenges," in *New Directions in Global Economic Governance: Managing Globalisation in the Twenty-First Century*, ed. John J. Kirton and George von Furstenberg (Aldershot: Ashgate, 2001), 171–187.
15 John J. Kirton, *G20 Governance for a Globalized World* (Aldershot: Ashgate, 2013).
16 Bayne, *Hanging in There*, 195.
17 FDL, NSA, Box 8, Memoranda of Conversation, Giscard-Ford, 15 December 1974.
18 Richard Cooper, *Almost a Century of Central Bank Cooperation*, BIS Working Papers No. 198, 25 February 2006.
19 N. Piers Ludlow, "Creating the Expectation of a Collective Response: The Impact of Summitry on Transatlantic Relations," in *International Summitry and Global Governance*, 138–151.
20 FDL, NSA, Box 8, Memoranda of Conversation, Giscard-Ford, 16 December 1974. On the rise of the European Council, see Emmanuel Mourlon-Druol, "Regional Integration and Global Governance: The Example of the European Council, 1974–1986," *Les Cahiers Irice* 1, no. 9 (2012): 91–104.
21 I explore the issue of G7/European Council coordination in more detail in Mourlon-Druol, "La Normalisation des Sommets: Rôle, Atouts et Limites des Sommets Institutionnalisés (G7 et Conseil Européen), 1974–1986."
22 Bonhomme and Mourlon-Druol, "Institutionalising Trust?"
23 FDL, NSA, Box 16, Rambouillet meeting (1975).
24 FDL, NSA, Box 16, Rambouillet meeting (1975).
25 FDL, NSA, Box 7, Memoranda of Conversation, Schmidt-Ford, 5 December 1974.
26 Nicolas Sarkozy, "Keynote Speech on Europe," 1 December 2011, www.ambafrance-uk.org/President-Sarkozy-s-keynote-speech.
27 José Manuel Barroso and Herman Van Rompuy, "G20 Summit: Improving Global Confidence and Support the Global Recovery," 23 July 2013, www.consilium.europa.eu/uedocs/cms_data/docs/pressdata/en/ec/138333.pdf.
28 Bonhomme and Mourlon-Druol, "Institutionalising Trust?"
29 Robert W.D. Boyce, *The Great Interwar Crisis and the Collapse of Globalization* (Basingstoke: Palgrave Macmillan, 2009), 5.

30 FDL, NSA, Box 8, Memoranda of Conversation, Schmidt-Ford, 29 May 1975.
31 FDL, NSA, Box 16, Rambouillet meeting (1975).
32 Archives du Ministère des Affaires Étrangères (thereafter AMAE), Direction des Affaires Économiques et Financières (thereafter DAEF), Box 2184, Telegram n°1374, Objet: Sommet de Versailles—déclarations de M. Hormats, 1 June 1982.
33 Andrew F. Cooper, "The G20 as an Improvised Crisis Committee and/or a Contested 'Steering Committee' for the World," *International Affairs* 86, no. 3 (2010): 741–757.
34 Margaret Thatcher Archive, Document 110941, Note of the first session of the conference at the Château de Rambouillet, 15 November 1975.
35 The National Archives (thereafter TNA), PREM 16/1223, Note of the first session of the Downing Street summit conference, 7 May 1977.
36 TNA, PREM 16/393, Nairne to Palliser, European Council, 29 July 1975.
37 FDL, NSA, Box 16, Rambouillet meeting (1975).

11 BRICS and re-shaping the model of summitry
Subordinating the regional to the global

Andrew F. Cooper

- **Contextualizing BRICS summitry**
- **Moving toward BRICS summitry**
- **Gaining momentum and facing constraints**
- **Conclusion**

At the core of summitry is self-selection. Summitry, unlike universalist-oriented forms of multilateralism, is not intended to tilt towards inclusivity. On the contrary, the focus of small, relatively intimate, meetings of government leaders is on a degree of exclusivity. With a heavy weight attached to dialogue and the exchange of views, some sense of a common identity is privileged.

Under these conditions it is not surprising that a good deal of the rise of summitry in the past 25 years has been concentrated at the regional level. Indeed, as noted in the Introduction to this volume, it is the massive increase in the summitry in the Americas and in comparative regional perspective that grabs attention and animates extended analysis.

At first glance, therefore, the Brazil, Russia, India, China, and South Africa (BRICS) summits appear to stand out as an exception to this generalized trend. The most distinctive feature about the emergence of a sustained process of BRICS summitry from 2009 lies in the lack and/or subordination of geographical connections. Unlike the rest of the processes examined in this volume, there is little or no salience of physical factors related to contact through proximity acting as the driver of summitry. To be sure, China and India share a border, but this component of the relationship is downplayed due to the disputed nature of this spatial condition. Nor can there be located in BRICS summitry a strong degree of "we" feeling, with a shared sense of belonging to a group with a distinctive regional or sub-regional identity.[1] China and India are most commonly framed as Asian countries, however nuanced in terms of the East or South Asian component. Brazil, South Africa, and Russia by way of contrast are viewed through a set of distinctive South American, African, and Eurasian lenses.

Yet, if containing many distinctive features, BRICS summitry also contains many other qualities that are at the core of the re-shaped model of summitry.[2] No less than in other forms of summitry examined in this volume, namely the G7/8/20, and East Asian and/or Asia-Pacific illustrations along with the detailed case studies with respect to the Americas, the BRICS is an explicitly political project, embedded in a geopolitical narrative. The choice of countries contained within the summitry process adheres to a particular, albeit multi-dimensional, rationale, and although not as contested as other summitry processes (above all on the nature of the political system for members), the choice of non-members also contains some *de facto* logic (no BRICS country, for example, is a member of the Organisation for Economic Co-operation and Development—OECD—although Russia was in accession negotiations until the Ukraine/Crimea crisis).

The operational dynamics around the summitry process reinforce the interplay between common features and major points of differentiation between the BRICS and the regional projects showcased in this book. All summits contain a high degree of leader-centrism, even if in most cases extensive background work is done by lower-ranked state officials. Credit for a successful launch of a new regionally based summit, whether narrowly or broadly defined, is commonly credited to a single head of government, whether Mexican President Carlos Salinas of Mexico in terms of the North American Free Trade Agreement (NAFTA), Australian Prime Minister Bob Hawke with respect to the Asia-Pacific Economic Cooperation (APEC), Brazilian President Fernando Henrique Cardoso on the original 2000 South American summit, or Venezuelan President Hugo Chávez in the case of the Bolivarian Alliance for the Peoples of Our America (ALBA). The BRICS is different in that no one leader jumps out as the prime catalyst for action. The fact that the first official BRICs summit at the leaders' level was hosted at Yekaterinburg in June 2009 by "caretaker" Russian President Dmitry Medvedev (not Vladimir Putin) further blurs the picture.

Moreover, unlike the regionally based summit processes, there was not a single launch of the BRICS through a well-defined and well-publicized meeting. Rather the BRICS followed what can be termed as the "global" model copied from the G20 model.[3] Without possessing a single take-off moment, therefore, the BRICS, akin to the G20, had an elevated roll-out process where an initial meeting at the ministerial level (foreign ministers in the case of the BRICS, finance ministers with the G20), before the move to the apex of power with the involvement of leaders. Equally, though, the BRICS deviated in some significant ways from the G20. Having felt a great deal of status deprivation from being mobilized as "outreach" partners via the G8, the BRICS refrained from building up any equivalent process to that of the G20—with other countries/regional groupings on an uneven basis. Alternatively, it moved on to add a new equal member—South Africa, in 2011, adding the capital "S" to BRIC—to the original construct of Brazil, Russia, India, and China.

This dual condition, with the BRICS paralleling certain aspects of the more numerous summitry processes at the regional level, but breaking away from that model on highly salient features, reveals the importance of the stretching of boundaries of what is taken to be the core set of cases of summits. The focus on the wide variety of institutional arrangements (or as Richard Feinberg would put it, "institutionalized multilateral summitry")[4] within the Americas and Asia-Pacific needs to be supplemented by analyses of projects that go beyond regional boundaries. While BRICS is the dominant illustration of this phenomenon, it should be mentioned that there are other cases, both in train as highlighted by the cross-cutting India, Brazil, and South Africa (IBSA) summit, and in the formative stages as illustrated by the move to create a forum of Mexico, Indonesia, South Korea, Turkey, and Australia (known as MIKTA) at the level of foreign ministers.

In overall terms the BRICS summit provides an ideal case study for expanding our understanding of summitry beyond regional experiences. The BRICS, akin to the G20, highlights the necessity of a return to older notions of hierarchy in terms of summitry. With the appearance of the G20, to overshadow the G7/8, the BRICS cannot be termed a classic counter-hegemonic construct in that the same countries are both in and out of the bigger club. Yet, given the existence of cross-cutting cleavages within the G20 and autonomous actions outside, the BRICS also cannot be located as simply a lobby group within the bigger club. What is more, even with its high degree of not only leader centrism but state centrism, the BRICS does not look like a variation of summitry exhibited by the global South in past eras (notably the 1955 Bandung conference). Although leaders are front and center in the project, as with the G20, there is space for other actions that shift some agency and attention beyond the state with the mobilization of elements *inter alia* of the business and think tank communities.

Above all, BRICS illustrates the ascendancy of informality in global summitry. Unlike many of the regional processes, there is no attempt either in the form of a sketchy outline or elaborate format to embed the rules of the game of summitry. Akin to the G summits (encompassing the G7/8 and G20), there is no constitution or charter. The mode of behavior by countries is not scrutinized either generally or in specific areas (for example, the adherence to some form of democratic principles). Plurality of membership is accorded value. Equality of membership is highly salient as well in the institutional culture, with a rotation of hosting functions and voice opportunities. What stands out, again in a similar manner to the G summits, is the level of improvisation. Unlike some of the regional summitry processes, there is no secretariat. What is different is that unlike the G summits, there is no clear delegation of power to other international bodies such as the International Monetary Fund (IMF) or World Bank.

Contextualizing BRICS summitry

BRICS summitry has been driven by the large economies of the original BRIC members. Indeed, it was because of economic size that the BRIC concept dramatically entered the public/intellectual domain in the early 2000s, becoming synonymous with economic growth, opportunities, and change. At the forefront of this privileging of the big emerging countries was Goldman Sachs. After all, it was the publication of the Goldman Sachs paper "Dreaming with BRICs: The Path to 2050" that attracted considerable attention and now serves as the key tag/description of the major emerging countries.[5] The economic projections of the future size of their economies paired with the (then unquestionable) reputation of the large investment bank, changed the popular image of those countries and started scholarly disputes on the accuracy and applicability of the model. Any discussion on the relative weight of the regional and global influence of the BRICS cannot ignore the underlying features of their economies.

From an economic perspective, focusing attention on the biggest four countries (Brazil, Russia, India, China)—the BRICs—which are (or promise to be) dynamic global motors of growth, has enormous appeal. On the basis of gross domestic product (GDP)/purchasing power parity, China (2), India (4), Russia (6), and Brazil (9) are all in the top ten. Mexico and Indonesia follow closely (11 and 15, respectively), with South Africa closing the ranks (25).[6] On the surface, it seems that their ever-deeper engagement and presence in the global economy is fairly recent, the beginning of the twenty-first century at best. However, focusing just on the most recent decade without looking at their economies in a longer historical perspective reveals that this view is often not correct.

Starting in Asia, China's economic success has its roots in the adoption of agricultural reforms in the mid-1970s, supplemented in the 1990s with large increases of foreign direct investment (FDI) in manufacturing. The average growth rate in China from the late 1970s stood at approximately 9.4 percent (with only two years' growth below 5 percent, in 1989 and 1990). In India, major policy reforms that started in the late 1980s triggered a higher growth rate, albeit slower than in China. After the period of "Hindu growth," India has experienced a sustained, high GDP growth of 4 percent to 8 percent annually, with an average of 5.8 percent over the past 20 years. Interestingly enough, even though the traditional thinking of developmental paths would suggest that the sources of increased growth of both countries are comparable and depend on trade in resources and basic manufacturing, growth in India has been led by the services sector, rather than exports of manufactures financed by FDI inflows as in China.

In the Americas, Brazil also enjoyed strong growth at approximately 7 percent annually from 1940 until the debt crises of the 1980s. Strong growth returned in the mid-1990s but was halted by the end of the decade with yet another currency crisis. Economic growth in Brazil remains volatile, although export growth in agriculture and natural resources as well as a fairly young population provide some advantages.

In general, the common features of the BRICS include large populations (collectively over 50 percent of the world's total), with a rapid increase of urban dwellers, low wage rates, episodes of sustained high growth, growing inflows and outflows of FDI, high rates of growth of trade and, consequently, growing domestic demand as a result of increases in individual incomes and overall economic development, and fast-growing demand for energy.

While the growth rates of the emerging powers tend to be unstable, they have remained, for the most part, significantly higher than those of the G7 and match or surpass the world average. Still, it is important to note that their economic successes may be hindered by population dynamics. As the cliché goes, China is at a great risk of becoming old before it becomes rich. India's high population growth will make this country the largest in the world within the next two decades, which may bring increased tensions over social security resources. On the other side of the scale, Russia has struggled with a shrinking population in recent years.

Differences notwithstanding, it seems clear that the economic and social transformation in the BRICS has underpinned a global shift in power relations. The big emerging powers benefited from the extraordinary increase in world trade in the second half of the twentieth century. Notwithstanding the internal differences of their economic development, their ever-closer integration into the global economy has played a major role in their economic success. By 2009 China's exports had overtaken the longstanding leader, Germany, exceeding those of the United States by close to US$100 billion, and leaving Japan behind.

Closely linked to increasing exports, the foreign exchange reserves of the BRICS are also a clear indication of their weight in global economy that has already proven problematic not only to individual countries (the United States in particular) but also the global system. In 2007, their combined reserves exceeded those of the G7 by over $800 billion and accounted for almost 40 percent of the world's total. It is also important to note the increase in foreign investment flowing from the emerging countries. Until recently, their biggest concern was how to attract investment from the industrialized countries in order to support the development of their industries. Now they are paying as much attention to creating an environment that would encourage the national companies to invest internationally and overcome the often unfavorable perceptions of their engagements abroad.

This large size across the board allows each of the BRICS to dominate its region. In a number of ways, it must be emphasized, each of the BRICS is either "too big" or uncomfortable with its immediate neighborhood. Such a sense of discomfort, however, far from inhibiting the BRICS, has encouraged the push outwards.

All the BRICS have demonstrated an impressive global reach in terms of their diplomatic profile. The stretch of China's international influence has been well documented.[7] For example, Beijing's concerted charm offensive toward Africa has been conducted not only bilaterally but also multilaterally through the convening of the impressive Forum on China–Africa Cooperation in November 2006.[8] Opening the 2012 meeting, President Hu Jintao announced $20 billion in loans to African countries over the next three years, "cementing an alliance that appears increasingly hostile to the west."[9] Similarly, New Delhi hosted its first India–Africa Summit in April 2008.

More generally, each of the BRICS has become a hub of diplomatic interaction—network as well as club diplomacy. Brazil under President Luiz Inácio Lula da Silva launched a number of high-profile diplomatic initiatives, from leadership of the G20 developing countries via the World Trade Organization (WTO), to the proposal for a global fund against hunger and a push on biofuel diplomacy using its sugar cane-based ethanol production. South Africa has shared an innovative partnership with India and Brazil—the IBSA Dialogue Forum—as well as playing a strong role in the G77, the African Union (AU), and

BRICS and re-shaping the model of summitry 199

the New Economic Partnership for Africa's Development (NEPAD), as well as the Brazil, South Africa, India, and China group (BASIC) on climate change.

The emergence of the BRICS thus moves beyond the traditional understanding of regional powers. It is the economic growth that has advanced these countries to the forefront of the global political economy. However, as suggested, size itself is not sufficient to explain their growing importance. On the flip side of the growing economic size of BRICS, supported by globalization and their ever-deeper involvement in international trade, are the international political and diplomatic structures. From the World Bank, to the IMF, to the United Nations Security Council, to the G7/8, more and more international institutions came under stress in the early 2000s because of their perceived double gap in legitimacy and efficiency. Much of the discussion about BRICS rests on economic indices, but diplomacy cannot be secondary to economics. Diplomacy around the BRICS demonstrates the centrality of the geopolitical implications (actual and potential) of the power shift from North to South and West to East.

The big emerging countries were targets of enhanced engagement by the old establishment. The initial response by the industrialized countries of the G7 was an opening up through a diffuse pattern of outreach. At the Evian Summit in 2003, France chose to showcase members of BRICS—with the leaders from China, India, and Brazil (along with those from another 20 potential members, including Mexico and Saudi Arabia). At Gleneagles in 2005, the United Kingdom, with a similar model in mind, invited the same core countries (albeit without Middle East representation) to discuss climate change. A similar framework was used in key ancillary bodies, most notably the G7 forum of finance ministers. Chinese and Indian finance ministers attended the two 2005 meetings in St Petersburg and London. So entrenched had this hub approach become that the exclusion of the O5 (discussed below) became a focus for reproach. French President Jacques Chirac publicly rebuked the United States for not being more inclusive of these regional hubs at the 2004 Sea Island Summit: "We cannot discuss major economic issues nowadays without discussing these issues with China, with India, Brazil, South Africa."[10]

Still such efforts proved frustrating. Concerted efforts to reform the G8 from the inside were directed through the so-called Heiligendamm or Outreach 5 (O5) process between 2005 and 2009, through which different members of the G8 took the lead in reaching out to five big emerging markets and regional hubs—four countries that moved over time to become the BRICS (Brazil, China, India, and South Africa), and Mexico. By the 2007 Heiligendamm summit, it was clear that major international challenges could not be addressed without the ongoing cooperation of the large countries of the global South. The formalization of the Heiligendamm process tried to accomplish this goal, if within clear boundaries.[11]

While Goldman Sachs is rightly given credit for coming up with the name of BRICS, in diplomatic terms this process proved to be the trigger for the consolidation of select big countries from the South into new habits of working together. Instead of consolidating the relationship between the big emerging countries and the G7/8, then, the Heiligendamm process consolidated the relationship between the big emerging countries themselves. In initiating the process, Chancellor Angela Merkel made it quite clear that "We don't want to turn the G8 into a G13." Rather, she explained to her parliament, "without the emerging economies, progress on issues such as climate change, the world trade round and intellectual property rights is unimaginable." Even so, the idea of establishing a dialogue between the G8 and the O5, and of creating a secretariat within the OECD (which caused some important developing countries some discomfort, as they view the OECD as itself an elitist Western club) to manage the developing G8-O5 contacts, suggested that the G8 was already reinventing itself "as a vehicle for informal problem-solving between the most powerful countries of today and tomorrow."[12] In addition to increasing the legitimacy of the G8, the informal dialogue was intended to create trust, bring more understanding of common responsibilities on global issues, and explore avenues for stalled negotiations in other international forums, especially the WTO Doha Round. The basic structure relied on a steering committee and four working groups (co-chaired by G8 and O5 countries) on investment, energy, development, and innovation—topics of most interest to the G8. Migration and governance, preferred topics of the O5, were excluded.

However, several mishaps at the launch of the Heiligendamm process, as well as the general approach to it as "outreach," did not contribute positively to the process. The most infamous incident was the release of the communiqué that announced the establishment of the process without any input from the O5 and before the emerging powers actually joined the G8 meetings.[13] Indian Prime Minister Manmohan Singh's remark—"We have come here not as petitioners but as partners in an equitable, just and fair management of the global community of nations, which we accept as reality in the globalized world"[14]—was seconded by a hopeful statement from China that the G8 Outreach would not be used as "a means of exerting pressure on developing countries."[15]

Although all the O5 countries became engaged in the process, this incremental approach was unlikely to have resulted in wider reform without a global shock such as the financial crisis. Traditionally focused on the formal, more inclusive structures (such as the United Nations), China never actively sought full membership in the G8. If comfortable with the language of dialogue, cooperation, and partnership, it had serious reservations about a tight embrace, potential attempts at "socialization" by the Western powers and the possibility of pressures on domestic policies, to which Beijing is very sensitive.[16] For India and Brazil, enlargement of the G8 was seen as a "consolation" prize for (and a stepping stone toward) UN Security Council permanent membership. All three of Brazil, China, and India have a strong self-image rooted in the developing world, expect more recognition of their growing role in the world, regard themselves as entitled to equal status in the G8, question the current global governance architecture, and push for comprehensive reforms. South Africa strongly supported the Heiligendamm process as a structured opportunity for expanding the Africa–G8 dialogue, but Pretoria's role as the representative of the "African cause" or "continental voice" on the international stage is somewhat awkward, with internal hesitation and African reservations. Another challenge for South Africa is "the interplay of three factors: costs, capacity, and global constraints." These are factors that no developing country, and no African country in particular, can ignore.[17]

Moving toward BRICS summitry

Since the Goldman Sachs publication, BRICS has moved from a laudatory account of the rise of four big emerging economies to a geopolitical reality with the original BRIC countries plus South Africa included. Such a shift indicates the extent to which we are moving into a more pluralistic world order. Although sharing some common characteristics in their diplomatic styles, the emerging states are more marked for their differences than similarities. Located in dissimilar regions, with unique historical circumstances, the group is by no means uniform.

Brazil, South Africa, and India are robust democracies and very active members of the WTO. Russia is a highly managed democracy with the legacy of empire and superpower status through the Cold War. China is a one-party state and a permanent member of the Security Council. As mentioned earlier, India has a fast-rising population. Russia and South Africa are in serious demographic trouble with a sharply reduced life expectancy. Brazil and Russia are resource rich. India and China are resource dependent. Although possessing multiple identities, all see themselves as being in between countries with a rising and a developing dimension. If coming from very different (albeit all problematic) neighborhoods, all possess accentuated global reach. Although all challenge the status quo to some extent, all to some degree want recognition by the established club membership of their ascendancy.

A forerunner of cooperation between a subset of BRICS is IBSA. Akin to the BRICS, the IBSA Dialogue Forum initially brought together the foreign ministers in Brasília in June 2003, and only in late 2008 broadened out to the leaders' participation. While IBSA has encouraged more trade between the parties, it is their shared identity in terms of their historical sense of victimization that draws most attention. The still relatively recent experiences of colonialism in India, apartheid in South Africa, and military dictatorship in Brazil resulted in a common position of champions against injustice and inequity on a global basis. In addition to the capacity for blockage came some policy alternatives. Most notably, there were early signs that the IBSA countries were increasingly committed to shaping some sort of joint vision of global action. They became strong advocates, for example, of the UN Millennium Development Goals and debt eradication for the least developed countries. Undoubtedly, IBSA proved an example of how commonality of interests and shared perceptions in a global grouping can lead to tangible benefits in trade and a strengthening of each other's diplomatic stance internationally. The main criticism of IBSA was what the grouping left out. By focusing on identity rather than on material attributes (if not interests), it distorted the relationship between economic clout and diplomatic will and skill. In comparison with the BRICs, IBSA lacks substance in its ability to act as a guide for future collective action: to break or bend the established global governance order.

What changed the situation was the relationship of the BRICS to the G summits, with the 2008 global financial and economic crises. Signs appeared that the concept of BRICs was being reconfigured as a grouping prior to the financial crisis. In October 2007 the foreign ministers of Russia, China, and India met in Harbin, China. In May 2008 all four BRICs foreign ministers met for a day in Yekaterinburg. Nevertheless, it was the global financial crisis that shifted the balance dramatically between the old establishment and the "rising" states. As noted, the first official BRIC summit was held in Yekaterinburg (June 2009), with subsequent meetings in Brasília (April 2010), Hainan

(April 2011), New Delhi (March 2012), Durban (November 2013), and Fortaleza (July 2014).

If still cautious about the goals for the BRICs summitry, there was from the outset no hiding the declaratory message of global transition. The June 2009 Yekaterinburg summit, following on the heels of a meeting of the Shanghai Cooperation Organization, was hailed as an "historic event" by Russia's President Medvedev, punctuated by its call for "[t]he emerging and developing economies [to] have a greater voice and representation in international financial institutions." President Lula da Silva, the host of the April 2010 summit, upped the ante by stating that "[a] new global economic geography has been born."[18]

One construction renders this move to formalize the BRICs as a grouping with a concern with equity and justice for the less powerful and those intended to curtail the restrictive unilateral or plurilateral/coalitional activity by the most powerful. The Yekaterinburg Joint Communiqué declared that: "We are committed to advance the reform of international financial institutions, so as to reflect changes in the world economy. The emerging and developing economies must have greater voice and representation in international financial institutions, and their heads and senior leadership should be appointed through an open, transparent, and merit-based selection process. We also believe that there is a strong need for a stable, predictable and more diversified international monetary system."[19]

A very different explication can point to this meeting as part of a more comprehensive process of realignment of power, with a new alternative concert of oppositional/adversarial states taking shape. Equally, though, there are strong counter-forces easing the expectation of new forms of interstate polarization. Each of the BRICs retains deep and specific ties with the pivotal/Northern countries in the general context of complex interdependence vis-à-vis the global economy. Of course rivalries also exist between the BRICs themselves: over borders, over resources, and over status (not least on the issue of Security Council membership). Realist scholars also signal the prospect of an alternative alignment with the United States/North if one of the BRICs rises faster and in a more antagonistic manner than the others. John Mearsheimer points in particular to "China's Unpeaceful Rise" as a catalyst for this type of balancing response.[20]

From the perspective of diplomatic practice, BRICS consists of a more formidable grouping of global states than IBSA. Yet in terms of coordination, the stakes for BRICS was higher. A key explanatory variable for the summitry process is the extent to which they have been able to engage effectively with the established international institutional order through traditional multilateral means and in the absence of these smaller network-hub forums. As Alden and Vieira point out, multilateralism provides an effective mechanism for countries within the formal institutional (IMF) and informal (G7/8) frameworks, but it is much more problematic for states outside it.[21] Marginalized countries of the global South have thus sought to innovate around the traditional exclusionary nature of the international system by establishing plurilateral network clubs amongst a grouping of like-minded states. IBSA's experimentation with trilateralism is a case in point.

BRICS are alternatively viewed as a diplomatic grouping constructed around economic weight. The inclusion of China and Russia (both nuclear powers and Security Council permanent members) within this forum indicates a different stratum within the international system. By these measures South Africa, Brazil, and even India in terms of Security Council membership, have a greater aspirational component. South Africa retains a pivotal status as a diplomatic actor and as a regional economic powerhouse, but it is at a markedly lower level in terms of its material capabilities. Not only is it left out of the Goldman Sachs BRIC group of countries, but it is also not a member of the second-tier Next 11, which includes among others Nigeria and Egypt. Brazil is also an outlier in several ways. As *The Economist* put it: "Unlike China and Russia it is a full-blooded democracy; unlike India it has no serious disputes with its neighbors. It is the only BRIC without a nuclear bomb."[22]

The image of a new form of bloc politics is accented according to this competitive scenario by the move of other countries from the global South into the BRICs forum. South Africa formally joined the BRICs/S grouping at the April 2011 summit in Hainan, China, and the possibility of other countries joining in the future is available, if unlikely.

ABroaders Yet the attractions for the BRICS appear more pragmatic than ideological. After all, South African President Jacob Zuma announced his interest in BRICs membership while conducting a massive trade tour to China accompanied by 13 Cabinet members and a delegation of 370 business people. Nor is South Africa's membership free of potential tensions, as brought to the fore by the case of the vote in March 2011 on Security Council Resolution 1973. Breaking from the common BRICS stance, South Africa supported "all necessary measures" to protect civilians in the escalating civil conflict in Libya, a declaratory move that was put into operation by the North Atlantic Treaty Organization (NATO).[23] At the same time, however, the salience of this move as a signifier of outlier status has been reduced after the April 2011 BRICS summit, with South Africa adhering to the stance of seeking a "political solution" to the conflict, and calling for a halt to the NATO campaign.[24]

Gaining momentum and facing constraints

At one level, in a similar but expanded manner to IBSA, the BRICS summit can be viewed as a useful means for members to share and learn from one another's development experiences. In addition to a shared sense of historical grievances and claims to represent the interests of all developing countries, the BRICS share a neo-Westphalian commitment to state sovereignty and nonintervention. They also combine a professed desire for a rules-based, stable, and predictable world order, with respect to the diversity of political systems and stages of development. Politically, the 2012 Delhi Declaration signals growing self-consciousness by the five BRICS that they have global weight and mean to begin using it. The BRICS statements on Syria and Iran clearly differentiate these countries from the West on contemporary global conflicts. To be sure, in the crucial vote on a draft Security Council resolution on Syria in July 2012, reflecting its identity as an open economy and a plural democracy, India sided with the West while China and Russia cast a double veto. Despite the differences in their mutual positions on various issues, though, the common interest on several global issues and the mutual willingness for coordination and cooperation have provided the BRICS members with some flexibility. Such flexibility is paradoxically the glue that binds the BRICS members together, notwithstanding their mutual differences, as Nikolas Gvosdev writes:

> ... One of the *advantages* of the BRICS process is that it remains a loose association of states with somewhat disparate interests, so no effort is made to force a common position ... But these states have also found a way to disagree on some key issues ... without torpedoing the entire enterprise.[25]

More ambitiously, this grouping of countries made a breakthrough with respect to the establishment of a BRICS development bank in the context of the 2014 Fortaleza summit, which highlights the group's ability to advance their common interest despite their mutual differences in its negotiations process. When India proposed the idea of the "South-South" bank in March 2012, Russia and Brazil expressed their reservations for the lack of a study on its feasibility. However, a special working group was formed in June 2012 to work out the details.

Subsequently, the Chinese government hosted officials, economists, and members of think tanks from BRICS countries in Chongqing to examine further the feasibility of the bank. Moreover, the BRICS finance ministers met in Tokyo around the IMF meetings in October, and later convened another meeting on the sidelines of the G20 summit of the finance ministers in November to discuss the bank idea further.[26]

There was pressure to finalize the proposal for a bank with a projected $50 billion capital at the 2013 Durban summit, and indeed the BRICS summit declaration outlined a bank with an initial $50 billion fund and a currency reserve agreement of $100 billion to weather any future financial crisis. Nonetheless, progress has been quite sluggish on the details about the bank. In fact, the BRICS finance ministers were still not able to decide on a host of sensitive issues concerning the bank, including its location.

That being said, the BRICS members have common interest in benefiting from the bank's mission. The BRICS development bank will benefit India with financial capital for critical domestic infrastructure development. China's interest lies in providing development loans to mobilize Chinese firms for infrastructure development in India and Africa. Also, the BRICS development bank would be beneficial for South Africa for its regional power status in the African continent. Moreover, the BRICS plan to put up an emergency bailout fund of up to $240 billion, which recently gained progress, would be beneficial for the emerging economies to weather any global financial crisis in future. The BRICS development bank and the emergency fund initiatives are similar to the regional measures initiated by other emerging economies, such as the Chiang Mai Initiative Multilateralized, Bancosur, etc., which demonstrate a growing multilayered "thick" international architecture of global governance, but also the ability of BRICS as a summit institution to furnish alternative global governance mechanisms apart from the core institutions of the old establishment.

Stepping back, nonetheless, some caution is warranted about the strength of these contours of transition in the international hierarchy. One explanation of the trajectory of the BRICS points to a comprehensive process of realignment of power, with a new alternative concert of oppositional/adversarial states taking shape. Equally, however, there are strong counter-forces to reconfigured interstate polarization and "overt balancing."[27] The most serious drag on the prospects of the BRICS being a major force in global governance is not resistance by the old order but serious differences of values and interests among the group's members that leave them open to the dismissive comment of being "bricks in search of cement."[28]

Certainly the BRICS have many rivalries over borders, resources, and status. With long and unsettled borders, India and Russia have problems with China. Two of the five are authoritarian states, although all of the three democracies have a tradition of reticence in global democracy-promotion efforts. They are divided on reform of the Security Council, with China's interest lying more in a bipolar than a genuinely multipolar global order, and on the global economic effects of China's currency value.

There are significant economic divergences between the BRICS countries as well. China's highly competitive exports inflict material harm on Brazil. In an environment of growing energy and food demand, China's and India's anxiety about rising prices must be set against Russia being a beneficiary, while Brazil is both a cause and beneficiary of rising food prices. India is vulnerable to internal and exogenous shocks, while South Africa's place at the table may make political sense but is economically less defensible. As featured in a highly publicized article in *Foreign Affairs*, there is a growing pessimism about the overall outlook with respect to the BRICS, as evidenced by signs of diminished growth due to the protracted impact of the financial crisis.[29]

Conclusion

The international system contains an intense push and pull between a consolidated form of institutional cooperation and competitive fragmentation. This duality accentuates very different modes of summitry. At one end of the spectrum, there is a wide number of regional summits that combine in different measures a degree of leader centrism with some technical dimension. However, these summit processes also contain some element of explicit and ongoing choice of membership, with an onus on exclusion. In some cases, countries that have been members are punished for a short or long time. In other cases, projects have been launched as counter-forms of mobilization to established summit processes. In most cases, this set of choices is underscored by some sense of shared identity based on contiguity, with connections built around a framework of neighborhood. Such identities, though, can be consolidated by images of ideological commonality.

BRICS contains some points of similarity with these regional projects in terms of the mix of leader centrism and technical focus, albeit even here there are some interesting departures. For not only is there the absence of a single prime founder—or for that matter, moment of creation—but the technical element took time to come into play. Such parallels nonetheless are trumped by the divergences. As rehearsed, the BRICS lack many of the core components of the regional forums. Not only is there no dimension of contiguity, but also there is no shared sense of regional connection or neighborhood.

The closer point of comparison, as suggested at the outset of the chapter, is not between the BRICS summitry and regional summits, but with global G summits. The fundamental question is less a sense of exclusion (or any form of punishment where for instance there are different voting patterns at the UN), than choices of inclusion. From one perspective, this question centers on whether the emerging big countries would be content to mobilize around the G7/8 (as some type of partnership group) or through the G20 via either IBSA or BRICS. In this competition BRICS has clearly won, with the choice of a larger and more diverse group but also one with more clout with the inclusion of China and Russia. As such, there is a tendency to argue that this is a recipe for greater economic—if not outright strategic—competition.

Such conclusions, through the lens of the relationship of the BRICS to the G20, are tempered. What the BRICS summitry process allows is a hedging of options. The BRICS can use their position as G20 insiders both to contest functional issues of national interest and in leveraging for great fairness and equality in other components of the global system, notably the IMF. At the same time the BRICS forum can be used as part of a diverse array of parallel or "routing around" initiatives.[30] There is a flexibility blending function and form in the BRICS lacking in other summit processes. With regard to form, although professing a shared vision of inclusive global growth, the BRICS are not tied to any fixed agenda. Nor, with their lack of a secretariat and inter-group bureaucracy, is there any fixed timeline. For sure, as seen by the protracted process related to the BRICS development bank (or the moveable dates for the Brazil 2014 BRICS summit), this flexibility can be seen as a weakness. Still, with the stakes high in terms of status, combined with the still impressive material prowess of the membership, there is a huge incentive for the BRICS to be seen as acting in a different way in terms of summitry, not only symbolically but in an instrumentally effective manner at the global level.

Notes

1 For background on the BRICS see Leslie E. Armijo, "The BRICs Countries (Brazil, Russia, India, and China) as Analytical Category: Mirage or Insight?" *Asian Perspective* 31, no. 4 (2007): 7–42; and Andrew F. Cooper and Ramesh Thakur, "The BRICS in the New Global Economic

Geography," in *International Organization and Global Governance*, ed. Thomas G. Weiss and Rorden Wilkinson (London: Routledge).
2. Richard Feinberg, "Institutionalized Summitry: When Leaders Matter," in *Oxford Handbook of Modern Diplomacy*, ed. Andrew F. Cooper, Jorge Heine, and Ramesh Thakur (Oxford: Oxford University Press, 2013).
3. Andrew F. Cooper and Ramesh Thakur, *The Group of Twenty (G20)* (London: Routledge, 2012).
4. Feinberg, "Institutionalized Summitry."
5. Dominic Wilson and Roopa Purushothaman, "Dreaming with BRICs: The Path to 2050," Global Economics Paper no. 99, Goldman Sachs, New York, October 2003, www.goldmansachs.com/our-thinking/archive/archive-pdfs/brics-dream.pdf. See the creation of the BRIC acronym in an earlier, 2001 paper on "The World Needs Better Economic BRICs," Global Economics Paper no. 66, Goldman Sachs, New York, November 2001.
6. CIA, The World Fact Sheet, 2008 estimates, www.cia.gov/library/publications/download/download-2008.
7. Andrew F. Cooper, Timothy M. Shaw, and Gregory Chin, "Emerging Powers and Africa: Implications for/from Global Governance?" *Politikon: South African Journal of Political Studies* 36, no. 1 (2008): 27–44.
8. See Ian Taylor, *The Forum on China–Africa Cooperation (FOCAC)* (London: Routledge, 2012).
9. David Smith, "China Offers $20bn of Loans to African Nations," *Guardian*, 19 July 2012.
10. G8, "Press Briefing by French President Jacques Chirac," Sea Island, 9 June 2004, www.g8.utoronto.ca/summit/2004seaisland/chirac040609.html.
11. Quoted in Hugh Williamson, "Great Powers Present and Future Try to Keep it Casual," *Financial Times*, 4 June 2007.
12. Williamson, "Great Powers Present and Future Try to Keep it Casual."
13. Hugh Williamson, "Emerging Powers Flex Muscles to Push for More Power in the G8," *Financial Times*, 4 July 2007.
14. Quoted in Praful Bidwai, "India's Clumsy Balancing Act," *Asia Times*, 26 June 2007.
15. Chinese Assistant Foreign Minister Tiankai Cui, quoted in F. Chen, "G8 Not Platform for Exerting Pressure," Beijing, 4 June 2007, www.gov.cn/misc/2007-06/04/content_636224.htm.
16. Madhav Nalapat, "G8 Must Make Way for New System," *China Daily*, 7 July 2010.
17. Brendan Vickers, "South Africa: Global Reformism, Global Apartheid and the Heiligendamm Process," in *Emerging Powers in Global Governance: Lessons from the Heiligendamm Process*, ed. Andrew F. Cooper and Agata Antkiewicz (Waterloo: Wilfrid Laurier University Press, 2008), 187.
18. Quoted in Pepe Escobar, "The BRIC Post-Washington Consensus," *Asia Times*, 17 April 2010. See also Andrew F. Cooper, "Consolidated Institutional Cooperation and/or Competitive Fragmentation in the Aftermath of the Financial Crisis," *Whitehead Journal of Diplomacy and International Relations* XIII, no. 2 (2011): 19–31.
19. Yekaterinburg Joint Communiqué, 16 June 2009, archive.kremlin.ru/eng/text/docs/2009/06/217963.shtml.
20. John J. Mearsheimer, "China's Unpeaceful Rise," *Current History* (April 2006): 160–162.

21 Chris Alden and Marco Antonio Vieira, "The New Diplomacy of the South: South Africa, Brazil, India and Trilateralism" *Third World Quarterly* 26, no. 7 (2005): 1079.
22 "Land of Promise", *The Economist*, 12 April 2007.
23 Department of International Relations and Cooperation, Republic of South Africa, "South Africa Welcomes and Supports the UN Security Council's Resolution on No Fly Zone in Libya," 18 March 2011, www.dfa.gov.za/docs/2011/liby0318.html.
24 "South Africa's Foreign Policy, All Over the Place: South Africa is Joining the BRICs Without Much Straw," *The Economist*, 24 March 2011, www.economist.com/node/18447027?story_id=18447027.
25 Nikolas Gvosdev, "The Realist Prism: What the U.S. Can Learn from the BRICS," *World Politics Review*, 22 June 2012, www.worldpoliticsreview.com/articles/12087/the-realist-prism-what-the-u-s-can-learn-from-the-brics.
26 Ananth Krishnan, "China's Caution May Slow BRICS Bank Plan," *The Hindu*, 10 October 2012.
27 Andrew Hurrell, "Hegemony, Liberalism and Global Order: What Space for Would-Be Great Powers?" *International Affairs* 82, no. 1 (2006): 1–19.
28 Joseph Nye, "BRICS Without Mortar," *The Moscow Times*, 7 April 2013, www.themoscowtimes.com/opinion/article/brics-without-mortar/478227.html.
29 Ruchir Sharma, "Broken BRICs: Why the Rest Stopped Rising," *Foreign Affairs* (November/December 2012), www.foreignaffairs.com/articles/138219/ruchir-sharma/broken-brics.
30 Naazneen H. Barma, Ely Ratner, and Steven Weber, "A World Without the West," *The National Interest* 90 (July/August 2007): 23–30; and Gregory Chin, "The Emerging Countries and China in the G20: Reshaping Global Economic Governance," *Studia Diplomatica* LXIII, no. 2 (2010): 105–124.

Part IV
Practitioners' point of view

12 The Summits of the Americas process and regional governance
A reflection

Marc Lortie

- **The 2001 Quebec City Summit of the Americas**
- **Role of civil society in summitry**
- **Indigenous peoples**
- **Regional organizations**
- **Follow-up**
- **Do summits have an impact on regional or global governance?**

As a practitioner of summitry during a diplomatic career that spanned four decades, I realized early on the importance of summits for regional and global governance. In international affairs it is important that leaders be involved from time to time in face-to-face encounters in order to achieve a greater degree of either integration or policy coordination.

My first participation at a summit was at the 1978 G7 Bonn economic summit. On his return to Canada, Prime Minister Pierre Trudeau announced, in the spirit of the Bonn declaration, major cuts to government expenditure without even consulting his Cabinet. In April 2001 at the Summit of the Americas in Quebec City, the acceptance of a "Democratic Clause" as a new criterion to allow nations to participate in the summit process and the agreement on a mandate to negotiate a "Democratic Charter of the Americas" could only have come from leaders gathered in a summit context.

However, summits are not a neat process of governance; they are often unwieldy political events. They take place in a highly political atmosphere with an attendant media circus and often against a backdrop of demonstrations or parallel events where opponents contest the legitimacy of democratically elected leaders. In this chapter, we will look at the Summits of the Americas and try to determine whether there is a future for this institution in regional governance of the hemisphere.

The 2001 Quebec City Summit of the Americas

In 2000, I was appointed "sherpa" by Prime Minister Jean Chrétien, with the responsibility to prepare the third Summit of the Americas, to be held in Quebec City in April 2001. The prime minister was determined to ensure that Canada be a full member of "la gran familia" of the Americas and a full partner in the growing prosperity of the region, as long as democracy and the rule of law prevailed in Latin American countries.

Over the previous two decades, the hemisphere had changed profoundly—politically, with the elimination of military dictatorships and the return to democratic rule, and economically, with the consolidation of market-based economies. The return of democracy and open economies were the political drivers that inspired US President Bill Clinton to invite leaders from the region to meet at a summit in Miami in 1994. It was on this occasion that the concept of a Free Trade Area of the Americas (FTAA) was launched. It was also on this occasion that Chile was officially invited to join the North American Free Trade Agreement (NAFTA), the "fourth amigo," as Prime Minister Chrétien said at the time.

In launching the preparation for the Quebec City Summit, the most serious challenge facing the region was democratic governance. This emerged at the annual June 2000 Organization of American States (OAS) General Assembly that Canada had hosted in the city of Windsor. Foreign ministers were confronted with President Fujimori of Peru's autocratic rule and the dilemma of how to respond. Although Peru was resisting what it called "outside meddling" in its domestic political situation, most leaders in the hemisphere wanted to send a strong signal that dictatorship was something of the past. It was clear that the forthcoming summit would have to address as a prime focus the state of the democratic situation in Peru. Should President Fujimori even be invited to attend the summit?

In setting the agenda for the summit, Prime Minister Chrétien believed it was important to consult his fellow leaders in a meaningful way. He embarked on a series of regional mini-summits with Central American and Caribbean leaders to seek their views and share his vision of greater integration in the region. It was particularly important to consult with leaders of small countries first because they had felt left out of previous summits. At these mini-summits, the leaders of Central America and then the Caribbean requested a free trade agreement with Canada. In both cases, the prime minister agreed to the request. During the same period, Chrétien hosted newly elected President Vicente Fox of Mexico, whose priority was further integration in

North America. Chrétien was much more cautious on the issue of North American integration, favoring a deepened economic relationship with Mexico to counterbalance the overwhelming relationship with the United States. The prime minister traveled to Washington to meet new US President George W. Bush just weeks after his inauguration, to brief him *inter alia* on the status of summit preparations.

Meanwhile, in my role as sherpa I convened a series of regular meetings with my counterparts from all 34 countries in order to develop an agenda and ensure that every one of them felt fully involved in the process. It is at the level of officials that much of the real grinding work of determining agendas, negotiating texts and resolving differences is achieved.

In November 2000, the situation in Peru changed when, on a trip to Japan, President Fujimori decided not to return home and sought asylum in Tokyo. A new chapter in the democratic life of Peru was opening up. For the upcoming summit this meant that a real opportunity was there to be seized to strengthen democratic governance in all the Americas.

In late 2000, four months before the summit, we officials at sherpa meetings developed the concept of a Democratic Clause and the Democratic Charter for the Americas. We decided that the clause should be clear in its formulation and its application: to belong to the summit process and to benefit from greater economic integration, participating states would have to respect the democratic rule of governance. This concept was not in fact new to the Americas. In 1996, when confronted with a potential *coup d'état* in Paraguay, participating countries in Mercosur had developed a democratic clause for all participants, present or future. It had an immediate major impact on the military establishment in Asunción. Likewise in Europe, in the 1980s the European Community had invited Greece, Spain, and Portugal to join its ranks only after they became democratic.

The first time I heard about a Democratic Charter was in December 2000 at a meeting with the new interim prime minister of Peru, Javier Pérez de Cuéllar, former secretary-general of the United Nations. In the course of our consultations he mentioned that he had just introduced in Congress the concept of a democratic charter as part of a new constitution for Peru. For my part, I mentioned the idea of introducing a democratic clause in the summit process. Soon after, Canadian and Peruvian diplomats began working together to engineer both concepts, the clause and the charter, in the Summits of the Americas process. Thus in April 2001 in Quebec City, hemispheric leaders not only agreed to a democratic clause for the summit process, but extended it to all pan-American organizations, including the Inter-American Development Bank (IDB) and the OAS. In addition, leaders instructed their foreign ministers to negotiate on an urgent basis a Democratic Charter of the Americas in order to consolidate and strengthen democratic governance in the region.

Ironically, the charter was accepted by foreign ministers in Lima, Peru, on 11 September 2001. Initially the date was chosen to coincide with the 1973 Pinochet coup in Chile, but the world changed that day, as terrorists attacked New York City and Washington. At the morning meeting, just as the dramatic news was arriving of the destruction of the World Trade Center, US Secretary of State Colin Powell in his speech to delegates expressed the view that the new charter would constitute the best answer the hemisphere could send to the terrorists attacking his country. The Democratic Charter was thus adopted unanimously in a mood of tense emotion, and to all those at the meeting there was a keen sense of history being made.

Role of civil society in summitry

The last two decades have seen a proliferation of nongovernmental organizations (NGOs) in most fields of activity, including human rights, indigenous rights, the environment, and many other important social and economic issues. In democracies, NGOs or civil society play an important role in understanding the major preoccupations and challenges facing a society. The return to democracy in many countries in the Americas was due in large part to the active role played by civil society.

Democratic politics demand a consensus-building approach, and reaching out to civil society helps build that consensus. For foreign policymakers it has become important to engage civil society in formal consultations on a wide variety of issues. Some degree of tension or frustration often emerges which is to be expected. Policymakers sometimes believe that they spend too much time in consultations, and civil society representatives believe that their perspective is not sufficiently taken into account by governments, but the dialogue is helpful to democratic governance. On occasion NGOs refuse to enter into consultations with governments and prefer to organize parallel events and issue their own communiqué. This is also part of democratic governance.

To develop a plan of action relevant to citizens and leading to regional governance, it is important to consult widely with business groups and labor organizations, and non-state actors such as think tanks, human rights groups, environmental groups, academics, or church groups. For example, Transparency International made an important contribution to the Summits of the Americas process by developing a series of criteria to prevent corruptive practices creeping into government procurement transactions. On political rights and fundamental freedoms, it was essential to consult with organizations such as Amnesty International, Human Rights Watch, the Carter Center, or the Inter-American Commission for Human Rights. These organizations were helpful to the summit process in addressing the challenge of consolidating good governance and democratic practices. During the preparation of the Quebec Summit, we consulted on a regular basis with more than 100 groups throughout Canada and more than 50 internationally. It was a time-consuming and sometimes onerous process but it was vital to the success of the enterprise.

Regional governance requires such consensus-building consultations with non-state actors. It has become important to reach out to civil society in the preparation of a summit. These consultations lead to a greater degree of acceptance of the decisions taken by leaders.

Despite our success in engaging civil society in a productive and meaningful dialogue, however, the anti-globalization movement, supported by some trade unionists and other activists, set out to create a major protest during the Quebec City Summit. These protesters were determined to express their opposition to trade liberalization and what they called the "neo-liberal" economic model of development. The majority of NGOs had intended to organize a peaceful march, hold a parallel summit, and issue an alternate communiqué, showing greater emphasis on human values. However, the presence of a small but highly organized group of unruly demonstrators attracted immense media attention and overshadowed both the parallel summit and the summit itself. As the summit began, the challenge for organizers was to contain the anti-globalization demonstrators whose objective was to perturb the summit just as they had derailed the World Trade Organization ministerial meeting in Seattle in 1999. Direct confrontation between this small minority and the police force dominated media reporting and the broadcast news. Major demonstrations at international summits had become the norm, diverting media attention and creating a significant security challenge for host governments.

Indigenous peoples

Given the fact that the Americas is a multi-ethnic and multicultural region with over 700 different indigenous peoples officially recognized by governments, and that most of them are part of the poorest and most marginalized streams of the hemisphere's population, we felt it was essential to integrate them in the planning of the Quebec City Summit. I discussed the idea with the heads of Canada's five National Aboriginal Organizations, who took the lead in the organization of the first Indigenous Leaders' Summit of the Americas. The results of that summit were communicated to the heads of state and government by its official host, Phil Fontaine, then national chief of Canada's Assembly of First Nations. This process was then repeated for successive summits that took place in Argentina and Trinidad and Tobago.

Regional organizations

Reaching out to NGOs and indigenous peoples was important in the Quebec City Summit process, but working closely with the established regional organizations was also a *sine qua non* requirement to achieve any degree of regional governance. These included the OAS, the IDB, the Pan American Health Organization (PAHO), the Caribbean Community (CARICOM), the Economic Commission for Latin America and the Caribbean (ECLAC), the Americas directorate of the World Bank, and the Development Bank of Latin America (CAF). The degree of knowledge about hemispheric issues in these organizations is unsurpassed. The challenge was to ensure that all of them worked together in a summit context. They all have their own mandate, traditions, and structure of governance. Summitry forces these organizations to adapt to a new environment. They are more than willing to do so as long as their contribution is sought and recognized. It is the role of the host country to engage them and to create, if necessary, a new structure to include them in the preparation and the follow-up of the summit. This was a key element in the success of the Quebec City Summit: every single regional organization considered the summit declaration and plan of action as the reference point in establishing its priorities.

Follow-up

To have an impact on regional governance, summits must have a system in place to ensure the implementation of the decisions taken. The Miami and Santiago Summits served as precedents for the Quebec City Summit. Sherpas know that the follow-up exercise constitutes the accountability factor that lends credibility to the whole summit process. As we have seen, the host country has a responsibility to set the agenda in consultation with its partners. The host country also has the responsibility to reach out to civil society and to engage regional organizations. The implementation phase remains crucial and must be done in a structured way. The Summits of the Americas process has developed such a system under the auspices of the OAS, and a special division within the organization has been assigned the responsibility to look into the implementation of the commitments of the various countries.

Do summits have an impact on regional or global governance?

In my opinion, the dynamic of leaders meeting periodically to discuss global or regional issues is irreplaceable in the modern management of international affairs. Summits matter, and exclusion from them undermines leaders. The recent suspension of Russia from the G7/8 summit process will have over time a negative impact for President Vladimir Putin. He and his country will be more isolated in world affairs.

Summits are unique occasions to tackle important international issues. For example, it is through summitry that apartheid in South Africa was stigmatized. In 1988 Canadian Prime Minister Brian Mulroney used his position of host of a Commonwealth summit, La Francophonie, and the G7 to orchestrate world condemnation of South Africa that led to the eventual release of Nelson Mandela. On the issue of economic assistance to the least developed countries, a series of successive summits tackled the problem of debt relief for the poorest of the poor, and proposed and implemented solutions such as debt forgiveness from donor countries. At the 2002 G8 Kananaskis Summit, leaders adopted the Africa Action Plan and injected new money in support of the New Partnership for Africa's Development (NEPAD). It was the beginning of a more trusted relationship with African countries. At the 2010 G8 Summit through the Muskoka Initiative more than US$7 billion was earmarked to mobilize global action to reduce maternal and infant mortality and improve the health of mothers and children in the world's poorest countries. In the 1970s and 1980s, annual world economic summits (G7) prevented the rise of economic nationalism and the resurgence of the kind of protectionist measures that had affected the world so dramatically in the 1930s. In 2008, French President Nicolas Sarkozy, in his capacity as president of the European Council (a body of the European Union), convinced President Bush to host a high-level meeting of world leaders to deal with the serious financial crisis facing the world. The end result was to create a much-needed approach to coordinate economic policies in an orderly fashion. The G20 was born.

On a regional basis, it is through summits that greater cooperation or integration has taken and can take place. In North America, in order to achieve any major agreement with the United States, it is essential that the White House be engaged. Prime Minister Mulroney was a master at involving US Presidents Ronald Reagan and George H.W. Bush in an effective effort to achieve Canadian objectives deemed of national interest. It was through presidential involvement that a Canada–United States free trade agreement and a treaty on acid rain were signed in the late 1980s. In Europe, greater integration follows a pattern of acute crises being resolved through regular summitry. In South America, Southern Common Market (Mercosur) summits have generated greater regional integration and the same could be said in Asia with the Association of Southeast Asian Nations (ASEAN) summits. In the case of the Summits of the Americas, there is no doubt that the first three meetings (Miami in 1994, Santiago in 1998, and Quebec City in 2001) provided a new vision of a more integrated hemisphere from the Arctic to Tierra del Fuego, and new norms on democratic governance were agreed upon.

However, summits also have their limitations. The grand design of greater economic integration in the hemisphere through an FTAA could not be rescued despite several leaders' meetings over the last decade. After years of negotiations (1995–2003), there were too many obstacles to be resolved and leaders were preoccupied by more pressing issues, and so talks were abandoned. The remark made by the then President of Uruguay Jorge Luis Batlle to President Bush in Quebec City in 2001 is still valid: the United States can import all the oil it needs from Venezuela, but Uruguayan cattle farmers are still awaiting free trade with North America. In the future, governments would be well advised to re-launch a project of economic benefits for the region.

Summits are political events and there is great pressure to produce concrete results. Public opinion and the media want results and it is not possible to show important results year after year. However, summits are not insignificant in the political life of leaders. President Jean-Bertrand Aristide of Haiti thought that merely receiving an invitation to attend the Quebec City Summit was an endorsement of his policies. He was shocked when leaders issued a specific resolution demanding that he implement promised democratic reforms immediately. Something comparable happened to Italian Prime Minister Silvio Berlusconi at the 2011 Cannes G20 Summit. French President Sarkozy and German Chancellor Angela Merkel joined forces with US President Barack Obama in demanding that Italy reduce its public debt. Despite his strong defense, Berlusconi returned home humiliated and defeated, and his prime ministership soon ended.

To achieve global or regional governance, trust and confidence between participating states and leaders must exist. Without that special ingredient regional governance cannot be achieved. In 2001 in Quebec City this trust existed and all leaders, with one notable exception, agreed with both the political declaration and the plan of action for greater coordination and integration in the hemisphere. President Hugo Chávez of Venezuela could not subscribe to the expression "representative democracy"; he favored "participative democracy." Chávez argued that citizens must be able to talk directly to their president, not through institutions. Neither could he agree to the FTAA as a way to further economic integration in the hemisphere. His approach did not augur well for the rest of the decade in the region. Although the élan of the first summits may have been lost in recent years, the hemisphere has witnessed the creation of a network of new sub-regional summits, the latest one being CELAC, gathering all countries of the Americas, including Cuba, with the exception of the United States and Canada.

Summitry leads to better understanding, stronger coordination and greater interdependence between nations, but summitry demands leadership and vision from leaders. In the case of the Americas, the process of summitry remains the occasion for active participation by parliamentarians, indigenous peoples, civil society, and business leaders, whose contribution strengthens cooperation and democratic governance. I would also argue that even if today's focus has shifted towards the Pacific region, the Summits of the Americas' value resides in being the only forum where the United States and Canada join the other democratic nations of the hemisphere to examine regional issues and strengthen cooperation with a view to creating prosperity. In the last decade democracy has been strengthened in many countries of the hemisphere and although serious challenges of poverty, inequality and social justice persist, the region has prospered under market-based economies. The summit process was conceived to celebrate the return of democracy in the Americas and to lead the way to greater prosperity. We should not let this institution falter because of a resurgence of a few populist regimes. At the same time, in an era of global communications the onus is on all governments in the Americas to find new ways and means to continue promoting democracy, the rule of law, and economic cooperation with a view to creating greater well-being and prosperity for the citizens of the hemisphere. Leadership is required.

13 Some thoughts on summit proliferation and regional governance

Carlos Portales

Summits have become a routine instrument of diplomacy in the Americas since the end of the Cold War. As of 1994, the Summit of the Americas process was able for a while to revive the old idea of Pan-Americanism: new policies were adopted, new institutions were created, and a far-reaching attempt was undertaken to establish a hemispheric system of free trade.

At about the same time, other summit processes emerged in the hemisphere and beyond. In Latin America, there was the Rio Group in 1986 and the Community of Latin American and Caribbean Nations (CELAC) in 2010; in the former Spanish and Portuguese colonies of Latin America, Ibero-American Summits have been held since 1991; in South America, the process initiated by Brazil in 2000 became the Union of South American Nations (UNASUR) in 2008. There have also been sub-regional initiatives, including the Central American Integration System (SICA), the Caribbean Community (CARICOM), the Andean Community, the Southern Common Market (Mercosur), as well as other groupings, like the Bolivarian Alliance for the Peoples of Our America (ALBA) and the Pacific Alliance with regular summits.

As a result, ten overlapping types of summits have taken place: one pan-American (without Cuba), one Latin American and Caribbean (without the United States and Canada), one Ibero-American (Spain, Portugal, and their former colonies), one South American (12 countries), four "sub-regional" processes and two "trans-sub-regional" groups. The total number of summit meetings among countries in the region increased from 31 between 1947 and 1989, to 303 from 1990 to 2012.

As a practitioner of summitry for more than two decades, I observed both the strength of this new tool of modern diplomacy and its potential to enhance regional governance, as well as the problems that have arisen concerning implementation and the diminishing returns resulting from proliferation and overlapping. I will highlight both aspects.

The Summits of the Americas process was initiated by the United States at the presidential level. The Organization of American States (OAS) was left aside in the preparations for the first summit in Miami. It was the US National Security staff who took the lead in assuring the participation of Latin American presidencies and foreign ministries. Only after the second summit, in Santiago, did the OAS play a more important role in coordinating the implementation. Afterwards, a Joint Summit Working Group (JSWG) was formed in Washington with 12 international organizations, in response to the need for a more coherent follow-up of summit commitments and in order to coordinate international tools for cooperation.

The pattern of decision making typical of the Ibero-American Summits and the Rio Group Summits, both more politically focused than other institutions, tends to concentrate on foreign ministries. The Ibero-American process was able to develop several areas of cooperation between Spain and Portugal and the Luso–Spanish American countries, but ideological differences began to vitiate the meetings, as was the case at the seventeenth summit in Santiago in 2007.

The Rio Group developed a voice for Latin America in the United Nations (UN). During the 1990s it cooperated in strengthening democracy in a manner comparable to what the inter-American process achieved, but here again differences emerged during the 2000s. The Rio Group Summits gradually came to include all Latin American and Caribbean countries. Inclusiveness would supplant strong consensus on principles as the basis for the new CELAC Summits that ultimately replaced the Rio Group Summits.

The most important benefits of establishing a periodic summit process are: to create spaces for dialogue, to foster agreement on common policies, and to help prevent/solve problems. The frequency of these opportunities for dialogue varies. Latin American heads of state attend four to six summits per year in comparison with three to four for Caribbean heads of government, while the leaders of the United States and Canada take part in only one meeting every three years with their Latin American and Caribbean counterparts. Common understanding is more easily forged among Latin American leaders, while the relationships with the US president and with the Canadian prime minister have been more formal.

The possibility for summits to exercise "peer pressure" very much depends on the social networks at work behind the scenes. Thus, during the twentieth summit of the Rio Group in Santo Domingo in 2008, the involvement of Latin American and Caribbean leaders facilitated a solution to the dispute triggered by the Colombian bombardment of the Ecuadorian border. The conflict prevention/resolution function has also been a feature of the UNASUR summits, particularly in the case of the first UNASUR Summit in Santiago (2008), which dealt with the struggle between the central and regional governments in Bolivia. The second and third UNASUR Summits in Quito and Bariloche (2009), moreover, were instrumental in the discussions concerning the regional effects of the announced project to enlarge the US military presence in Colombia. Direct diplomacy among heads of state was decisive in seeking accommodation and avoiding conflict. Other UNASUR special meetings were called to deal with crises in Ecuador, Paraguay, and Venezuela, and to support (with unequal results) the governments of these countries. In practice, UNASUR has now replaced the OAS as a crisis management forum for South American countries.

The purpose of summits, as stated in the Introduction to this volume, is to allow leaders to identify central issues and to set a course of action for national bureaucracies and international organizations. Certain countries influence the agenda-setting process in specific ways, starting with the *originators* of the summit process.

The Summits of the Americas process began with US President Bill Clinton's invitation to renew the Inter-American system. This had a major impact for a ten-year period that saw strong US involvement, generalized support for democratic regimes, and widespread acceptance of market principles and fiscal restraint in economic policies. To a large extent, this initial success of hemispheric summitry was possible thanks to the engagement of US diplomacy.

The Ibero-American Summits were launched in 1991 by Spain in collaboration with Mexico. Historical and cultural affinities between the Iberian countries and their former colonies in the Americas served as the basis for a new foreign policy platform for the Spanish democracy at a time of business expansion. For many years it was the sole regional summit in which Cuba was allowed to participate. Not only does Spain act as a mover in the process, but it bears most of the financial burden. Furthermore, Madrid is where the headquarters of the summit entities (the Ibero-American Cooperation Secretariat, and the Ibero-American General Secretariat) and of other Ibero-American organizations are located. Since the beginning of the twenty-first century, the relative importance of this summit has diminished because of the emergence of Latin and South American summitry and Spain's economic crisis.

UNASUR Summits stem from a Brazilian initiative in 2000, the South American Summits, which was replaced in 2004 by the South

American Community of Nations, whose mission was to encourage convergence among Mercosur, the Andean Community, Chile, Guyana, and Suriname. This process was modified following a proposal made by Venezuelan President Hugo Chávez at the Energy Summit of Margarita Island (2006): the project was transformed into a more political one and trade integration goals were left aside. Negotiations among presidents were decisive. Brazil and Venezuela have been important players in this South American game. The role of the high-profile, but weak, UNASUR secretary-general remains to be clarified, as agreement on nominations has been hard to reach and the secretariat's budgeting and staffing process has been slow.

The CELAC Summit process, created in 2010, has resulted from the convergence of the already all-inclusive Rio Group (headed at the time by Mexico) and the Brazilian Summits of Latin America and the Caribbean (CALC) on integration and development. Since this new process did not have a single originator but grew out of a compromise, single-country influence is more diffuse. CELAC lacks a permanent secretariat and is managed by successive pro tempore presidents.

Along with the originators of summitry, summit *organizers* also play an important role. Countries that host the meetings propose the central theme of the agenda (not necessarily the centerpieces of the debates), finance the organization of the event, and become the temporary secretariat or head of the intergovernmental group in charge of following up on summit decisions. Of the 71 regional summits held from 1986 to 2014 in the Americas, 53 have been organized by only 11 countries: Chile and Brazil (seven summits each); Argentina, Mexico, and Peru (five each); Bolivia, Colombia, and Venezuela (four each); Ecuador, Panama, Paraguay, and Spain (three each). Large and medium-sized American countries—as well as Spain—tend to take on the organization of summits because this enhances their government's influence in regional affairs and because a summit may serve to endorse national policies.

Summits, especially the Summits of the Americas, have been instrumental in setting agendas and creating negotiation and coordination mechanisms crucial for implementation. However, they have been effective only to the extent that a basic consensus was maintained, as shown by several examples. The Inter-American Democratic Charter was not fully applied because views on democracy became much more controversial after it was adopted. The creation of a "special rapporteur for freedom of expression"—a summit mandate—was followed by political conflicts over the role of this new institution within the inter-American human rights system. The new concept of security in the region was never fully implemented because of differences on drug issues.

The Ibero-American Summits have had more limited goals, but they have established a network of cooperation that includes a great number of ministerial and high-level meetings, in addition to spaces for business and cultural cooperation. Nevertheless, the decision to hold meetings every two years rather than once a year may reflect the limits of this process. CELAC, meanwhile, is still in its early years. It has a recognized voice in a region where different outlooks exist, but it lacks negotiation frameworks and structured follow-up mechanisms.

Each summit process thus has its own mandates and implementation schemes. Small countries and even some medium-sized ones lack the resources to participate fully in these processes. International organizations often cooperate in implementation, but they read the mandates through the lenses of their governing bodies (composed of countries that in some cases have not participated in the summits), have different priorities, and do not follow "direct instructions" of the summits' leaders. These situations limit the possibilities of coordinating regional governance.

There is a great deal of overlap among different summit processes. Parallel ministerial and high-level meetings cover similar issues. There are 15 ministerial meetings in the Summits of the Americas process, 25 ministerial and high-level meetings in the Ibero-American Summits, 12 Ministerial Councils in UNASUR, and ten less formalized ministerial meetings held within CELAC. Among the 32 issue areas that these ministerial and high-level meetings examine, three areas are covered by all five ministerial processes, five areas by four processes, eight by three processes, and five by two processes. There are only 11 areas where no overlap exists. To say the least, this complex setting increases the possibilities of duplication, contradiction, and lack of coordination.

Summits have been widely used instruments for conducting international relations in the Americas in the last quarter of a century. They have tried to enhance regional governance by taking advantage of "smaller worlds." To be effective, summits need to achieve consensus on objectives and have the ability to implement them. This may happen on occasion, but the design of these new instruments, the continued support of the leaders for mobilizing domestic and international resources, and the capacity to implement agreements are absolutely critical. The proliferation of summits and parallel procedures of implementation has made some of their goals incompatible and effective action more difficult. Limited resources, including bureaucratic ones, have been stretched because of overlapping institutions. On the other hand, frequent dialogue among heads of state has strengthened socialization among them and, in many cases, facilitated conflict resolution.

Summits can therefore have a significant impact on regional governance, provided there are clear common goals and member states mobilize their "political energy" in order to implement decisions. The erosion of their commitment to realize the goals they have agreed on may lead to conclusions like the one President José Mujica of Uruguay formulated when a journalist asked him what decisions the heads of state had made at the last Mercosur Summit: "I do not know ... We agree on a statement." We might add that at the last Summit of the Americas not even a final statement was agreed upon.

14 Conclusion

Summitry and governance—an assessment

Gordon Mace, Jean-Philippe Thérien, Diana Tussie and Olivier Dabène

- The functions of summitry
- The future of summitry

Regular summits of heads of state and government, except for the Commonwealth, did not exist before the first oil crisis of 1973. Summitry became a common feature of multilateral cooperation as of 1975, when presidents and prime ministers found it useful to meet regularly in order to address vital problems requiring prompt attention in turbulent times and for which the large-scale multilateralist machinery was too slow. Regular summits also became possible because of fundamental transformations in communications technologies and in the practice of diplomacy itself. Indeed, world leaders increasingly saw themselves as diplomats-in-chief; they wanted to overcome the bureaucratic gridlock, respond to specific issues in a timely manner, and assert their leadership.

Forty years on, summitry has become a fixture of international affairs and has spread from the global arena to regional forums all over the world. In the Americas, for instance, leaders of mid-sized to large states generally attend between four and eight summits each year. Summits typically end with a communiqué, a group photo, and the assurance that the meeting has been quite useful and extremely productive. However, has summitry really contributed to governance and, if so, in what ways?

The literature on summitry, as highlighted in the Introduction to this volume, is rich and diversified and includes high-quality case studies and historical narratives. What this book adds to the corpus is a hitherto neglected comparative focus. We have used the comparative approach to try to understand how summitry has or has not impacted regional governance. To this end, contributors were asked to center their analyses on a number of functions that the literature attributes to summitry: dialogue/socialization, agenda setting/orientation, negotiation/coordination, and legitimation. The next part of the conclusion highlights our main findings with regard to these functions. This will be followed by some reflections on the future of summitry.

The functions of summitry

Socialization and dialogue are certainly the functions best fulfilled by summitry in all contexts. In Chapter 10, Emmanuel Mourlon-Druol reminds us that the model for the Rambouillet Summit was the fireside chat, where like-minded leaders who had previously had little face-to-face contact would meet in a relatively intimate setting to discuss world affairs and initiate actions. Such intimacy was somehow lost as the G7 became the G8 and the G20 was created. The idea persisted, however, that these summits provided an opportunity for leaders to get to know each other, exchange ideas, and better understand the worldviews of their peers.

Furthermore, in his discussion of the "ASEAN Way" in Chapter 9, Richard Stubbs shows how informality, common values, and consensus building characterize summitry inside the Association of Southeast Asian Nations (ASEAN). Consensus in ASEAN does not necessarily mean unanimity, but it does presuppose extensive consultation before decisions are made. The longevity of leaders and the importance of dynastic political families are also important contributing factors to the socialization process in ASEAN summits.

In the Americas, similarities exist between the cases of the Southern Common Market (Mercosur) and the Caribbean Community (CARICOM), two institutions that began as trade agreements, and where dialogue and socialization are now permanent features. In Chapter 6, Marcelo de Almeida Medeiros and his co-authors show how ideological solidarity was a central component of the socialization process in Mercosur between 2003 and 2014, when member states were led by left-leaning presidents. With regard to CARICOM, Jessica Byron in Chapter 5 underlines how summits act as an important space for dialogue and socialization because these meetings serve to transmit community traditions and values to incoming participants. Interestingly enough, this involves inviting newcomers to present their visions of CARICOM and to exchange with other leaders ideas about community goals and practices. Kindred interests can thus be articulated in global forums even though a unified front may be unattainable.

Socialization remains an important dimension of summitry even when values and interests collide, as was true of the Summits of the

Americas process from 2004 to 2014. Gordon Mace and Jean-Philippe Thérien point out in Chapter 3 that the last two hemispheric summits at least made possible a civil exchange of views between President Barack Obama and the leaders of the Bolivarian Alliance for the Peoples of Our America (ALBA), despite fundamental differences regarding inter-American relations. This divergence of approach was probably one of the factors leading to the creation of the Union of South American Nations (UNASUR) and the Community of Latin American and Caribbean Nations (CELAC) as alternative regional forums. It is telling, however, that hemispheric dialogue and socialization have remained strong enough to contribute to the recent reversal of US policy regarding Cuba. This historic shift, along with Cuba's participation in the 2015 Summit of the Americas in Panama, is bound to reshape inter-American relations.

Indeed, all the case studies included in this volume demonstrate that the experience of summitry has significantly helped to advance the functions of socialization and dialogue. Especially when confronting crises, summits are effective diplomatic vehicles for gaining formal validation of policies and catalyzing the policy process, but they have not met with the same degree of success when it comes to agenda setting and orientation. Most summits naturally end with the publication of a communiqué summarizing the discussions and highlighting the points of agreement, but few of them make public a plan of action or even an overview of follow-up measures.

This is understandable in the case of the Brazil, Russia, India, China and South Africa group (the BRICS)[1] and G20 summits, because these meetings bring together member states evolving in different contexts and having diverse interests. In these instances, as Andrew Cooper notes in Chapter 11, summits serve to propose strategies or convey messages concerning—in the case of the BRICS, for example—a global transition to a new world order. This also applies to the G7 and G8 meetings, even if membership is more limited. However, according to Mourlon-Druol, what makes G7/8/20 summits distinctive is their psychological dimension. During economic or political crises, such as the global financial meltdown of 2008–09, these summits played a central role in catalyzing coordinated action among member countries and in fostering trust in the international community.

At the regional level, there exists a broad spectrum of experiences. At one end are the Central American Summits and the North American Leaders' Summits, which, according to Kevin Parthenay and Greg Anderson—in Chapters 7 and 8, respectively—are somewhat dysfunctional with regard to agenda setting and orientation because the leaders of the two regions have never considered them major forums for integration. Variable geometry and pragmatic disinterest in Central America, and asymmetry in North America are among the reasons for the weak impact of these summits on regional governance.

At the other end of the spectrum, one finds the Summits of the Americas process and, perhaps, the emerging summits of the Pacific Alliance, which are in a special category with regard to agenda setting and orientation. In both instances, summits generally end with a declaration and a plan of action designed to guide the in-between-summits process. As we suggest below, plans of action certainly do not guarantee implementation, but they do provide a roadmap for civil servants once summits are concluded.

As to the function of negotiation/coordination, former sherpa Marc Lortie points out that summitry is far from a neat process of governance. The apparent harmony displayed at summit meetings masks the grueling consultation and negotiation work that officials have to accomplish beforehand. In some cases, the leaders' meeting will approve a creatively worded initiative that reduces conflict or postpones it until the implementation stage. This diplomatic procedure avoids the twin evils of confrontation and stalemate, allowing for degrees of consensus and incremental progress. Sometimes, as Diana Tussie demonstrates in Chapter 4 with regard to UNASUR, delicate top-level negotiations are conducted, potentially altering the balance of contending forces *within* countries and thus directly affecting regional governance. This was the situation from 2008 to 2010, which she identifies as UNASUR's "golden period," when the union had to manage crises brought on by domestic troubles in Bolivia and Ecuador. In both cases, leaders successfully supervised mediation efforts that had a clear impact on regional stability.

Summits rarely have to turn themselves into crisis management committees, but this has happened a few times over the past 40 years. The negotiations that precede summits generally do not involve the same degree of drama and urgency as did the UNASUR experience or certain situations that at one time or another have arisen in the G8 and the G20. However, negotiation has always been an intrinsic part of summitry, and the way in which it is conducted generally determines the success or failure of summits.

A smooth and efficient negotiation process, however, is only one of the conditions needed to ensure a successful summit. Another essential factor concerns coordination—more specifically, the implementation of summit decisions by regional and national bureaucracies. It is in this area that summitry has been the most deficient. Most contributions included in this volume point in the same direction: there is a wide gap between the objectives laid out in summit communiqués and concrete results. Among the reasons for this implementation problem, one of the most important is certainly the lack of resources. This conclusion is especially obvious when summits have produced clear and detailed plans of action, as was the case with the Summits of the Americas, but it is also documented in other instances, such as Mercosur and CARICOM. Undoubtedly, repeated lack of implementation undermines the contribution that summitry can make to regional governance and widens the credibility gap.

The function of legitimation, finally, can be examined in relation to two of its primary dimensions. The first concerns the diffusion of norms and values, a process that is particularly strong at the regional level. In fact, summits are often considered the most visible manifestation of a regional project as well as a vehicle for norm generation and transmission, and this is particularly the case in the Americas. Through the Democratic Charter, the Free Trade Area of the Americas project, and the concept of multidimensional security, to cite a few examples, the Summits of the Americas process has been a major norm entrepreneur and a promoter of values such as democracy, human rights, free trade, and multifaceted security. Summitry as practiced by Mercosur and CARICOM was also instrumental in extending and interiorizing the idea of democracy. Meanwhile, the summits of UNASUR promoted the concept of regional stability. Overall, summits spread an ethos of collective identity and then create traction for policies that strengthen that identity. If one considers the example of CARICOM, summitry also served to promote shared values and the need for a Caribbean Community itself. In a word, summits provide leverage for specific policies and thus constitute significant instruments of regional governance.

Although summitry quite successfully generated norms and promoted values for most regionalist projects, especially in the Americas, it was much less effective with respect to democratic access, the other dimension of legitimation.[2] In this connection, Jan Aart Scholte correctly remarks that summits are executive clubs *par excellence* and epitomes of top-down governance, but this is not to deny the progress made, most notably by the Council of Europe, Mercosur, and the Summits of the Americas process. In each instance, documents are made available before the summit, resources are deployed to facilitate the participation of organizations in summit meetings, and support is made available for civil society participation in regional activities between summits.

Still, by and large, all summit experiences have left the impression that there is a "democratic deficit." Civil society organizations complain about limited access, and parliamentarians tend to be excluded from the process—one rare exception being Mercosur, where governors from federal countries and selected legislators are invited to summit meetings. This general lack of openness has to do with, among other factors, the longstanding political tradition in many countries of treating foreign policy as the private reserve of the executive and, more and more, of presidents and prime ministers. Another factor is the dearth of resources to support civil society participation. This is particularly true when summits include numerous countries located in a large and diversified geographical area, such as Asia or the Americas, an environment that makes it difficult for civil society to represent all social groups and interests and to effectively influence decision makers. Finally, civil society organizations often complain of the lack of interest on the part of government representatives when they meet face to face at summit events. As Scholte observes in Chapter 1, new structures or practices such as scrutiny by national parliaments, suprastate parliaments, and multi-stakeholder agencies would be needed if governments ever chose to encourage more democratic participation in summits.

This overview of the functions assigned to summitry indicates that its contribution to international and regional governance is uneven. On one hand, summitry has been particularly successful with regard to socialization. By bringing together heads of state and government on a regular basis to exchange views, summits contribute to improving governance; they create occasions for face-to-face contacts where leaders get to know each other and come to better understand the context and rationale behind the views expressed by each member state. As a result, summits help defuse conflicts, prevent problematic situations from becoming unmanageable, facilitate collective decision making, and provide traction for policies.

On the other hand, summitry's record is less positive when it comes to orientation and coordination. Summits have not been particularly useful for managing regional affairs and paving the way for collective action. The implementation of summit decisions has generally been a failure, and, with few exceptions, summits have produced limited concrete results.

Finally, with regard to legitimation, the glass is only half full. Summitry has achieved some success in the area of norm diffusion and the transmission of values, but it needs to do more to bring about a real opening in favor of democratic participation. At the same time, however, legitimacy requirements vary from region to region and from state to state, and there is no homogeneous view of legitimacy within civil society. The predominant view among researchers and policy practitioners alike is that civil society participation will increase the democratic legitimacy of global governance, yet it seems very difficult to make any sort of generalization about the role that civil society has played or should play in summits.

The future of summitry

Summits of heads of state and government have now become part of political leaders' toolbox for managing international affairs. Though it is clear that summits help to spread an ethos and disseminate ideas, their overall contribution to governance is mixed. The simple fact of meeting face to face with other leaders is certainly a positive element of summit diplomacy, but as far as outcomes are concerned, measuring the direct impact of summit decisions on the conduct of international relations remains an elusive goal. Despite this difficulty, however, Richard Feinberg is probably right to argue that because of the emergence of multipolarity, summitry has become "a vital feature of modern diplomacy." This means, Feinberg adds, that summitry "is here to stay."[3]

That said, summitry faces a number of challenges, three of which are particularly important in regions such as Asia and the Americas, which are characterized by multiple institutions. The first of these challenges is overlap. Granted, Olivier Dabène's findings in Chapter 2 suggest that the problem of overlap may not be highly significant, at least when only agenda is taken into account. His analysis of the summit meetings of Mercosur, UNASUR, and the Andean Community for the period 2000–13 shows that there is more complementarity than overlap with regard to these institutions' respective agendas. Dabène's analysis thus supports the view that the increasing diversity of summits may engender what has been called "regional governance complexes."[4] However, Carlos Portales, drawing on his experience as Chilean sherpa for hemispheric, regional, and transregional summit meetings, suggests in Chapter 13 that proliferation of such meetings is indeed a threat in Latin America. Leaders' participation in various types of summits raises the very real possibility of duplication and even contradiction among the positions adopted by the states. In short, overlap may not be an inescapable curse of summit diplomacy, but it is certainly a permanent risk.

Another challenge is the cost entailed by a state's participation in summits. In 2015, for example, the Mexican president is scheduled to take part in no fewer than seven regional and international summits, and the president of Brazil in at least nine such events. These numbers do not include bilateral meetings. The cost must be measured not only in time and money, but also in the bureaucratic resources needed to formulate the country's positions and plan the strategy for each meeting. Furthermore, as the number of summits increases, involvement in summitry risks diverting leaders' attention away from important domestic and international problems.

Finally, there is the challenge of democracy, an issue discussed earlier in relation to the legitimation function. It can be argued, of course, that summit participants are elected leaders and, as such, represent their populations' values and points of view. Yet the fact remains that if citizens knew—in addition to summitry's problem-solving capacity, efficiency and contribution to stability—that they were truly being listened to, summits would be even more effective. Outside Europe, however, mechanisms promoting legislative or civil society participation in summitry are extremely limited and not very effective. While business leaders, through business forums, often have direct access to leaders during summits, the same cannot be said about legislators, subnational governments, and civil society organizations. If summitry is to gain greater legitimacy as an instrument for regional and international governance, the process clearly needs to become more democratic and create more opportunities for all the stakeholders to be heard.

Nevertheless, all the case studies in this volume, with the exception of those dealing with North America and Central America, conclude that summits have had a positive effect on governance, at least as a space for dialogue. By enabling face-to-face meetings between leaders, summits have been able to defuse threats, foster trust, and promote stability, particularly in times of crisis. However, if summits are to contribute more effectively to governance, particularly at the regional level, certain conditions must be fulfilled.

As both practitioners' chapters have pointed out, for summits to be effective, a basic requirement is that leaders must share the core components of a common vision on how to address problems. A lack of confidence and of a common vision clearly debilitates summitry, as evidenced by the Summits of the Americas process after 2004. Another requirement is leadership as to where a region should be headed. Given their resources and expertise, larger states and originators of summitry processes have a special responsibility in this connection. These actors are the movers of summitry, and the process needs their constant interest and involvement to move forward. Finally, following up on summit decisions is essential if summitry is to succeed and improve governance. Participating governments must have, and maintain, the political energy necessary to implement summit decisions and facilitate the ever-growing politics of interdependence.

Summits have become an institutionalized instrument of regional and global politics. Our comparative analysis shows that their contribution to governance is multifaceted. Depending on context and circumstances, summitry frames discourses, charts courses of action, fosters trust, and facilitates networking among leaders and interdependence among countries. As a result, and in spite of all their shortcomings, summits do indeed play a positive role in world affairs.

Notes

1 The BRICS, nevertheless, have adopted concrete measures such as the BRICS Bank, which is part of a grand strategy.
2 Legitimacy and legitimation are complex notions involving access to, control of, and performance by an institution. By focusing only on access in this volume we certainly miss an important aspect of legitimation and we are clearly aware that access may not be perceived in the same way by actors in the North as by those in the global South. Assessments must therefore be as nuanced as possible.
3 Richard Feinberg, "Institutionalized Summitry," in *The Oxford Handbook of Modern Diplomacy*, ed. Andrew F. Cooper, Jorge Heine, and Ramesh Thakur (Oxford: Oxford University Press, 2013), 316.
4 Detlef Nolte, "Latin America's New Regional Architecture: A Cooperative or Segmented Regional Governance Complex?" EUI Working Papers RSCAS 2014/89, 2014.

Bibliography

Bayne, Nicholas and Robert D. Putnam, *Hanging in There: The G7 and G8 Summit in Maturity and Renewal* (Aldershot: Ashgate, 2000). Examines the first 25 years of summitry in the context of globalization and institutional change.

Berridge, Geoff R., *Diplomacy: Theory and Practice*, 4th edn (Basingstoke: Palgrave Macmillan, 2010). Essential reading on diplomacy containing what became an influential typology distinguishing between serial, ad hoc, and high-level summits.

Chrestia, Philippe, "Les Sommets Internationaux," *Études Internationales* 31, no. 3 (2000): 443–474. A contribution of francophone literature on summitry offering a general assessment of the phenomenon.

Dunn, David H., ed., *Diplomacy at the Highest Level: The Evolution of International Summitry* (New York: Palgrave Macmillan, 1996). A classic on summitry, with an important introduction by the editor. His definition of summitry has widely circulated.

Feinberg, Richard E., "Institutionalized Summitry," in *The Oxford Handbook of Modern Diplomacy*, ed. Andrew F. Cooper, Jorge Heine, and Ramesh Thakur (Oxford: Oxford University Press, 2013), 303–318. A significant contribution on the reasons explaining the rise of summitry by an academic who was also deeply involved in the organization of the first Summit of the Americas.

Galtung, Johan, "Summit Meetings and International Relations," *Journal of Peace Research* 1, no. 1 (1964): 36–54. A piece by one of the first scholars to have foreseen the future importance of summitry in the conduct of international affairs.

Jarque, Carlos M., Maria Salvadora Ortiz, and Carlos Quenan, eds, *América Latina y la Diplomacia de Cumbres* (Madrid: Secretaría General Iberoamericana, 2009). One of two volumes produced under the aegis of the secretariat of the Organization of Ibero-American States with contributions from scholars as well as practitioners, as applied mostly to Latin America.

Kirton, John J., *G20 Governance for a Globalized World* (Aldershot: Ashgate, 2015). Comprehensive, theoretically based study on the evolution and impact of the G20 by one of the foremost scholars in the field.

Mace, Gordon and Hugo Loiseau, "Cooperative Hegemony and Summitry in the Americas," *Latin American Politics and Society* 47, no. 4 (2005): 107–134. One of the few scholarly analyses on the relationship between summitry and the governance of inter-American relations.

Malamud, Andrés, "Presidential Diplomacy and the Institutional Underpinnings of Mercosur: An Empirical Examination," *Latin American Research Review* 40, no. 1 (2005): 138–164. Another study on the link between summitry, as an important channel for presidential diplomacy, and regional governance in South America.

Melissen, Jan, "Summit Diplomacy Coming of Age," *Discussion Papers in Diplomacy* No. 86, Netherlands Institute of International Relations Clingendael, 2003, 1–21. A widely read contribution contextualizing international summits at the start of the twenty-first century.

Mourlon-Druol, Emmanuel and Federico Romero, ed., *International Summitry and Global Governance: The Rise of the G7 and the European Council, 1974–1991* (London: Routledge, 2014). Using recently released archival material, the volume offers a detailed study of the emergence of G7 and Council of Europe summitry and seeks to understand the historical context favoring the development of these summits.

Reynolds, David, *Summits: Six Meetings that Shaped the Twentieth Century* (New York: Basic Books, 2007). A major historical contribution focusing on six high-level summits that influenced the evolution of world affairs from 1938 to 1985.

Rojas Aravena, Francisco and Paz V. Milet, *Diplomacia de Cumbres: El Multilateralismo Emergente del Siglo XXI* (Santiago de Chile: FLACSO-Chile, 1998). Written by two leading Latin American international relations experts, this book examines the new role of summitry in the framework of Latin American multilateralism.

Index

Abe, Shinzo xviii
ACP (Asia, Caribbean, and Pacific group of states) 94, 95
agenda interaction 30–51; agenda duplication 31, 32, 35, 39, 47 (hard duplication 32, 49; soft duplication 32); aggregation 32; CAN strategy regarding the SA-CSN-UNASUR agenda 38–9; innovation 31–2, 34–5, 39, 41, 47, 48; left turn in South America 40, 41, 43, 48, 50; Mercosur strategy regarding the SA-CSN-UNASUR agenda 36–8; multilayered summitry 31, 32–3, 36, 47; recommendations for further research 48; regional integration 34–5, 47; SA-CSN-UNASUR/Mercosur-CAN agenda interaction 33–6; subsidiarity 31–2, 34, 35, 49; synergy 32, 34, 39, 40, 41, 47; typology of agenda interactions 31–2, 33; *see also* CAN; CSN; Mercosur; UNASUR
agenda setting and orientation xix, 3, 6, 16, 31, 33, 48, 113, 224, 230; CARICOM 100; Central American summits 130, 134, 137, 230–1; consensus 65–6; Mercosur 113–15, 120; multilateral summitry 179, 181–2, 183, 188; SOA 59–62, 66, 225; *see also* summitry, functions of
ALBA (Bolivarian Alliance for the Peoples of our America) 73, 194, 222; SOA 63, 65, 230

ALC/UE (Latin America, the Caribbean, and the European Union Summits) 49
Amnesty International 217
Anderson, Greg 141–56, 230–1
Anthony, Kenny 96
APEC (Asia-Pacific Economic Cooperation) 165, 171, 175, 194; XXVI Asia-Pacific Economic Cooperation Summit, 2014 xviii
Argentina 107; Falkland Islands 113, 120
Arias, Oscar 74, 126
Aristide, Jean-Bertrand 98, 220
ASA (Africa and South America Summits) 49
ASEAN (Association of Southeast Asian Nations) 159–76; 2008 ASEAN Charter 160, 162, 163, 166, 168; AEC 167; AFTA 163, 166, 167; ASEAN Civil Society Conference/ASEAN People's Forum 25; ASEAN Community 162, 166, 168; 'ASEAN minus X' principle 163; ASEAN Secretariat 162; 'ASEAN Way' 160, 164, 165, 173, 229; criticism 160, 166, 168–9, 172; free trade 167; lessons for others 173; membership 159, 160, 166, 171, 175 (dynastic political families 169–70, 229; longevity in power 169, 171, 229); origins 159–60; regional governance 168, 171; regional prosperity 166, 168, 170, 171, 172, 173; stakeholder

240 *Index*

democracy 24; *see also* ASEAN summitry
ASEAN summitry 159–64, 173; 1976 Bali 160–1, 164; agenda 164–8; APT 160, 162, 169, 170, 171; ASEAN + One 160, 162, 171; ASEM 165; consensus 163–4, 165, 169, 173, 229; consultations 162–3, 229; cooperation 165–6, 167; EAS 160, 162, 165, 168, 169, 171; implementation 167, 168; informal summit 160; legitimacy 171, 172, 173; socialization 170, 173, 229; success 159, 165, 168–73, 220; summitry functions 173; TAC 161–2, 164, 165–6, 173; *see also* ASEAN
ASPA (Summits of South American and Arab countries) 49
Assange, Julian 83–4
Attali, Jacques 177
AU (African Union) 198
Azcona del Hoyo, José 126

Ba, Alice 166, 169
Bachelet, Michelle 44, 50, 78
Ball, George 2
Barroso, José Manuel 185
BASIC (Brazil, South Africa, India, and China group) 199
Batlle, Jorge Luis 220
Bayne, Nicholas 181, 182
Berlusconi, Silvio 220
Berridge, Geoff 102
Bird , Lester 96
Blair, Tony xxi
Bohlen, Charles xxii
Bolivian crisis 43, 76, 78–9, 231; 'Pando killings' 78, 79
Brazil 225; Mercosur 36, 107, 118, 120, 121; SOA 65; UNASUR 39, 46, 65, 73, 74–5, 84, 224; *see also* BRICS
BRIC (Brazil, Russia, India, and China group) 196, 201, 202–203, 204; 2009 Yekaterinburg 194, 202, 203
BRICS (Brazil, Russia, India, China, and South Africa group) 193–210; 2008 global crisis 202, 207; Brazil 194, 196, 197, 198, 201, 204; BRICS Bank 87, 205–206, 208, 230; China 193, 196, 197, 198, 201, 203, 204; diplomatic global reach 198–9, 203; economic growth 196–8, 199, 204; flexibility 205, 208; G summits 199; 208; geopolitical shift 201, 203; India 193, 196, 197, 201; lack of geographical connection 193–4, 208; Libya 204–205; membership 196 (great differences and rivalries 201–202, 206–207; regional dominance of each member 198); O5: 199–201; power (realignment of power 203, 206; shift in power relations 197–8, 199); Russia 194, 196, 204; South Africa 194, 195, 198–9, 201, 204–205; state sovereignty and nonintervention 205; Syria 205; UN Security Council 201, 203, 204–205, 207; *see also* IBSA; BRICS summitry
BRICS summitry 230; coordination 203–204; 'global' model 194; similarities/differences regarding other summitries 194–6, 207–208 (G20, similarities 194–5; informality 195–6, 208; leader-centrism 194, 195, 207; state centrism 195; technical focus 207); *see also* BRICS
bureaucracy 1, 3, 59, 146, 171, 226, 228, 235; Mercosur 106, 117
Burnham, Forbes 90, 91, 100
Bush, George H.W. 56, 57, 149, 220
Bush, George W. 215, 219, 220
Byron, Jessica 88–105, 229

C4 (El Salvador, Honduras, Guatemala, and Nicaragua) 137
CABEI (Central American Bank for Economic Integration) 129
CACM (Central American Common Market) 126, 134
CAF (Development Bank of Latin America) 218
CALC (Latin America and the Caribbean Summits) 49, 225
CAN (Andean Community) 36, 49; CAN13: 38; CAN strategy

regarding the SA-CSN-UNASUR agenda 38–9; convergence 39; criticism 73; democracy 34; membership 37, 49; overlapping 31, 39; *see also* agenda interaction
Canada 220; *see also* NAFTA; NALS; SOA
Cardoso, Fernando Henrique xxi, 44, 73, 86, 194
CARICOM (Caribbean Community) 88–105, 218, 222; 1989 Grand Anse Declaration 94, 95; 1997 Charter for Civil Society 19, 98; admittance to opposition politicians 97–8; Assembly of CARICOM Parliamentarians 21, 96, 98; bodies and agencies 91–2; CARICOM Bureau 89, 91, 96, 103; CARICOM Secretariat 89, 91, 92, 98–9; CARICOM SG 91, 92; CCJ 96, 97; CHG Conference 24, 88, 90, 91, 92, 96, 100, 102, 104; civil society 95, 96, 97, 98, 104; Community Council 91, 92; CSME 92, 94, 95–6, 97–8; democracy 19, 20, 24, 93, 99, 232; an 'elite rapport' 88; FTAA 95, 99; Haiti 93, 95, 97, 98; membership 88, 93, 94, 96, 102; objectives 89; origins 88–9; private sector 95; regional integration 96, 98–9, 100; RNM 95; security issues 97; shortcomings 100, 101, 102, 105; SOA 99; sovereignty 95, 96; Treaty of Chaguaramas 89, 90–1, 97; *see also the entries below for* CARICOM; agenda interaction
CARICOM summitry 89, 102; agenda setting and orientation 100; CARICOM/Cuba summits 102; closed session 92; coordination and negotiation 93, 99, 101, 102; crisis management 95, 98, 99; dialogue and socialization 99–100, 101, 229; evolutionary phases 89, 92–9 (1973–76: 89, 92; 1982–89: 89, 93–4; 1990–2000: 89, 94–6; 2000 onwards 89, 96–9, 104); implementation 89, 91, 96, 100, 103, 104; institutionalization of 91;

Intersessional Summit 91, 103; legitimation of domestic policies 101; other functions 101–102; plenary 92; US/CARICOM special summit 95; *see also* CARICOM
Carter Center 217
CELAC (Community of Latin American and Caribbean Nations) 49, 72, 102, 222, 223, 225, 226, 230; 2015 First Ministerial Forum xviii; Brazil 65; SOA 65, 67, 221
Central American summits 124–40, 230; alternative instruments of regional diplomacy 127–30 (Extraordinary Summit of Central American Presidents and Heads of State 128; Partial summits 128); crisis of 125, 127–37, 139; crisis management 125, 129, 138; democracy 126–7, 129; failure to fulfil summitry functions 125, 130, 230–1 (agenda setting 130, 134, 137, 230–1; evolution of 130; interdependence 127, 128, 129, 135, 137; origins 125–7; minimal effectiveness 127, 130–2; pragmatic alienation 127, 134–5, 231; presidential diplomacy 125 ('power of chair' 124; presidential attendance 134–5, 139); socialization 137; success 126, 137, 138; typology 128–9 (differentiated summits 129; extraordinary summits 129, 130; ordinary summits 128, 130; suboptimal decision making 127, 135–7; summits with third parties 129); variable geometry integration 127, 132–4, 231; *see also* Central American summits, crisis of; ODECA; SICA
Cerezo, Vinicio 126
Charles, Eugenia 90, 100, 105
Chávez, Hugo 43, 44, 45, 46, 50, 75, 119, 221; ALBA 194; death 82, 83; Lula/Chávez rivalry 73, 74, 85; Mercosur 73, 119, 123; Uribe/Chávez difficult relationship 80
China *see* BRICS
Chirac, Jacques 199

Chrestia, Philippe 102
Chrétien, Jean 214–15
Churchill, Winston xix, xx
civil society 6, 24, 221, 232, 235; 2001 Quebec City Summit 217; CARICOM 95, 96, 97, 98, 104; democracy 67, 216, 217, 233–4; G8, civil society forum 25; Mercosur 112–13, 116, 232; role in summitry 216–17, 218
Clinton, Bill xxi, 58–9, 214, 224
Colombia: Colombian crisis 43, 47, 75, 76, 223–4; ELN 75; FARC 75; US/Colombia defense agreement 43, 75, 79–80, 87, 224
comparative analysis 4, 5, 6–7, 228, 236
Concert of Europe 22, 26
constructivism 5
Cooper, Andrew F. 89, 193–210, 230
Cooper, Richard 183
coordination and negotiation 3, 6, 13, 15, 33–4, 35, 184, 231; BRICS 203–204; CARICOM 93, 99, 101, 102; Central American summits 137; consensus 65–6; IBSA 203–204; Mercosur 115–17, 120; multilateral summitry 179, 183–4, 185, 187–8, 189; SOA 59, 62, 66, 225; *see also* summitry, functions of
Correa, Rafael 43, 44, 45, 79, 80–1
Council of Europe 232
CSN (Community of South American Nations) 33, 49; CSN1: 34, 35, 41, 42; CSN2: 34, 41; CSNex 41, 43; participation 40, 44–5; *see also* agenda interaction
Cuba 55, 221, 224; CARICOM/Cuba summits 102; reintegration in the inter-American system 63; shift in US policy toward Cuba 67, 230

Dabène, Olivier 1–8, 30–51, 126, 228–36
democracy 7, 16–17, 119; democracy in polycentric governance/statist governance 17–18; democratization 57, 170; OAS 216 (Inter-American Democratic Charter 62, 225); positive effects and values 17; *see also* summitry and democracy
demonstration 19, 26, 213, 217
dialogue and socialization xix, xxii, 3, 6, 7, 16, 109–110, 193, 223, 226, 229–30; ASEAN 170, 173, 229; the best fulfilled functions 229; CARICOM 99–100, 101, 229; Central American summits 137; Mercosur 109–113, 119–20, 229; multilateral summitry 179–81, 183, 184, 187, 188, 229; SOA 59, 62, 63, 64–5, 66, 67, 229–30; success 230, 233; UNASUR 71, 76, 84, 230; *see also* summitry, functions of
diplomacy xx; BRICS 198–9, 203; from 'club' to 'network diplomacy' xxii; Westphalian diplomacy 14; *see also* presidential diplomacy; summit diplomacy
drug issues 35, 63, 74, 75, 83, 225
Duarte, José Napoléon 42, 44, 126
Duhalde, Eduardo 42, 44
Dunn, David 2

EAI (Enterprise for the Americas Initiative) 56, 57–8
ECLAC (Economic Commission for Latin America and the Caribbean) 136, 218
Ecuador: Assange Affair 83–4; Ecuadorian crisis 43, 46, 47, 76, 80–1, 224, 231
EEC (European Economic Community) 180
EU (European Union) 18; ACP-EU relations 94, 95; cosmopolitan federalism 23; stakeholder democracy 24
European Commission 181, 185
European Council 23, 184, 185, 188, 219

Feinberg, Richard 195, 234
Ferreira Cabral, Maria Eduarda 106–23
Ford, Gerald 180, 182, 183, 184–5, 186, 187, 189
forum shopping 30

Fox, Vicente 214–15
free-trade 40, 47; ASEAN 167; FTA 36; Mercosur 107, 115; OAS 56; pro-free trade group of presidents 40, 50; SOA 58, 62, 65; trade liberalization 146, 147, 151, 217; *see also* FTAA; NAFTA
Frizzera, Guilherme 119
FTAA (Free Trade Area of the Americas) 36, 71, 73, 112, 214, 220, 232; CARICOM 95, 99; Mercosur 113, 115, 120; SOA and FTAA break-down of negotiations 57, 58, 62, 63, 65, 66, 221
FTAAP (Free Trade Area of the Asia-Pacific) xviii
Fujimori, Alberto 214, 215
Fukuda, Takeo 187–8

G3 (Group of Three) 102
G6 (Group of Six) 189
G7 (Group of Seven) 1, 15, 230; 1975 Rambouillet Summit 178, 180, 182, 184–5, 186, 187, 189, 224, 229; 1978 Bonn Summit 182, 213; BRICS 199; criticism 179, 181, 182; difficult interpersonal relationships 187; origins 178, 183, 189; results of the G7 summits 182–3, 185, 219; Russia 219; *see also* multilateral summitry
G8 (Group of Eight) 1, 219, 230; civil society forum 25; O5: 199–201; origins 189; polycentric governance 18; Russia 219; stakeholder democracy 24; *see also* multilateral summitry
G20 (Group of 20) 1, 15; 2009 London 182; 'global' model 194; membership 189; origins 184, 187, 189, 219; polycentric governance 18; summitry impact 3, 22, 220, 230; *see also* multilateral summitry
GATT (General Agreement on Tariffs and Trade) 57
GFATM (Global Fund to Fight AIDS, Tuberculosis and Malaria) 23–4
Giscard d'Estaing, Valéry 179, 180, 181, 183, 184, 187

Global Counter-Terrorism Forum 18
globalization 5, 7, 14, 16, 21; as reason for summitry proliferation xxi, 1, 3, 106
Goldman Sachs 196, 200, 201, 204
Gorbachev, Mikhail xx
governance: current transformation of 13–16, 27–8, 76; democratic governance 216; polycentric governance 14–15, 16–20, 21, 24, 25, 27, 28; Westphalian era 13–14; *see also* regional governance; summitry and regional governance
Gvosdev, Nikolas 205

Haiti 46, 47, 220; CARICOM 93, 95, 97, 98; MINUSTAH 50
Hale, Geoffrey 147
Hampson, Fen Osler 120
Hawke, Bob 194
hegemony: counter-hegemonic resistance 20, 26–7, 195; US hegemony 58, 145
Heine, Jorge xviii–xxii
Held, David 119
Hormats, Robert 186–7
host country 101, 217, 218, 225
Humala, Ollanta 42, 45, 46, 50, 82
Human Rights Watch 217

IASB (International Accounting Standards Board) 18
Ibero-American Summits 49, 129, 222, 223, 224, 226
IBSA (India, Brazil, and South Africa group) 195, 198, 202, 205, 208; coordination 203–204; criticism 202; *see also* BRICS
ICANN (Internet Corporation for Assigned Names and Numbers) 18
IDB (Inter-American Development Bank) 37, 59, 136, 216, 218
IIRSA (Initiative for the Integration of the Regional Infrastructure in South America) 34–5, 37–9
ILO (International Labour Organization) 23
IMF (International Monetary Fund) 180, 181, 184, 196, 199, 204, 206, 208

244 *Index*

implementation of summit decisions 17, 83, 213, 222, 227, 231–2, 233, 236; ASEAN 167, 168; CARICOM 89, 91, 96, 100, 103, 104; consensus, need of 226; failure 7, 233; international organization 226; lack of resources 66, 232; SOA 59, 62, 218–19, 225; success 231; *see also* summitry effectiveness
India *see* BRICS
Inter-American Commission for Human Rights 217
interdependence 87, 146, 152, 185–6, 221, 236; Central America 127, 128, 129, 135, 137; management of 5, 30, 102; as reason for summitry proliferation xxi, 1, 3, 102, 106, 159, 189; shift of paradigms xxii
International Competition Network 18

Kennedy, John F. xix
Khruschev, Nikita xx
Kirchner, Cristina 44, 45
Kirchner, Néstor 42, 43, 44, 64, 75, 80, 81
Kohl, Helmut 180–1
Krasner, Stephen 151–2

Lagos, Ricardo xxi
leadership 8, 89, 93, 221, 228, 235; Central America 134; differences between leaders 73–4, 110, 128, 187; originators of summitry 224–5, 235; women 100; *see also* president, presidential diplomacy
League of Arab States 22
left turn in South America: agenda interaction 40, 41, 43, 48, 50; Mercosur 115, 118, 229; UNASUR 76
legitimation xix, 1, 3, 6, 16, 118, 232, 233–4; ASEAN 171, 172, 173; CARICOM 101; Central American summits 131, 132, 134, 135, 137–8; democratic access 232, 233, 235, 236; diffusion of norms and values 232, 233, 236; media 118; Mercosur 118–19, 120; SOA 232; *see also* summitry, functions of

Legler, Thomas 5
liberalization 57, 62, 89; trade liberalization 146, 147, 151, 217; *see also* free-trade
Libya 204–205
Lortie, Marc 7, 213–21, 231
Lugo, Fernando 42, 44, 45, 46, 81–2
Lula da Silva, Luiz Inácio 43, 44, 45, 46, 80, 198, 203; Lula/Chávez rivalry 73, 74, 85

Mace, Gordon 1–8, 55–70, 228–36
Maduro, Nicolás 45, 46, 50, 85
Malamud, Andrés 108
Mearsheimer, John 203
Medeiros, Marcelo de Almeida 106–23, 229
media and summit coverage xx, 6, 19, 182, 213, 217; demonstrations 217; legitimation 118
Medvedev, Dmitry 194, 203
Melissen, Jan 3, 160
Mercosur (Southern Common Market) 49, 102, 106–123, 222; 1991 Asunción Treaty 108, 110; 1994 Ouro Preto Protocol 108, 110; Argentina 107; autonomy 107, 113, 117; Brazil 36, 107, 118, 120, 121; bureaucracy 106, 117; CCM 108, 116; civil society 112–13, 116, 232; crisis 73; criticism 73; democracy 24, 34, 37, 47, 113, 119, 123, 215; free trade 107, 115; FCCR 119; FCES 24, 119; FOCEM 37–8, 49, 112, 115, 121–2; FTAA 113, 115, 120; institutional design 106, 107–108, 116–17, 118, 119; GMC 108, 117; low institutionalization 107, 108, 119, 120; membership 36, 37, 49, 110, 111, 118, 120, 121; MERCOCIUDADES 35, 49; origins 107; overlapping 31, 32, 35, 49; Paraguay 110, 112, 119, 122, 215; Parlasur 21, 23, 119; presidential diplomacy 106, 107, 113, 115, 116, 117, 120; private sector 112; SA-CSN-UNASUR agenda 36–8; security issues 47, 114–15; shortcomings 112, 116, 119, 120; 'spill-around'

integration 107–108; Uruguay 112, 122; Venezuela 37, 73, 110, 112, 119, 120, 123; *see also the entries below for* Mercosur; agenda interaction

Mercosur, CMC summits 106, 108, 114–15, 220; agenda-setting and orientation 113–15, 120; consensus and ideological cohesion 110, 112, 115, 229; coordination and negotiation 115–17, 120; council Decisions 111, 112, 114, 115–17, 120; dialogue and socialization 109–113, 119–20, 229; the greatest promoter of summits in the region 108, 109, 121; high politics/low politics 106, 116–17, 118; importance for Mercosur's governance 107, 108, 120; legitimation 118–19, 120; Mercosur27: 36; Mercosur40: 37; representativeness of 110, 111, 118, 119, 120, 121; *see also* Mercosur

Merkel, Angela 187, 200, 220
Mesquita de Souza Lima, Rafael 106–23
Mexico *see* NAFTA; NALS
Miki, Takeo 182, 186
MIKTA (Mexico, Indonesia, South Korea, Turkey, and Australia group) 195
MINUSTAH (United Nations Mission in Haiti) 46, 47, 50
Mitterrand, François 177, 180–1, 187
Modi, Narendra xxi
Morales, Evo 43, 44, 45, 46, 75, 76, 78, 79
Moravcsik, Andrew 21
Morin, Jean-Frédéric 30
Mourlon-Druol, Emmanuel 1–2, 177–92, 229, 230
Mujica, José 227
Mulroney, Brian 219, 220
multilateral summitry: blurred boundaries in the G7/8/20 functions 183–5; distinguishing the outcome and the process 177, 179, 187, 188; functions 178–9, 188–9, 230 (agenda setting 179, 181–2, 183, 188; coordination/cooperation 179, 183–4, 185, 187–8, 189; socialization 179–81, 183, 184, 187, 188, 229; trust 179, 183, 184–5, 187, 188, 230); institutionalized multilateral summitry 195; outcomes: results of the G7 summits 182–3; processes: G7/8/20 as a diplomatic instrument 179–82, 189; regularity 180, 187, 188; sherpa 7, 180, 181, 186, 214, 215, 218, 231, 234; *see also* G7; G8; G20

multilateralism 5, 30, 204; democracy 21–2; as reason for summitry proliferation 2, 3

NAFTA 58, 143–8, 167, 194, 214; anti-summitry of North American integration 141, 145–6, 152–3; asymmetry 143–8; dependence of Canada and Mexico on US 145, 148, 149; free trade 146–7, 148; negative integration 148; sovereignty 145–6, 147, 148; theory of the firm 144–5; US hegemony 145; *see also* NALS

Nairne, Patrick 188
NALS (North American Leaders' Summit) 230; 9/11 attacks 148; 2005 Waco 141, 149; 2014 Toluca Summit 141, 150–1; anti-summitry of North American integration 141, 152–3; asymmetry, sovereignty, and the security/economics agenda 147, 148–51, 231; Canada 142, 146; Mexico 142, 146; North American integration 142, 147, 152–3, 231; rationale for 146; sovereignty 142; SPP 141–2, 147, 149–50, 151; summitry 150–1; undermined by rebilateralization of North American relations 150; US 142, 146–7, 151, 230–1; weak institutionalization 141, 142, 153; *see also* NAFTA

NATO (North Atlantic Treaty Organization) 204–205; Colombia/NATO agreement 82
neoliberal institutionalism 5

246 Index

NEPAD (New Partnership for Africa's Development) 199, 219
Nesadurai, Helen 167
NGO (nongovernmental organization) 97, 216, 217, 218; *see also* civil society

O5 (Outreach 5 process) 199–201
OAS (Organization of American States) 55–6, 49, 218, 223; Bolivian crisis 76, 78–9; democracy 216 (Inter-American Democratic Charter 62, 225); diminished legitimacy 55; economic integration and cooperation 55–56, 58; free trade 56; membership 57; US 71, 78–9; *see also* SOA
OAU (Organization of African Unity) 88
Obama, Barack xviii, 63, 141, 220, 230
ODECA (Central American States Organization) 125–6
OECD (Organisation for Economic Co-operation and Development) 180, 194, 200
Onuki, Janina 116
Orsini, Amandine 30
Ortega, Daniel 126

Pacific Alliance 37, 40, 47, 49, 72, 222, 231
PAHO (Pan American Health Organization) 218
Panyarachun, Anand 163
Paraguay: Mercosur 110, 112, 119, 122, 215; UNASUR, Paraguayan crisis 81–2, 224
Parlatino (Latin American Parliament) 23
Parliamentary Confederation of the Americas 21
Parthenay, Kevin 124–40, 230–1
Peña Nieto, Enrique xviii
Pérez de Cuéllar, Javier 215
Piñera, Sebastián 42, 44, 45, 50
political mobilization 25, 26–7, 81
polycentrism 14–15, 16–20, 21, 24, 25, 27, 28; challenges 73; regulation, outsourced to private governance 18; stakeholder democracy 24; statist/polycentric governance distinction 15, 18; *see also* governance
Portales, Carlos xix, 7, 222–7, 234
presidential diplomacy 1, 74; attendance to summits 39–40, 44–5, 50, 134–5, 139, 223, 228; Central American summits 124, 125, 134–5, 139; differences between leaders 73–4, 110, 128, 187; Mercosur 106, 107, 113, 115, 116, 117, 120; president/prime minister as 'diplomat-in-chief' xxi, 228; 'presidentialization' of foreign/regional policy xxi, 74, 125, 233; regional integration 125; SICA 124, 125, 127–8; *see also* summit diplomacy
private sector 221; CARICOM 95; Mercosur 112
Putin, Vladimir xviii, xxi, 219
Putnam, Robert 181, 182

Quiroga, Jorge 42, 44

Reagan, Ronald xx, 180, 220
regional governance: definition 4–5; region, definition 4; regional governance and stability 84; *see also* governance; summitry and regional governance
regional integration 34–5, 47, 219, 220; CARICOM 98–9, 100; leftist conception of/'new model of integration' 40, 41, 43, 47; North American integration 142, 147, 152–3, 215; OAS 55–56, 58; post-trade integration 39, 47; presidential diplomacy 125; *see also* SICA and Central American integration
regionalism 57; fourth wave of 30, 32; *hacia afuera* regionalism 107; post-hegemonic regionalism 71
regionalization 14, 16, 21
Reynolds, David 169
Rio Group 43, 49, 50, 95, 222, 223, 225
Rodríguez, Eduardo 42, 44

Roosevelt, Franklin Delano xx
Rousseff, Dilma 45, 46
Russia, suspension from the G7/8 summit 219; *see also* BRICS

SA (South American Summit) 33, 35, 36, 37, 47, 49, 194, 224; extraordinary summits 43; participation 40, 44–5; SA1: 33–4, 36, 38; SA2: 34, 36, 42; SA3: 34, 36, 39; *see also* agenda interaction
SADC (South American Defense Council) 74–5, 82
SAFTA (South American Free Trade Agreement) 34, 36, 40
Salinas, Carlos 146, 194
Sanahuja, José 136
Santos, Juan Manuel 44, 45, 75, 80, 87
Sarkozy, Nicolas 185, 219, 220
Schmidt, Helmut 185, 186, 187
Schmitter, Philippe 107–108
Scholte, Jan Aart 13–29, 232, 233
security issues 74, 225; CARICOM 97; Mercosur 47, 114–15; multidimensional security 62, 66, 232; UNASUR 74–5, 76, 84
Shaw, Timothy 89
sherpa 7, 180, 181, 186, 214, 215, 218, 231, 234
SICA (Central American Integration System) 23, 222; 1991 Tegucigalpa Protocol 124, 127, 130, 132, 133, 139; Central American Court of Justice 133, 136, 137; consensus 135–6; Consultative Committee 24; criticism 130–2; democracy 19, 24; institutionalization 138; Parlacen 23, 136, 137; pillars 133, 138; presidential diplomacy 124, 125, 127–8; reform 136–7; shortcomings 127, 130–1; SICA PTP 128, 129; *see also* Central American summits
SICA and Central American integration 124–5, 126–7, 128; differentiated integration 133; 'intervention without integration' 133; maximalism/minimalism 136, 139; regional pragmatism 135;

weakening of regional interdependence 128, 129, 135; *see also* Central American summits; SICA
Singh, Manmohan 200
SOA (Summits of the Americas) 55–70, 224; 1994–2003, years of consensus 58–62, 66; 2003–15, years of confrontation 58, 63–65, 66; 2001 Quebec City Summit 56, 62, 213, 214–19, 220; ALBA 63, 65, 230; Brazil 65; CARICOM 99; CELAC 65, 67, 221; civil society 217; democracy 214, 220 (representative democracy/participative democracy 221); Democratic Charter of the Americas 213, 215, 216, 232; Democratic Clause 213, 215–16; disaffection toward the SOA process 64; failure 62, 64–5, 66; free trade 58, 62, 65; follow-up 218–19; FTAA, break-down of negotiations 57, 58, 62, 63, 65, 66, 221; JSWG 59, 223; indigenous peoples 217–18; multidimensional security 62, 66, 232; origins 56–8, 223, 224; recommendations for the future for 67; regional governance 232; regional organizations 218; SIRG 59; success 62, 66, 220–1, 231; UNASUR 63, 65, 67; US 56, 57, 58, 65, 66–7, 113, 221, 223, 224; *see also the entries below for* SOA; OAS
SOA summitry: 1994 Miami Summit 56, 59, 62, 214, 218, 220, 222, 223; 1996 Santa Cruz Summit 56; 1998 Santiago Summit 56, 62, 218, 220, 223; 2004 Monterrey Summit 56; 2005 Mar del Plata Summit 56, 63, 64; 2009 Port-of-Spain Summit 56, 63, 64; 2012 Cartagena Summit 56, 63, 64, 67; agenda setting 59–62, 66, 225; coordination 59, 62, 66, 225; dialogue and socialization 59, 62, 63, 64–5, 66, 67, 229–30; implementation 59, 62, 218–19, 225; legitimation 232; *see also* SOA; SOA, 2001 Quebec City Summit
Solís, Luis Guillermo 133

Sonnenfeldt, Helmut 178–9, 182
Sotillo, José 136
South Africa, apartheid 219; *see also* BRICS
sovereignty 21, 22, 143; BRICS 205; CARICOM 95, 96; NAFTA 145–6, 147, 148; NALS 142; sovereignty vs. regional integration 96; UNASUR 79, 83–4; Westphalian sovereignty 148; *see also* state
Spain 224, 225
Spencer, Baldwin 97
Stalin, Josef xx
Stubbs, Richard 159–76, 229
summit: definition/use of the term xix–xx, 2; typologies of 2; *see also* summit diplomacy; summitry
summit diplomacy 228; BRICS, diplomatic global reach 198–9, 203; criticism of xx–xxi; democracy 67; G7/8/20 as a diplomatic instrument 179–82, 189; misaligned incentives in summit diplomacy xx; practitioner's point of view on summitry 7; summitry, a diplomatic tool xix, 4, 7, 222, 226; summitry, a vital feature of modern diplomacy 234; *see also* diplomacy; presidential diplomacy
summitry xx, 228; a central feature of world politics 1, 228, 234; challenges 234–5; criticism of xx–xxi; dysfunctional aspects of summitry xx–xxi, 3; exclusion from 207, 208, 219; exclusivity 193, 207; future of summitry 234–6; host country 101, 217, 218, 225; limitations 220; literature on 2–4, 228; modes of 207; opposition to xx, xxii; organizers 225; originators of 224–5, 235; reputation xx, 225; summit, a political event 85, 213, 220; *see also the entries below for* summitry; agenda interaction; summit; summit diplomacy
summitry and democracy 16–29; 2001 Quebec City Summit 214, 220 (Democratic Charter of the Americas 213, 215, 216; Democratic Clause 213, 215–16; representative democracy/participative democracy 221); CAN 34; CARICOM 19, 20, 24, 93, 99, 232; Central American summits 126–7, 129; civil society 67, 216, 217, 233–4; democracy as a challenge to summitry 235; democratization of summitry 13, 20–7, 28, 233 (communitarianism 20–1, 28; cosmopolitan federalism 20, 22–3; counter-hegemonic resistance 20, 26–7, 28; deliberative democracy 20, 25–6, 28; multilateralism 20, 21–2, 28; stakeholder democracy 20, 23–5, 28, 233); Mercosur 24, 34, 37, 47, 113, 119, 123, 215; potential of summits for democracy enhancement 19; shortfalls in democracy 18, 19–20, 28, 232 (democratic deficit 233; no access to summits for opposition politicians 20, 79, 97); SICA 19, 24; sovereignty 21, 22; Spain 224; summit diplomacy 67; UNASUR 19, 24, 38, 74 (Democratic Protocol 19, 74, 81); *see also* democracy
summitry and regional governance 4–5, 30, 65–6, 213, 219–21, 222–7, 232, 234; ASEAN 168, 171; consensus-building consultations with non-state actors 217; consensus, need of 65–6, 225, 226, 231; functions of summitry 6, 109; mixed results 7; SOA 232; South America 30–1; summitry, positive effect on governance 235; *see also* summitry, functions of
summitry effectiveness 1–2, 3, 16, 213, 231, 234; ASEAN 159, 165, 168–73; benefits of establishing a periodic summit process 223; Central American summits 127, 130–2; consensus, need of 65–6, 225, 226, 235; disappointing results 8, 16; distinguishing the outcome and the process 1, 177, 179, 187, 188; G20 3, 22, 220, 230; institutionalization of summits 3; peer pressure 223; success 67, 231 (determinants of

Index 249

summit success 102); summitry, positive role in world affairs 235; *see also* implementation of summit decisions
summitry, functions of xix, xxi, xxii, 3, 6, 178, 224, 228–9; 'action-trigger' mechanism xix, 16; a central instrument of multilateralism 3; control in a more complex governance 13, 14, 16; cooperation 183–4, 187, 219 (Ibero-American Summits 226; UNASUR 76, 83, 84, 85); crisis management xix, 20, 31, 33, 43, 223–4, 226, 228, 230, 231, 233 (CARICOM 95, 98, 99; Central American summits 125, 129, 138); institutionalist perspective 5–6; managing interdependence 102; policy formulation and execution 16; shift from 'national interest' to 'a balance of interests' xxii; summitry and governance 6, 109; summitry success and functions of summitry 67; trust 179, 183, 184–5, 187, 188, 220–1; *see also* agenda setting and orientation; coordination and negotiation; dialogue and socialization; legitimation; multilateral summitry; summit diplomacy; summitry and regional governance; UNASUR, crisis management
summitry proliferation xix, xx, 1, 222–7; the Americas 4, 33, 49, 71, 193, 228, 234; overlapping 31, 222, 226, 234; proliferation as a threat 234–5; reasons for proliferation xxi, 1, 2–3 (control in a more complex governance 13, 14, 16, 27–8; globalization xxi, 1, 3, 106; interdependence xxi, 1, 3, 102, 106, 159, 189; multilateralism 2, 3); regional governance 30; regional level 193;
Syria 83, 205

terrorism 115, 168, 182; 9/11 attacks 65, 115, 148, 216
Thérien, Jean-Philippe 1–8, 55–70, 228–36

Toledo, Alejandro 42, 43, 44
Transparency International 216–17
Trudeau, Pierre 187, 213
Tussie, Diana 1–8, 71–87, 228–36

UN (United Nations) 18; Rio Group 223; UN Security Council 201, 203, 204–205
UNASUR (Union of South American Nations) 33, 49, 71–87, 102, 222, 224–5, 230, 232; 2008 UNASUR Treaty 35, 36–7, 72, 73; ALBA 73; Bancosur 38, 46, 50, 206; Brazil 39, 46, 65, 73, 74–5, 84, 224; CELAC 72; challenges 74–5; Colombia 75; convergence 35, 37; councils 35, 49, 74, 81; democracy 19, 24, 38, 74 (Democratic Protocol 19, 74, 81); membership 49, 72, 82; 'new model of integration' 41 (post-hegemonic regionalism 71); overlapping 31, 32, 35, 39, 43, 46, 47, 49; Petrosur 38, 46, 50; a 'post-trade' agreement 39; presidential diplomacy 71, 72, 73–4, 76 (core group of five presidents 43); security issues 74–5, 76, 84; SICA PTP 128–9; SOA 63, 65, 67; South American Parliament 23; success 76, 83; Venezuela 39, 41, 46, 72, 82, 83; *see also the entries below for* UNASUR; agenda interaction; SADC
UNASUR, crisis management 43, 46, 47, 72, 73, 76–82, 83, 85, 224, 231; Bolivian crisis 43, 76, 78–9, 231; a collective safety net 72, 76, 79, 84; Colombian crisis 43, 47, 75, 76, 79–80, 87, 223–4; Ecuadorian crisis 43, 46, 47, 76, 80–1, 224, 231; neutralizing the US 84; non-intervention and respect for sovereignty 79, 83–4; Paraguayan crisis 81–2, 224; Venezuela 76, 80, 84, 85, 224; *see also* UNASUR
UNASUR summitry 72, 73–6; I UNASUR 41, 73, 77, 224; VI UNASUR 35, 83; VII UNASUR

35, 83; cooperation 76, 83, 84, 85; dialogue and socialization 71, 76, 84, 230; evolution of summits 77–8; extraordinary summits 43, 46, 72, 77, 82, 83; participation 40, 44–5, 46; *see also* UNASUR
UNFCCC (UN Framework Convention on Climate Change): COP 15
United Kingdom 84, 113, 120
Uribe, Álvaro 42, 43, 44, 80
Uruguay 112, 122
US (United States): 1954 US-supported coup in Guatemala 55; 1965 intervention in the Dominican Republic 55; foreign policy 55, 63, 65, 66 (shift in US policy toward Cuba 67, 230); NALS 142, 146–7, 151; OAS 71, 78–9; SOA 56, 57, 58, 65, 66–7, 113, 221, 223, 224; US/CARICOM special summit 95; US/Colombia defense agreement 43, 75, 79–80, 87, 224; US hegemony 58, 145; war on terror 63, 66; *see also* NAFTA; NALS

Van Rompuy, Herman 185
Venezuela 225; champion of summit attendance 46; crisis 82, 83; Mercosur 37, 73, 110, 112, 119, 120, 123; UNASUR 39, 41, 46, 72, 82, 83 (Venezuelan crisis 76, 80, 84, 85, 224)
Ventura, Deisy 116

Washington Consensus 58
Weilemann, Peter 109
World Bank 199, 218
World Social Forum and Occupy 25
WTO (World Trade Organization) 95, 198, 200, 201; civil society forum 25; Uruguay Round 56–7

Xi Jinping xviii

Yalta conference xx
Young, Oran 30

Zedillo, Ernesto xxi
Zelaya, Manuel 85, 113
ZOPFAN (Zone of Peace, Freedom and Neutrality) 161
Zuma, Jacob 204

Routledge Global Institutions Series

112 The United Nations as a Knowledge System (2015)
by Nanette Svenson (Tulane University)

111 Summits and Regional Governance (2015)
The Americas in comparative perspective
edited by Gordon Mace (Université Laval), Jean-Philippe Thérien (Université de Montréal), Diana Tussie (Facultad Latinoamericana de Ciencias Sociales), and Olivier Dabène (Sciences Po)

110 Global Consumer Organizations (2015)
by Karsten Ronit (University of Copenhagen)

109 Expert Knowledge in Global Trade (2015)
edited by Erin Hannah (University of Western Ontario), James Scott (King's College London), and Silke Trommer (University of Helsinki)

108 World Trade Organization (2nd edition, 2015)
Law, economics and politics
by Bernard M. Hoekman (European University Institute) and Petros C. Mavroidis (European University Institute)

107 Women and Girls Rising (2015)
Progress and resistance around the world
by Ellen Chesler (Roosevelt Institute) and Theresa McGovern (Columbia University)

106 The North Atlantic Treaty Organization (2nd edition, 2015)
by Julian Lindley-French (National Defense University)

105 The African Union (2nd edition, 2015)
by *Samuel M. Makinda (Murdoch University),*
F. Wafula Okumu (The Borders Institute),
David Mickler (University of Western Australia)

104 Governing Climate Change (2nd edition, 2015)
by *Harriet Bulkeley (Durham University)* and
Peter Newell (University of Sussex)

103 The Organization of Islamic Cooperation (2015)
Politics, problems, and potential
by *Turan Kayaoglu (University of Washington, Tacoma)*

102 Contemporary Human Rights Ideas (2nd edition, 2015)
by *Bertrand G. Ramcharan*

101 The Politics of International Organizations (2015)
Views from insiders
edited by *Patrick Weller (Griffith University)* and
Xu Yi-chong (Griffith University)

100 Global Poverty (2nd edition, 2015)
Global governance and poor people in the post-2015 era
by *David Hulme (University of Manchester)*

99 Global Corporations in Global Governance (2015)
by *Christopher May (Lancaster University)*

98 The United Nations Centre on Transnational Corporations (2015)
Corporate conduct and the public interest
by *Khalil Hamdani and Lorraine Ruffing*

97 The Challenges of Constructing Legitimacy in Peacebuilding (2015)
Afghanistan, Iraq, Sierra Leone, and East Timor
by *Daisaku Higashi (University of Tokyo)*

96 The European Union and Environmental Governance (2015)
by *Henrik Selin (Boston University)* and
Stacy D. VanDeveer (University of New Hampshire)

95 Rising Powers, Global Governance, and Global Ethics (2015)
edited by *Jamie Gaskarth (Plymouth University)*

94 Wartime Origins and the Future United Nations (2015)
edited by Dan Plesch (SOAS, University of London) and
Thomas G. Weiss (CUNY Graduate Center)

93 International Judicial Institutions (2nd edition, 2015)
The architecture of international justice at home and abroad
by Richard J. Goldstone (Retired Justice of the Constitutional
Court of South Africa) and Adam M. Smith (International Lawyer,
Washington, DC)

92 The NGO Challenge for International Relations Theory (2014)
edited by William E. DeMars (Wofford College) and
Dennis Dijkzeul (Ruhr University Bochum)

91 21st Century Democracy Promotion in the Americas (2014)
Standing up for the Polity
by Jorge Heine (Wilfrid Laurier University) and
Brigitte Weiffen (University of Konstanz)

90 BRICS and Coexistence (2014)
An alternative vision of world order
edited by Cedric de Coning (Norwegian Institute of International
Affairs), Thomas Mandrup (Royal Danish Defence College), and
Liselotte Odgaard (Royal Danish Defence College)

89 IBSA (2014)
The rise of the Global South?
by Oliver Stuenkel (Getulio Vargas Foundation)

88 Making Global Institutions Work (2014)
edited by Kate Brennan

87 Post-2015 UN Development (2014)
Making change happen
edited by Stephen Browne (FUNDS Project) and
Thomas G. Weiss (CUNY Graduate Center)

86 Who Participates in Global Governance? (2014)
States, bureaucracies, and NGOs in the United Nations
by Molly Ruhlman (Towson University)

85 The Security Council as Global Legislator (2014)
edited by Vesselin Popovski (United Nations University) and Trudy Fraser (United Nations University)

84 UNICEF (2014)
Global governance that works
by Richard Jolly (University of Sussex)

83 The Society for Worldwide Interbank Financial Telecommunication (SWIFT) (2014)
Cooperative governance for network innovation, standards, and community
by Susan V. Scott (London School of Economics and Political Science) and Markos Zachariadis (University of Cambridge)

82 The International Politics of Human Rights (2014)
Rallying to the R2P cause?
edited by Monica Serrano (Colegio de Mexico) and Thomas G. Weiss (The CUNY Graduate Center)

81 Private Foundations and Development Partnerships (2014)
American philanthropy and global development agendas
by Michael Moran (Swinburne University of Technology)

80 Nongovernmental Development Organizations and the Poverty Reduction Agenda (2014)
The moral crusaders
by Jonathan J. Makuwira (Royal Melbourne Institute of Technology University)

79 Corporate Social Responsibility (2014)
The role of business in sustainable development
by Oliver F. Williams (University of Notre Dame)

78 Reducing Armed Violence with NGO Governance (2014)
edited by Rodney Bruce Hall (Oxford University)

77 Transformations in Trade Politics (2014)
Participatory trade politics in West Africa
by Silke Trommer (Murdoch University)

76 Rules, politics, and the International Criminal Court (2013)
by Yvonne M. Dutton (Indiana University)

75 Global Institutions of Religion (2013)
Ancient movers, modern shakers
by Katherine Marshall (Georgetown University)

74 Crisis of Global Sustainability (2013)
by Tapio Kanninen

73 The Group of Twenty (G20) (2013)
by Andrew F. Cooper (University of Waterloo) and Ramesh Thakur (Australian National University)

72 Peacebuilding (2013)
From concept to commission
by Rob Jenkins (Hunter College, CUNY)

71 Human Rights and Humanitarian Norms, Strategic Framing, and Intervention (2013)
Lessons for the Responsibility to Protect
by Melissa Labonte (Fordham University)

70 Feminist Strategies in International Governance (2013)
edited by Gülay Caglar (Humboldt University, Berlin), Elisabeth Prügl (the Graduate Institute of International and Development Studies, Geneva), and Susanne Zwingel (the State University of New York, Potsdam)

69 The Migration Industry and the Commercialization of International Migration (2013)
edited by Thomas Gammeltoft-Hansen (Danish Institute for International Studies) and Ninna Nyberg Sørensen (Danish Institute for International Studies)

68 Integrating Africa (2013)
Decolonization's legacies, sovereignty, and the African Union
by Martin Welz (University of Konstanz)

67 Trade, Poverty, Development (2013)
Getting beyond the WTO's Doha deadlock
edited by *Rorden Wilkinson (University of Manchester) and James Scott (University of Manchester)*

66 The United Nations Industrial Development Organization (UNIDO) (2012)
Industrial solutions for a sustainable future
by *Stephen Browne (FUNDS Project)*

65 The Millennium Development Goals and Beyond (2012)
Global development after 2015
edited by *Rorden Wilkinson (University of Manchester) and David Hulme (University of Manchester)*

64 International Organizations as Self-Directed Actors (2012)
A framework for analysis
edited by *Joel E. Oestreich (Drexel University)*

63 Maritime Piracy (2012)
by *Robert Haywood (One Earth Future Foundation) and Roberta Spivak (One Earth Future Foundation)*

62 United Nations High Commissioner for Refugees (UNHCR) (2nd edition, 2012)
by *Gil Loescher (University of Oxford), Alexander Betts (University of Oxford), and James Milner (University of Toronto)*

61 International Law, International Relations, and Global Governance (2012)
by *Charlotte Ku (University of Illinois)*

60 Global Health Governance (2012)
by *Sophie Harman (City University, London)*

59 The Council of Europe (2012)
by *Martyn Bond (University of London)*

58 The Security Governance of Regional Organizations (2011)
edited by *Emil J. Kirchner (University of Essex) and Roberto Dominguez (Suffolk University)*

57 The United Nations Development Programme and System (2011)
by Stephen Browne (FUNDS Project)

56 The South Asian Association for Regional Cooperation (2011)
An emerging collaboration architecture
by Lawrence Sáez (University of London)

55 The UN Human Rights Council (2011)
by Bertrand G. Ramcharan (Geneva Graduate Institute of International and Development Studies)

54 Responsibility to Protect (2011)
Cultural perspectives in the Global South
edited by Rama Mani (University of Oxford) and Thomas G. Weiss (The CUNY Graduate Center)

53 The International Trade Centre (2011)
Promoting exports for development
by Stephen Browne (FUNDS Project) and Sam Laird (University of Nottingham)

52 The Idea of World Government (2011)
From ancient times to the twenty-first century
by James A. Yunker (Western Illinois University)

51 Humanitarianism Contested (2011)
Where angels fear to tread
by Michael Barnett (George Washington University) and Thomas G. Weiss (The CUNY Graduate Center)

50 The Organization of American States (2011)
Global governance away from the media
by Monica Herz (Catholic University, Rio de Janeiro)

49 Non-Governmental Organizations in World Politics (2011)
The construction of global governance
by Peter Willetts (City University, London)

48 The Forum on China-Africa Cooperation (FOCAC) (2011)
by Ian Taylor (University of St. Andrews)

47 Global Think Tanks (2011)
Policy networks and governance
*by James G. McGann (University of Pennsylvania) with
Richard Sabatini*

46 United Nations Educational, Scientific and Cultural Organization (UNESCO) (2011)
Creating norms for a complex world
by J.P. Singh (Georgetown University)

45 The International Labour Organization (2011)
Coming in from the cold
*by Steve Hughes (Newcastle University) and
Nigel Haworth (University of Auckland)*

44 Global Poverty (2010)
How global governance is failing the poor
by David Hulme (University of Manchester)

43 Global Governance, Poverty, and Inequality (2010)
*edited by Jennifer Clapp (University of Waterloo) and
Rorden Wilkinson (University of Manchester)*

42 Multilateral Counter-Terrorism (2010)
The global politics of cooperation and contestation
by Peter Romaniuk (John Jay College of Criminal Justice, CUNY)

41 Governing Climate Change (2010)
*by Peter Newell (University of East Anglia) and
Harriet A. Bulkeley (Durham University)*

40 The UN Secretary-General and Secretariat (2nd edition, 2010)
by Leon Gordenker (Princeton University)

39 Preventive Human Rights Strategies (2010)
by Bertrand G. Ramcharan (Geneva Graduate Institute of International and Development Studies)

38 African Economic Institutions (2010)
by Kwame Akonor (Seton Hall University)

37 Global Institutions and the HIV/AIDS Epidemic (2010)
Responding to an international crisis
by Franklyn Lisk (University of Warwick)

36 Regional Security (2010)
The capacity of international organizations
by Rodrigo Tavares (United Nations University)

35 The Organisation for Economic Co-operation and Development (2009)
by Richard Woodward (University of Hull)

34 Transnational Organized Crime (2009)
by Frank Madsen (University of Cambridge)

33 The United Nations and Human Rights (2nd edition, 2009)
A guide for a new era
by Julie A. Mertus (American University)

32 The International Organization for Standardization (2009)
Global governance through voluntary consensus
*by Craig N. Murphy (Wellesley College) and
JoAnne Yates (Massachusetts Institute of Technology)*

31 Shaping the Humanitarian World (2009)
*by Peter Walker (Tufts University) and
Daniel G. Maxwell (Tufts University)*

30 Global Food and Agricultural Institutions (2009)
by John Shaw

29 Institutions of the Global South (2009)
by Jacqueline Anne Braveboy-Wagner (City College of New York, CUNY)

28 International Judicial Institutions (2009)
The architecture of international justice at home and abroad
by Richard J. Goldstone (Retired Justice of the Constitutional Court of South Africa) and Adam M. Smith (Harvard University)

27 The International Olympic Committee (2009)
The governance of the Olympic system
by Jean-Loup Chappelet (IDHEAP Swiss Graduate School of Public Administration) and Brenda Kübler-Mabbott

26 The World Health Organization (2009)
by Kelley Lee (London School of Hygiene and Tropical Medicine)

25 Internet Governance (2009)
The new frontier of global institutions
by John Mathiason (Syracuse University)

24 Institutions of the Asia-Pacific (2009)
ASEAN, APEC, and beyond
by Mark Beeson (University of Birmingham)

23 United Nations High Commissioner for Refugees (UNHCR) (2008)
The politics and practice of refugee protection into the ~ twenty-first century
by Gil Loescher (University of Oxford), Alexander Betts (University of Oxford), and James Milner (University of Toronto)

22 Contemporary Human Rights Ideas (2008)
by Bertrand G. Ramcharan (Geneva Graduate Institute of International and Development Studies)

21 The World Bank (2008)
From reconstruction to development to equity
by Katherine Marshall (Georgetown University)

20 The European Union (2008)
by Clive Archer (Manchester Metropolitan University)

19 The African Union (2008)
Challenges of globalization, security, and governance
by Samuel M. Makinda (Murdoch University) and F. Wafula Okumu (McMaster University)

18 Commonwealth (2008)
Inter- and non-state contributions to global governance
by Timothy M. Shaw (Royal Roads University)

17 The World Trade Organization (2007)
Law, economics, and politics
*by Bernard M. Hoekman (World Bank) and
Petros C. Mavroidis (Columbia University)*

16 A Crisis of Global Institutions? (2007)
Multilateralism and international security
by Edward Newman (University of Birmingham)

15 UN Conference on Trade and Development (2007)
*by Ian Taylor (University of St. Andrews) and
Karen Smith (University of Stellenbosch)*

**14 The Organization for Security and
Co-operation in Europe (2007)**
by David J. Galbreath (University of Aberdeen)

13 The International Committee of the Red Cross (2007)
A neutral humanitarian actor
*by David P. Forsythe (University of Nebraska) and
Barbara Ann Rieffer-Flanagan (Central Washington University)*

12 The World Economic Forum (2007)
A multi-stakeholder approach to global governance
by Geoffrey Allen Pigman (Bennington College)

11 The Group of 7/8 (2007)
by Hugo Dobson (University of Sheffield)

10 The International Monetary Fund (2007)
Politics of conditional lending
by James Raymond Vreeland (Georgetown University)

9 The North Atlantic Treaty Organization (2007)
The enduring alliance
*by Julian Lindley-French (Center for Applied Policy,
University of Munich)*

8 The World Intellectual Property Organization (2006)
Resurgence and the development agenda
by Chris May (University of the West of England)

7 The UN Security Council (2006)
Practice and promise
by Edward C. Luck (Columbia University)

6 Global Environmental Institutions (2006)
by Elizabeth R. DeSombre (Wellesley College)

5 Internal Displacement (2006)
Conceptualization and its consequences
by Thomas G. Weiss (The CUNY Graduate Center) and David A. Korn

4 The UN General Assembly (2005)
by M. J. Peterson (University of Massachusetts, Amherst)

3 United Nations Global Conferences (2005)
by Michael G. Schechter (Michigan State University)

2 The UN Secretary-General and Secretariat (2005)
by Leon Gordenker (Princeton University)

1 The United Nations and Human Rights (2005)
A guide for a new era
by Julie A. Mertus (American University)

Books currently under contract include:

The Regional Development Banks
Lending with a regional flavor
by Jonathan R. Strand (University of Nevada)

Millennium Development Goals (MDGs)
For a people-centered development agenda?
by Sakiko Fukada-Parr (The New School)

The Bank for International Settlements
The politics of global financial supervision in the age of high finance
by Kevin Ozgercin (SUNY College at Old Westbury)

International Migration
by Khalid Koser (Geneva Centre for Security Policy)

Human Development and Global Institutions
by Richard Ponzio

The International Monetary Fund (2nd edition)
Politics of conditional lending
by James Raymond Vreeland (Georgetown University)

The UN Global Compact
by Catia Gregoratti (Lund University)

Institutions for Women's Rights
by Charlotte Patton (York College, CUNY) and
Carolyn Stephenson (University of Hawaii)

International Aid
by Paul Mosley (University of Sheffield)

The Changing Political Map of Global Governance
by Anthony Payne (University of Sheffield) and
Stephen Robert Buzdugan (Manchester Metropolitan University)

Coping with Nuclear Weapons
by W. Pal Sidhu

Global Governance and China
The dragon's learning curve
edited by Scott Kennedy (Indiana University)

The Politics of Global Economic Surveillance
by Martin S. Edwards (Seton Hall University)

Mercy and Mercenaries
Humanitarian agencies and private security companies
by Peter Hoffman

Regional Organizations in the Middle East
by James Worrall (University of Leeds)

Reforming the UN Development System
The Politics of Incrementalism
by Silke Weinlich (Duisburg-Essen University)

The International Criminal Court
The Politics and practice of prosecuting atrocity crimes
by Martin Mennecke (University of Copenhagen)

BRICS
by João Pontes Nogueira (Catholic University, Rio de Janeiro) and Monica Herz (Catholic University, Rio de Janeiro)

The European Union (2nd edition)
Clive Archer (Manchester Metropolitan University)

Governing Climate Change (2nd edition)
Peter Newell (University of East Anglia) and Harriet A. Bulkeley (Durham University)

Protecting the Internally Displaced
Rhetoric and reality
Phil Orchard (University of Queensland)

The Arctic Council
Within the far north
Douglas C. Nord (Umea University)

For further information regarding the series, please contact:

Nicola Parkin, Editor, Politics & International Studies
Taylor & Francis
2 Park Square, Milton Park, Abingdon
Oxford OX14 4RN, UK
Nicola.parkin@tandf.co.uk
www.routledge.com